The Indian State Since Independence

The Indian State Since Independence
70 Years

C.P. Bhambhri

SHIPRA

(2022, First Published in 2017)

Rs. 1600; US$ 64

ISBN: 978-93-86262-41-7

2026 Imp., PoD

The Indian State Since Independence—70 Years

Published by:
SHIPRA PUBLICATIONS
LG 18-19, Pankaj Central Market
I.P. Ext., Patparganj, Delhi 110092, India
11 47322068; 96500 28065, 98105 22367
info@shiprapublication.com
www.shiprapublication.com

Preface

It is a formidable task for any individual scholar to construct the history of seventy years of Indian state because in the absence of original source material, a scholar has to depend on available secondary sources for the understanding of extremely complex social dialectics of contemporary state of India. Has the Indian state been successful in establishing its legitimate authority over well-defined territorial boundaries of the whole country? How has the central authority of government of India managed conflict situations in the periphery especially in Jammu and Kashmir and some regions of North East India? Has the Indian state succeeded in establishing its ideological hegemony over highly diverse and plural society of India? Has the India state been able to strengthen "the basic structure" of democratic, plural, secular and federal system of governance during the last seventy years of its journey? The Indian state succeeded in accommodating challenges to its authority or has it exercised its excessive coercive powers to suppress dissent? What is the explanation for the birth of Hindu Ideological State beginning with 2014? A few important questions as mentioned above have been answered in this brief study of seventy years of the Indian state.

Acknowledgments

Thanks are due to D. Kumar, publisher, Shipra Publications, for persisting in his efforts to bring out a new and completely updated edition of the book. Thanks are also due to journals and other publications where some of the material contained in the book was earlier published. Thanks are to:

a) Social Scientist (New Delhi)
b) People's Democracy (New Delhi)

C.P. Bhambhri
Jawaharlal Nehru University
New Delhi
14th July, 2017

Contents

1

Seventy Years of Indian State (1947-2017): An Introduction

India had been described as the 'most important jewel in the British Crown', however, the British colonizers by consciously following ruthless policies of economic plunder and exploitation had left behind a legacy of underdevelopment, mass poverty and deprivation and the greatest challenge faced by the post-independence state was to eradicate mass poverty and undertake programmes for economic development of the whole underdeveloped society and regions of this vast country of continental size. Economic underdevelopment of India was not the only legacy of the colonial rulers, the leadership of newly Independent decolonized country was confronted with anarchic and chaotic social situation created by the Partition of India and the retreating colonial power had handed over the task of rehabilitation of transfer of populations from India to Pakistan and Pakistan to India and thus maintaining 'law and order' in highly disturbed society became the first priority of the Indian state after August 15, 1947. The story of challenge faced by India just after independence does not end here because the nationalist leadership had always claimed that it had won freedom on the basis of struggles based on "Non-violence and Satyagraha", the same leadership asked Indian army to fight war like situations in Jammu and Kashmir and Telangana where Communist party led armed struggle of peasant classes was posing a challenge to the newly independent state of India. It is the above mentioned context which explains that the colonial state apparatus, army, civil and police bureaucracy, got legitimized in Independent India and this coercive and governing apparatus created by the colonizers was not only inherited, it was legitimized because of its engagement while dealing with 'armed challenges' to the newly independent state of India. Not only this. If on one hand, the inherited coercive state apparatus has been brought under 'democratic control', on the other, Army, civil and police bureaucracy has strengthened its roots by establishing its pre-eminence as protectors and defenders of the Indian state. India has third or fourth professional standing army in the world and it is well-equipped with all the latest weapon system which is available to the advanced NATO Country's Army.

Table I: Estimated strength of Central Government Select Ministries/ Departments

Ministry/Depts.	*2015*	*2016*	*2017*	*2018*
Police	10,28,077	10,07,366	10,94,135	11,13,689
Income Tax	46,400	46,236	80,082	80,082
Custom & Excise	50,100	50,638	91,756	91,756
Railways	13,26,437	13,31,433	13,31,433	13,31,433
External Affairs	8,913	9,294	11,373	1,403
I&B	4,141	4,012	6,258	6,258
Cabinet	900	921	1203	1218
Total	**33,05,646**	**32,84,714**	**35,38,016**	**35,67,574**

(All 55 Government departments., excluding three defence forces).

Note: The figures above are strength of the department mentioned as on March 1 of that year. Statistics for 2015 and 2016 are as per actual and for 2017 and 2018 are as estimation.

Source: Union Budget 2017-18.

The central and state governments are largest employers of civil and police personnel in India and the Central government is also expanding para-military forces like the Central Reserve Police Force, the Border Security Force, et al for performing functions of armed forces as second line of defence in 'disturbed' areas like Jammu and Kashmir, or North East especially Nagaland, Manipur or states and regions which are infected by Left Extremism or Maoism or Naxalism. The 'defence and security' of the state and its territorial boundaries is given a very high priority not only by employing large number of personnel for the Army and para-military armed forces, but also by enacting Special Laws which curb fundamental rights of citizens especially Armed Forces Special Protection Act which is in force in areas considered 'disturbed' by the Indian state. Further, the Indian state has acquired 'extraordinary powers' to curb individual or group activities which are considered a 'threat' to the safety and territorial integrity of the country. If on one hand, the Indian state has not repudiated or repealed law on Sedition or Public Safety Act which it inherited from the colonial state, on the other, during the last seventy years it has enacted new tough laws like Preventive Detention Act to Unlawful Activities Anti-Terrorist Act to curb the activities of individuals or groups considered 'dangerous' by the state. The Civil liberty groups and defenders of human rights consider that democratic state of India has many 'undemocratic' features and these 'libertarians' characterize this state as 'coercive' and 'authoritarian'. This approach to the study of Indian state has been followed by some scholars and 'libertarian' groups who consider that as a continuation of foreign colonial oppressive state, the decolonized India has given more coercive powers to the functionaries of Indian state and during the last seventy years while continuing with the policies of coercion followed by the erstwhile colonisers the Indian state has more resources and power to effectively enforce its coercive laws and curb freedoms of citizens. This approach of 'libertarians' to project the coercive face of the Indian state as the only 'reality' is not only partial presentation of the essence of Indian state after independence, it is quite flawed because while emphasizing 'continuities' of the colonial state, the real significance of the Transfer of Power in 1947 from British colonizers to Indian nationalist leadership is not properly understood. The real meaning of the Transfer of Power in 1947 is that the colonial rulers were forced to quit India because of the pressures built by powerful anti-colonial mass struggle for independence,. The new rulers of the Indian state were patriots who had not only fought against colonial oppression, they also had a pride in Independent India. The nationalist leadership of the Indian state in 1947 came to power with a commitment to build a new 'democratic, sovereign, secular, Republic of India on the basis of a constitution prepared by the Constituent Assembly of India. The real meaning of the Transfer of Power in 1947 is that India witnessed a 'break with the past' inspite of the fact that some 'continuities' of the colonial oppressive state apparatus can be pointed out but these 'continuities' of the colonial past have to be seen in the context of fundamental 'change' which took place when foreign rule was replaced by the state of the natives. Continuities with change is the essence of the Transfer of Power of 1947 and its best example is that coercive apparatus of the state came under the full control of the nationalist leadership who unlike the colonial rulers, were democratically elected to govern the country. The Constitution of India prepared by the Constituent Assembly of India placed state power in the hands of 'democratically' elected representatives who were accountable for governance and every activity of the coercive apparatus of the state like Army, Civil and police functionaries. The approach to the study of state by these academicians who consider that post- 1947 state is a 'continuity' of the colonial state system is completely flawed and deserves to be rejected because post-independence Indian state which begins its journey from August 15, 1947 should be studied by one of the following 'approaches' which help in understanding the 'reality' of post-independence state.

Liberal-Democratic-Pluralist Approach

John Locke, John Stuart Mill and many other western scholars and theoreticians of capitalist democracy have approached the study of state by focusing attention on 'individual rights and freedoms' and institutions of governance which can ensure that human freedoms are protected and promoted. The state according to liberal-democratic-pluralist theoreticians acts as a neutral umpire while dealing with multiple and diverse problems of sections of society and while resolving inter-group or inter-community conflicts in a plural society, the state in a democracy tries to maintain equilibrium among social groups with the sole purpose of providing equal protection to every individual citizen and social group. Liberal theoreticians beginning with John Locke to John Rawls have been engaged in internal debates about the meaning of Individual liberties and rights and inspite of such debates, all liberal-democratic theoreticians have agreed that the right to own private property is fundamental for the enjoyment of individual freedoms. If individual citizens have a right to elect their representatives and hold them accountable while governing human society, such an elected government has a fundamental duty to protect private property owned by individual citizens. Further, liberal democracies have evolved institutional mechanisms of governance where power is not concentrated in any one institution and it is shared and divided among many institutions of governance of the state. Western democratic state systems have adopted institutional system for protecting rights and liberties of individual citizens and inspite of different kind of institutions which have been working in different western democratic state systems, the common factor in all democracies is that the state is considered as protector and guardian of individual liberties and rights and every individual has institutional protection if his rights are violated by the functionaries of the state. A fundamental criticism of liberal democracy, its theory and praxis, has been put forward by defenders of 'human equality' who have argued that capitalist democracy of liberal theoreticians is like an empty shell because without 'human equality' individual freedoms are like bones without flesh and blood. Capitalism and inequality in human society create conditions where real freedoms are enjoyed by the owners of means of production for private appropriation and profit and the majority of working and labouring classes are promised liberty which is empty and without any substance. The idea of individual liberty hangs in the air in capitalist democratic states because rights and freedoms of exploiters cannot be equal to the so-called rights of the exploited majority of citizens. Social corrections have been suggested by those who recognize that inequality in society creates real road blocks and obstacles in the way of individuals who have been guaranteed freedoms but pre-conditions for the enjoyment of freedoms do not exist because the absolute majority of labouring classes do not have any share in the wealth of society. The idea of welfare state has been put forward by those who want to reconcile to some extent the problems created by capitalism in democracy and some capitalist countries have tried to pursue social welfare and social security policies and programmes for creating some essential conditions for everyone to participate in democratic processes of governance and enjoy to some extent freedoms provided by democratic state systems. The welfare state in a capitalist country acts as a midwife by creating some conditions for deprived citizens so that they can enjoy some freedoms. However, the basic issue of liberty in an unequal capitalist society remains unresolved because the fundamental feature of capitalism is that private appropriation for profit by the owners of means of production creates 'inequality' and liberty in an 'unequal' society remains an empty promise for the real producers of wealth, the labouring classes.

Marxist Approach to the Study of State

If liberal theorists of capitalist democracy have advocated the idea of individual freedom and rights as the foundational principle of a democratic state in capitalist societies, Karl Marx had offered a fundamental critique of capitalism by pointing out that the institution of private property in capitalism creates fundamental social inequalities because those who own the means of production by appropriating and accumulating surplus and profits generated by millions of laboring classes create divisions between the 'exploiter' and the 'exploiting' classes. A capitalist society is divided into 'classes' based on 'unequal social relations', the private owners of the means of production need to control the state for private accumulation of surplus and profits. The state in class-divided capitalist societies is an 'instrument' in the hands of dominant capitalist classes and such a state exercises coercive authority over the sellers of labour so that the interests of private capitalist appropriators are fully protected and safeguarded. The state is an agency of the dominant exploiting classes and its basic function is to serve the interests of the exploiters and also maintain social conditions for the functioning of such an 'unequal' society. An issue which is worth examining is the relationship between democracies which took strong roots in many advanced capitalist societies of the west especially during the 20th century and capitalist state which acts as a protector and guardian of the exploiting capitalist classes which dominate over the whole society under the protective umbrella of the state. If democratically elected governments claim that real power is derived from people's vote and support and because these governments are elected on the basis of universal franchise, they are 'accountable' to the citizens who have elected them. Democratically elected governments claim that power is exercised for the development and welfare of multiple sections of society and because the elected governments are ultimately responsible to the society at large, such elected governments cannot be just an agency or an instrument in the hands of dominant exploiting capitalist classes. While this debate on the relationship between formally elected representative governments and the dominant role played by powerful capitalist classes which control the state for the advancement of their own class interests continues, one issue which is settled once for all is that in an 'unequal society' which is the logical product of laws of motion of capitalism, power in society is also unequally distributed. The state in an unequal society even in a democracy cannot provide equal services and protection to all the citizens because if society is divided basically on the basis of ownership of the means of production for private appropriation, the state has to 'protect the interests of private property owners' and ensure that conflicts which may arise in socially unequal society are resolved basically by guaranteeing the rights of dominant capitalist classes. If liberal democratic state system in a capitalist society cannot ensure individual liberties and rights for every citizen, Marx intervenes and argues that these individual liberties can be ensured only in a society based on equality and Marx further argues that capitalism cannot ensure equal enjoyment of rights and liberties for every citizen, its alternative is socialism where equality and liberty of human beings can be really enjoyed. It is only in socialism according to Karl Marx the idea of social equality can be harmonized with individual liberty and rights. Such a reconciliation is not possible under capitalism and the state which is an agency of capitalist unequal social order cannot be considered 'neutral' while dealing with social class conflicts.

Special and Salient Features of Indian State: 70 Years

The first and foremost specific feature of the Indian state inspite of its commitment to election based representative democracy is that it has actively promoted Indian capitalism and its direct involvement in laying down firm foundations for the development of capitalism has not stopped inspite of India's transition from the era of economic planning to the launching of New Economic Policy in 1991. India had inherited some indigenous capitalist industries on the eve of Independence, and this process of industrialization had to be accelerated by laying down the foundations of robust infrastructure for economic development of the country. Not only this. The new agenda for the acceleration of processes of industrialization was also linked with the modernization of agriculture because India had to feed its own people by raising the levels of productivity of its agriculture. The system of economic planning and the model of mixed economy which was followed by post-independence state of India created a situation where the state was in the centre stage of economic development of agriculture and industry and it was the state which was actively engaged in building public and private sectors of economy. This activist role of the state in every major sector of economy created a social base for its relative autonomy form powerful social classes whether landlords or private owners of industry, commerce and trade. Dominant social classes in post-independence India looked towards the state for performing crucial and critical role for the development of public and private sectors of economy.[1] The state enjoyed relative autonomy with the consent of the dominant classes and from 1947 to 1991, these classes had substantially benefited from state intervention in economy. There was hardly any opposition from the socially dominant classes when in the beginning of 1990's democratically elected political executive decided to break with the past model of state regulated economy to New Economic Policy of 'deregulation, liberalization, privatization and globalization'. The New Economic Policy beginning with the 1990s showed great preference for free market economy model for domestic capital and this new policy, unlike the past (1947 to 1991) openly welcomed foreign private capital for investment in multiple sectors of Indian economy. India has been fully integrated with world capitalist system and during the last about three decades of the 'opening' of Indian economy to foreign capital has provided an opportunity to Indian capitalists to invests in foreign markets and foreign capital investors to freely operate in Indian market. The New Economic Policy has given birth to a new state which is openly encouraging Indian private capitalists to collaborate with foreign private capital investors. The Indian state of today is a full-fledged capitalist state and Indian capitalist classes find the state very hospitable because it facilitates capitalist classes to operate in the Indian market and also invest in foreign markets. However, this is only one special feature of the Indian state.

The State in an Unequal Society

Capitalism in India has developed very strong roots during seventy years of post-independence of country's journey and capitalist development has given birth to the emergence of most 'unequal' society. A few salient facts about the prevalence of inequality in India deserve to be mentioned with a view to highlight the social consequences of capitalist development.

I. 'Between one-third and one-fourth of Indians live in absolute, sub-human poverty'.[2]

II. Top concentration of Wealth.[3]
   a) 2000 top 1 per cent hold 37 per cent of the wealth of the country and it has increased to 53 per cent by 2016.
   b) Between 2001 and 2016 top 1 per cent cornered 61 per cent of all the increase in wealth estimated at US$ 2.28 trillion.
   c) Forbes mentions that "US dollar billionaires were only 2 in 1995 however, "extremely high net worth individuals were 46 persons in 2012, 55 persons in 2014".
   d) One hundred top richest in India are all billionaires in US Dollar terms.[4]

III. Along with these billionaires, India has population of 300 to 350 multi-millionaires including rising professional, technocratic middle and upper middle classes. It is based on a credit Suisse Global Wealth Survey.[5]

This survey informs that nearly 250 million of world's poorest people are in India. Further, this survey mentions, referring to 2012, that top 22% of Indians owned 77.6% of wealth and the top one percent controlled 25%, while the bottom 70% of the population owned just 13.6% of wealth in India. The total wealth in the country is estimated at US$ 3 trillion and just 57 billionaires in India have the same wealth (US$ 216 billion) as that of the bottom 70% of their country. If on one hand, the ruling classes and capitalist state is focused on accelerating the rate of economic growth, on the other, in the absence of any redistribution plan, social inequalities have grown and deepened in India. India was always socially an 'unequal' society, however, it was expected that under democratic pressures the state will follow schemes for redistribution so that concentration of wealth, assets and incomes in the hands of a few owners of means of production would not take place, unfortunately, it has not happened and inequalities have increased in society.[6]

India is faced with serious social challenges arising out of social inequality and regional and sectoral imbalances. If some regions are engaged in insurgency and violent uprisings against the Indian state, the other regions or so-called mainland of India is still seeking solutions through democratic methods of elections and participations in parliamentary democratic politics.

Ideological Shifts in Politics and Society

The state and the ruling classes have to establish their ideological hegemony over every strata of society so that their authority to rule is willingly accepted by everyone. The only test of acceptance of ideological hegemony by every section of society is that citizens accept that this is their own state and this state is their real protector and well-wisher. Liberal-Democratic theorists maintain that by ensuring people's participation through elections in governance of a country a democratic state can create conditions for the willing acceptance of authority of the state. The western democratic states of advanced capitalist countries seem to have established ideological hegemony by strengthening the institutions of democratic participation by voters in regular, free and fair elections. If citizens in a democracy accept this fact that an elected government is their own because it is accountable to them it has been suggested that one can assume that the state has established its ideological hegemony and the citizens of such a state have come to accept willingly the authority of the state. The story of Indian state is quite different. The British colonial state had established its authority over India by following policies of coercion and suppression of anti-colonial liberation struggles and movements. When the colonial rulers realized especially beginning with 1940s that policies of suppression and coercion were becoming counter-productive and the coercive state apparatus of colonisers was unable to suppress popular feelings for freedom, they decided to quit in 1947. Anti-colonial movements and struggles launched by Indians became very strong from 1920s to 1940s and the British colonial state gradually accepted the fact that their days are numbered and popular struggles for freedom could not be suppressed and policies of coercion followed by the colonisers could not succeed, and hence the decision to quit India was taken by the British. The idea of nationalist leadership to 'delegitimize' the colonial state in the minds of the people became strong and popular, the British had to quit because they realized that the nationalist leadership had succeeded in mobilizing the mass of peasantry, laboring and middle classes against 'the foreign rule', the British had no option but to quit. The idea that the colonial state is not 'ours' and it is 'foreign' rule made people come on the streets and this mass opposition eroded the foundations of oppressive colonial state. The sum and substance of above narrative is that when a state loses its legitimacy, it either becomes very oppressive and authoritarian or like the illegitimate British colonial state, the option of leaving the colony is exercised. The new independent state of India had 'legitimacy' and 'ideological' acceptability because the mass of people recognized a fact that our independent state is a product of our struggles and sacrifices and it is not something 'foreign' like the British colonial state. The new independent state was accepted as 'ours' and led by the people and the new constitution of India was accepted as our Constitution prepared by our Constituent Assembly which consisted of our representatives. Thus, Indian nationalism acted as 'legitimizer' of the new state of India. However, during the last seventy years,

Indians have witnessed many ideological contests on the basis of which different ideological groups have competed against one another with a view to establish their ideological hegemony over the state.

The Idea of Ideological State: Hindu Rashtravad

Traditionally the state has been studied by following one of the three approaches mentioned above i.e. approach of Libertarians or Liberal-Democratic theories of the state or Karl Marx's approach to the study of state, however, some new social and political developments which have taken place in the Arab Islamic world have led some scholars to study this phenomenon of Islamisation of the state by suggesting that these Islamist states are Ideological as distinguished from other state systems of Asia, Africa or advanced Western capitalist countries. The essence of an Ideological state lies in the fact that while performing traditional law and order and developmental-welfare functions, an ideological state is primarily guided by its dominant ideology of promoting and protecting Islam as enshrined in the Holy Quran by Prophet Mohammad and as interpreted by Mullahs and Maulvis. One of the best example of an ideological state is Iran, where only Ayatullah, a chief Islamic theologian, can rule the country. The Islamists are also trying to revive Caliphate, an anachronism, where pure Islamic ideological state system can be established and the rulers are bound by the dictates of Holy Quran and the teachings of Prophet Mohammad. Mullahs as custodians of Islam and the teachings of Prophet Mohammad shall not only be guided by an ideology, it will implement and enforce all the fundamental principles of Ideology and ensure that every citizen of such a state, without any exception, follows the ideological principles an laid down by Islam. It is only an ideological state which has strict laws on 'blasphemy' and a person or a group which is alleged to be breaking the fundamental principles of ideology shall be declared 'blasphemous' and the state shall inflict severe punishment on such a violator of supreme ideology. While every modern state is committed to the implementation of some basic social and human values while governing a society, however, unlike other modern states, the ideological state functions under the umbrella of a supreme ideology and it has to defend 'purity' of its ideological principles and inflict severest punishments on those who deviate from the fundamentals of ideology. The state has to be guided by a supreme ideology and it has to act as a 'guardian' of purity of Ideology just as Islam. Unislamic activities by a citizen cannot be tolerated by an ideological state and Mullahs and Maulvis as custodians of Islam are expected to decide about 'unislamic activities' and the state as guardian of purity of Ideology will announce punishments. In sum, the state is guided by the principles of a supreme ideology and all its activities are expected to conform with the fundamentals of ideology and any deviation from any fundamental principle shall invite severe punishment.

It is argued here that India is witnessing an ideological shift and the Indian state is gradually moving away from liberal–democratic values enshrined in the Republican Constitution of India and Hindu Rashtravadis represented by Rashtriya Swayamsevak Sangh and its 44 affiliates including its political face—the Bharatiya Janata Party are moving forward to capture the India state with the sole purpose of making it an ideological Hindu state. The sole agenda of BJP-RSS is to capture state power through electoral process and exercise this power to establish a Hindu state. K.B. Hedgewar, M.S. Gowalkar to Mohan Bhagwat as Sarsanghchalak or supremo of the RSS have worked very hard to create a strong para-military like disciplined organization of Swayamsevaks (cadre)and Pracharaks of the RSS are deployed to inculcate the ideology of greatness of Hindus of India among the 'young' recruits to the RSS. The aim of such an ideological traning by the RSS is to inculcate great pride among its cadre about the glorious past of the Hindus and the RSS recruits are asked to work hard with dedication and devotion to spread this message of greatness among the Hindus who are expected to revive their own glorious past based on traditions mentioned in Vedas, Mahabharata and Ramayana. Brahmans are very important for the RSS because on the basis of their knowledge of Sanskrit language, they can transmit Hindu values as enshrined in ancient Hindu religious scriptures. The RSS is committed to work for the unity of Hindus so that they can defend Hindu Rashtra from external and internal enemies. Leadership of the BJP is in the hands of RSS Pracharaks who work under the guidance and instructions of the RSS. RSS and BJP are indistinguishable and BJP-in-government is committed to the implementation of the ideology of Hindu Rashtravad in unity with RSS and its 44 affiliates like Vishwa Hindu Parishad, Bajrang Dal, Akhil Bharatiya Vidyarthi Parishadet all. BJP-in-government in reality means that India is ruled by the Sangh Parivar Hindu Family.[7]

The Indian state ruled and controlled by the BJP-RSS is an ideological state which is guided by a supreme idea of making India a united Hindu Rashtra for the sole purpose of promoting and protecting Hindus and their holy places or holy animals like cow. The BJP and RSS are committed to protect the 'purity' of Hindu race by preventing Hindu girls from marrying Muslims or Christians. It is a part of ideological role of the Indian state currently under the BJP government at the Centre that vigilante groups are operating without any fear and punshing, even killing, suspected killers of holy cow of the Hindus or punishing Muslims who marry Hindu girls by proclaiming that Muslims have launched a 'Love Jihad' against Hindus. The state is quite indifferent to the activities of gau-rakshaks or Love Jihadis because as a Hindu ideological state it approves of these actions because they are undertaken to defend Hindu religious beliefs. A normal law-based state committed to the principles of Rule of Law would punish illegal activities of groups like Bajrang Dal or gau-rakshaks or those who spread hatred against other religious communities but an ideological state of Hindus would not take any punitive action because these groups are performing ideological role of the state.

Dominant Hindu society as interpreted by the rulers is at work and the latesr example is that the Modi led BJP government is engaged in pursuing this ideology is that on May 23, 2017, a notification was issued by the central government asking all the 29 states and 7 Union Territories of India to implement the regulations of lives stocks market rules framed under the Prevention of Cruelty to Animals Act of 1960 requiring "animal market committees to be formed in every distinct to ensure that the purchaser of the cattle does not further sell the animal for purpose of slaughter'. The detailed rules for the sale and purchase of animals and the list of animals mentioned in this notification in reality attempt to prohibit the sale and purchase of holy cow, mother to a section of high caste Hindus, from falling in the hands of butchers and those who run slaughter houses. BJP-led governments are engaged in protecting the holy cow because it is considered sacred by a section of high caste Hindus. Not only this. Hindus consider River Ganga sacred and in normal circumstances a secular and routine agenda for any government of India but cleaning of holy Ganga river water is an agenda for serving the cause of Hindus who consider taking a bath in Ganga River water a holy and sacred activity. This is the reason that Hindu ideological state led by BJP-RSS is concentrating on the cleaning of dirty water flowing in holy Ganga River so that Hindu worshippers can take bath in clean water at the holy river. Yogi Adityanath, BJP Chief Minister of Uttar Pradesh observed on My 21, 2017 that 'the holy river belongs to everyone and a symbol of *Sanatan Sanskriti'* It is everyone's mother and people have to save it. Any insult to the river can never be tolerated and it is equal to 'rashtradroh' (anti-nationals). There are many examples to substantiate the argument that Hindu ideological state like Islamist state is fundamentally committed to promote and protect religious beliefs either of Hindus or of Muslims. And in reality, the primary goal of these ideological states is to implement religious beliefs of either Hindus or Muslims. Hindu or Islamist states are distinguished from other modern states because for the former state systems religion defines their whole world view and comprehensively lays down the basic functions which these states have to perform. Hindu Ideological State legitimizes its ban on cow slaughter or construction of Ram Temple at Ayodhya because the Hindu state has to be guided by matters concerning Hindu faith and Hindu sentiments has to be respected by such a slate.

Summing Up

I. Indian Capitalism and the State

Social classes are formed in a specific historical context and formation of Indian capitalist classes and its relationship with the state cannot be an exception to this general rule of class formation. Indian trading and business communities and classes struggled very hard to emerge as capitalist classes because British colonial state had followed very negative and obstructionist policies towards indigenous emerging capitalist classes. The colonial context in which new capitalist mode of production was emerging led new capitalists to identify their interests with anti-colonial struggles led by nationalist leadership. After

Independence, the state leadership consciously promoted the class interests of private industrial and entrepreneurial classes and in this project of nation-building, the state and capitalist classes worked in harmony with one another especially because the individual private industrial capitalists had recognized that without the active support and involvement of the state any industrialization of India was just not possible. The state and capital have worked in almost complete harmony during the last seventy years of post-Independence India and because of this closeness between the state and capital, not only resource base of Indian economy has increased, individual capitalists have also joined the ranks of big industrial groups and many of them are monopoly capitalists. India has emerged as a full-fledged capitalist state and Indian capitalist classes with the full support and encouragement of the state have become very powerful and prosperous. This is the first feature of the Indian state which deserves to be noticed and India is a new developed emerging economic power of the countries of the South and the economic resource base of the state and private capitalist industrial and entrepreneurial strata of society has increased to an extent that Indian monopoly capitalists and the state have without any hesitation interpreted themselves with global monopoly finance capital and transnational corporations.

II. Consolidation of Power

A modern state has to ensure safety and security of its citizens and it is expected to create powerful and effective infrastructure and apparatuses of the state to defend its borders and legally defined territorial boundaries. During the last seventy years, the Indian state has fought four wars with Pakistan and Indian army was also engaged in war with China in 1962 on the issue of disputed boundaries. During the last seven decades of post-independence journey, India has strengthened its war machine and also civilian police and para-military forces have been strengthened to defend the territorial integrity of the country and maintain domestic law and order.

III. Ideology of the State

The state legitimizes its rule by winning over the loyalty of its citizens and the citizens willingly obey the authority and laws of the state if they believe that their state is working for their interests. Ideology thus plays the legitimizing function and this is the reason that every modern state tries to win over the loyalty of its citizens by establishing institutions which promote values and ideology of the state. Liberal-Democratic states legitimize themselves by promoting the idea of individual freedom as their main ideology and most important social value. The state is guardian and protector of rights and liberties of the citizens and it is the duty of citizens to obey the liberal-democratic state because only such a state can ensure freedom to individuals. This ideological message is given to every citizen through every institution of ideology maintained by the state, the most important role is played by educational institutions and the media.

The Constitution of India has laid down the foundations of the state based on ideology of liberal, pluralist and secular value system. This ideology of liberalism as enshrined in the constitution is not acceptable to the Hindu Sangh Parivar of the Rashtriya Swayamsevak Sangh and Bhartiya Janata Party. India is witnessing great 'ideological contest' between the idea of liberal-democratic state and the idea of Hindu Rashtravad of the RSS. Is India moving away from the ideological framework of liberal, democratic, plural, secular state as mentioned in the Constitution of India or to the making of Hindu ideological state? What is the social base of organizations and leaders desiring to establish a Hindu ideological state for India? Ideological shifts of fundamental character can take place if some powerful social classes and groups support new ideology. Narendra Modi led BJP government at the centre and BJP governments in North and North-Western India have obviously come to power with the support of voters during the elections but this is only one part of the explanation in favour of the votaries and believers of the ideology of Hindu state. It is just one observable fact but the real issue is to find out the social support base for Hindutva. Dominant Hindu social groups like big industrial houses, merchants and traders and the emerging professional, entrepreneurial and technocratic upwardly mobile middle and other middle classes of about 300 to 350 million in the income group of multi-million US dollar are a powerful social constituency which is aggressively supporting the idea of Hindu ideological state as propagated by the RSS and BJP. Big or medium or small private property owners in urban India are under the influence of Brahmanical-ritual based Hinduism and these Hindu-religious believers are providing conscious support to the parties of Hindutva. It should not be concluded that every practitioner of some kind of Hindu rituals and believer stands up in support of the BJP-RSS ideology of Hindu State. However, a large number of Hindus across the length and breadth of the country are providing social base to expanding RSS-BJP which stands for the creation of Hindu State. Hindu trading classes and Brahman castes were always attracted to RSS-BJP's ideology of Hindu state, but from 2017, new social classes and groups have joined the ranks of Hindutva. Incidentally, social soil of India seems to be quite fertile for those forces, movements and leaders who are determined to exploit Hindu religious sentiments and one important reason for the success of appeals in the name of Hindu religion among mass of Hindus is that Hinduism and its different religious sects were never 'attacked' and 'delegitimized' by any powerful group which stood for enlightenment, rationality and humanism and Rama Swamy Naikar in Tamil Nadu had launched a movement against Hindu ritual based religiosity and propagated the idea of 'atheism' but even in Tamil Nadu, the home of anti-Brahman movement, ritual based, temple focused Hindu religion is going strong and BJP-RSS is expanding its roots in that state/region also. The best example of three years of the functioning of ideologically-oriented Hindu state is that Rajasthan, Haryana, Uttar Pradesh, Madhya Pradesh, Gujarat, Maharashtra et al is that the protection of holy cow which is considered holy by Hindus especially of the upper castes has emerged as the most important agenda of the forces of Hindutva. Islamist Ideological States punish their citizens on charges of 'blasphemy' if they are found dishonouring Holy Quran. Hindu Ideological State considers protection of holy cow as its priority and inflicts severe punishment on an individual who is suspected of harming the holy cow. India is at the cross roads because such a fundamental 'ideological' shifts in national history has never occurred without 'violence'. Is India witnessing the end of liberal-democratic project launched after independence and its substitution by the establishment of Hindu ideological state?

NOTES

1. Land reforms were not implemented and agrarian social and productive relations were not restructured because the landed classes were an integral part of the ruling class coalition.
2. Amit Bahadur; "Danger Zones of High Economic Growth". *Economic and Political Weekly*, Bombay, October 22, 2016, pp. 14-15.
3. Global Wealth Databook, 2014.
4. Rukmani (2014) "India's staggering Wealth Gap in Five Charts", *Hindu*, Chennai, December 8, 2014.
5. *The Economic Times*, New Delhi, Dcember 15, 2016. p. 4.
6. Also see, Francois Bourguignon: The Globalisation of Inequality. Princeton: 2015. Also see, Joseph Stiglitz: The Price of Inequality: How Today's Divided Society Endangers Our Future: (2012).
7. See Dhirendra K. Jha: Shadow Armies: Fringe Organisations and Foot Soldiers of Hindutva: 2017: New Delhi: Juggernaut.

2

Global Capitalism and Peripheral Capitalist Democratic Nation-State Systems

Professor Samuel Huntington (1991) and Fukuyama (1992) celebrated the emergence of democracy at the global scale because of the collapse of the centralized socialist state systems of Eastern Europe. Philosophical and social discourse of the 1990s centred on the values of liberal-democratic institutions for governance, proven failure of the state to manage economies and virtues of market-based capitalist civil societies. The main thrust of the intellectual concerns of the Western scholars in the 1990s has been around the virtues of market-based capitalist liberal-democratic pluralist institutions for governance and minimal role for the state and maximalist role for the autonomous institutions of civil society and voluntary community institutions for the management of social relations. State has been equated with statism and ridiculed, and freedom of individuals has been glorified in market-led societies. Even Keynesian prescriptions based on welfare capitalism has few takers in the West and special contract between capital and labour based on welfarism has been denounced as statist and a plea has been made to extend individual freedoms by allowing the freeplay of 'rational public choices' in market capitalism. Since capitalism is global, Western liberal democratic, pluralist institutions for governance are also a role model for every country in the world. The collapse of socialist state systems has been interpreted by the Western scholars and their ruling elite as a testimony for victory of their institutions for governance for every country in the world. If World War II was fought to 'save democracy', the Western agenda for 1990s is "export of capitalism and democracy" as a model for freedom-loving human beings around the world.

It is suggested here that the Western scholars have misread the meanings of 1990s and all celebrations in favour of market-based capitalism and liberal-democratic-pluralist institutional systems for governance are not only premature but a complete misrepresentation of social and political reality of the closing years of the twentieth century.

The main contention here is that liberal-democratic-pluralistic values and institutions are based on totally flawed liberal theory from John Locke to John Rawls. Further, liberal democratic theory with all its conceptual innovations is at a dead end because it cannot help us in interpreting and explaining the social reality of the erstwhile decolonised countries which are in the process of building peripheral capitalist democratic nation-state systems under the present phase of global capitalism. Every premise, assumption and conceptual baggage of liberal democratic theory is faulty while grappling with the social, economic, cultural and political developments of newly emerging capitalist democracies.

Karl Marx had sensitised us that capitalism as distinguished from other modes of production, is global because the logic of capitalism is to maximise accumulation by expanding markets and by breaking boundaries of the so-called territories occupied by different states. We are concerned with the latest phase of capitalist globalization where direct colonial control of capitalist-imperialist states has been formally replaced by independent state systems in the erstwhile colonised Asia, Africa and Latin America. The latest phase of global capitalism is characterised by the globalization of finance and financial markets, production facilities and capitalist North and peripheral developing capitalism in the countries of the South are structured on the basis of an international division of labour managed by the following institutions of global capitalism: (i) G-7 countries, (ii) International Monetary Fund, (iii) International Bank for Reconstruction and Development (World Bank), (iv) The Bank for International Settlements, (v) The General Agreement on Tariffs and Trade, (vi) World Trade Organization, (vii) Organization for Economic Cooperation and Development. These institutions which are effectively controlled and managed by the super-capitalist states act as supra-state and supra-national institutions while dealing with peripheral, developing capitalist state systems. Its impact has been felt and the real issue, which has emerged in a big way, is concerning the very existence, even relevance of nation-state, whether democratic or authoritarian, in peripheral developing capitalist countries.

Roland Axtmann sums up the present agenda for Liberal-Democratic Theory. He observes:

> "A global economy has emerged which has become institutionalized through global capital markets and globally integrated financial systems, global trade and global production networks. In such a 'global economy', the patterns of production and consumption in the world are increasingly interdependent; income and employment are determined at a global level; and national macro-economic management is becoming increasingly anachronistic and doomed to failure..., however, it is the cartels and joint ventures amongst transnational and multinational corporations that are the most important element of economic [self] governance."[1]

The caravan of global capitalism is moving at a fast speed to achieve its goal of complete integration of various countries under the hegemony of centres of global capitalism by integrating peripheral capitalist countries in regional organizations led by the powerful capitalist countries of the West. Important regional organizations have emerged which consist of either developed capitalist countries or peripheral countries led by advanced capitalist countries, i.e., European Union, the North American Free Trade Organization of United States, Canada and Mexico, the Association of South East Asian Nations, the Asian Pacific Economic Co-operation, etc. Regionalization of countries is an answer of the capitalist countries for extending their hegemony and this development erodes the sovereignty of nation-states.

The central issue concerning liberal democratic theory at the end of Twentieth Century and the beginning of the Twentyfirst Century is to relate democracy with global capitalism and new threats to the very sovereignty of democratic nation-states of the peripheral developing capitalist countries. John Locke's, *Two Treatises of Government* (1689), John Stuart Mill's, *Considerations on Representative Government* (1861), John Rawls', *Political Liberation* (1993), and Amitai Etzione's, *The Spirit of Community* (1993), represent the last intellectual tradition of liberal democratic theory in the West. It is worth examining fundamental questions about democratic nation-states of peripheral developing capitalist countries like India. John Locke asks a question: "What makes a Government legitimate?" And, my answer is: "The consent of the governed." John Locke observes that: "All men are naturally in that state [of nature] and remain so till, by their own consent, they make themselves members of some political society."[2]

Consent makes state legitimate is the running theme of liberal theorists. An individual exercises his democratic rights and on the basis of his own free choice elects a Parliament and this provides legitimacy to a democratic-state. While all theorists are mirror images of their own Age, classical or neo-classical liberals are firmly committed to the principle of legitimacy of democratic state which is the result of autonomously expressed consent of the individual citizens. Individualism and consent-based legitimacy in politics remain the pillars of liberal theoretical enterprise. Fred O'Augustino observes:

> "...within a broad contractualist framework, these institutions are legitimate which are or which would be chosen by (specifically) autonomous choosers. Or, within a teleolgical tradition, these institutions are legitimate which are conducive to the cultivation of a capacity for autonomy. This idea of autonomy plays a crucial role, then, in setting liberal standards of legitimacy. Without some such idea, the liberal political theorist does not know what, institutionally, to recommend or reject."[3]

Liberal theorists suggest that in the institutional milieu of market for civil society, state institutions and family should be constituted in a manner where individual 'choices' are respected as 'sovereign'. Adam Smith who laid down the foundations of theory of economic liberealism and John Stuart Mill, who refined and defined theory of political liberalism along with many other liberal thinkers of the 20th century who are re-inventing liberal theory, are all agreed that individual's sovereign right is the legitimising first principle of democratic society and governance. Free market institutions, popularly elected parliaments and social milieu, which maximise areas of individual freedom and choices, are essentials of liberal democratic society. Many inconvenient questions were ignored by the founder of Liberal Theory and the result was that J.S. Mill ended up as an empty liberal and an abstract individual and all recent developments in Liberal Theory made by the growing tribe of theorists have felt shy of addressing themselves to the questions of imperialism, nationalism, patriotism, and democratic anti-imperialist struggles. Rights of the oppressed colonised societies have not been theoretically integrated in liberal theoretical intellectual tradition. From Adam Smith (1776) to John Rawls (1993), every liberal theorist has either been blind to the question of nationalism and rights of individuals in colonies or he has acted as 'liberal' in his own society and apologist of 'imperialism' in other societies. Plamenatz hits the nail at the head of all liberal theorists, classical or new *Avtars* of liberalism in the 20th century in his writing about John Stuart Mill. He observes that:

> "His liberalism requires democracy, but does not make an ideal of it. And it is not incompatible with imperialism, if by imperialism is meant the deliberate and presistent endeavour of a wealthy and self-governing people to fit other people to govern themselves in the way that enlarge individual freedom...Mill seems a kind of mirror of his Age... John Stuart Mill was at once the most characteristic and most remarkable Victorian philosopher-economist and political theorist."[4]

John Locke was very clear that while free consent of an individual legitimized the authority of the state, he also considered private property as a fundamental institution of liberal society. Liberal democratic theorists have not been able to reconcile properly the rights of an individual as a free citizen with the power of accumulators of surplus value and profits. Political liberalism has no answer to the questions raised by the exercise and distribution of power in a capitalist society.

The upshot of above discussion is that liberal democratic theory is totally flawed because all its theoretical abstractions get knocked down before the central question of power distribution in capitalist society and its impact on the exercise of rights of individuals. This theory further fails to provide explanations regarding the rights of colonised people and the emerging national capitalisms in the decolonised continents of Asia, Africa and Latin America. If popularly elected parliaments are legitimate to exercise power of governance over its own territorially defined area, the Indian parliament should have full autonomy to legislate for the whole country. Is it happening in the present global reality of distribution of power among nations? Does liberal democratic theory, with all its variants and re-inventions, help us in asserting that democratic liberal institutions of India have equal power over Indian society as enjoyed by the democratically elected governing institutions of the advanced capitalist-imperialist countries? If the answer is in the negative, what happens to Lockean principle of consent as the basis of legitimacy of democratic states?

What happens to the concept of autonomy of an individual which is so dear to the Liberal Theorists? What is the quality of rights of individuals in a peripheral developing capitalist democratic nation-state of India and the rights of individuals enjoyed by a United States' citizen? It is further maintained that liberal democratic theory is at the dead end to offer any satisfactory explanations on the basis of its first principles while dealing with the problems of globalization, quality of democracy in capitalist centre, and the status of democracy in newly emerging peripheral capitalist nation-states like India.

While the liberal democratic theory has been keeping under the carpet the real problems of capitalism and their impact on "the first principles" of liberalism, we will like to relate the problematic of democratic state of India in the context of global capitalism which is operating under the leadership of advanced capitalist countries represented by the group of seven (G 7) like the United States, the United Kingdom, France, Germany, Japan, Italy, Canada and now the emerging European Union. Since the essence of capitalism in its every stage lies in Accumulation Process this issue continues to be central inspite of the changing nature of capitalism in the 20th century. Two pillars of present phase of capitalism are around the role of finance capital. Finance capital has taken march over industrial capital or commercial capital. Further, finance capital is global and it has subsumed within itself not only all other forms of production but also every country of the world has come under its direct control and supervision. Linked with information technology and economy, global finance capital has made global financial markets subservient to the centres of capitalist power. The result is that "...the globalization of production and finance has undermined the ability of economic policy makers to manage national economic activity effectively, at least insofar as policies are attempted that do not fit into the international framework set by the extra-national (or transnational) global force".[5]

One issue, which has emerged in a big way, concerns with the concept of national sovereignty, popular sovereignty, and individual rights because new global capitalism at the end of 20th century has made capitalist centre as sovereign and all capital receiving countries as dependent. What are the rights of citizens of dependent democratic nation-states of the peripheral capitalism?

The second issue, which has also emerged along with the role of financial capital at the global level, is the pervasive crisis of capitalism in all the OECD countries. The main indicators of crisis of capitalism in developed countries are the rising levels of unemployment and poverty. The concrete expression of crisis of capitalism is found in the attacks against welfare state and foreign workers in the West. The rolling back of the state has emerged because the crisis-ridden capitalism cannot honour its social contract with labour because this social contract was mediated by capitalist welfare states. Reagan-economics in US or Thatcherism in UK were right wing responses in the context of crisis of capitalism, and race riots are reflective of social divide created by crisis situations in European Union or the United States. In this age of crisis of advanced capitalism, the global integration of crisis-ridden peripheral developing capitalist states like India makes social situation quite complex because the centres of capitalism are trying to resolve their crisis by transferring their problems to the peripheral capitalist countries. Since the 1990s, the Indian ruling classes and state political leaders have openly declared their intention to integrate with world capitalist system to resolve the crisis of Indian capitalism. Indian crisis has not been resolved even by changing the path of development by the class votaries of global integration because global capitalism is itself in crisis. French philosopher Etienne Balibar observes: "...if we think of a 'crisis' of the world order, of which the collapse of the 'socialist' semi-periphery could be the signal, is it not because, among other things, we are faced with the disturbing impression that most 'peripheries' remain desperately peripheral, while the 'central position of the traditional 'centres' is not so secure."[6]

Indian democratic state is facing a serious crisis of accumulation of capital and its prescription of global integration has not at all helped in the resolution of basic crisis of developing capitalism in India. While the Indian state has not been able to resolve its basic economic crisis in spite of its 'opening' to the advanced capitalist countries, the autonomy of Indian state vis-a-vis global capitalism has been eroded. Indian democratic state stands at a cross-road because the logic of global capitalism has been allowed to operate wherein all principles enshrined in the liberal-democratic constitution of India have been abandoned under the weight of superior state systems of advanced capitalism.

Our contention is that liberal democratic theory cannot defend its 'first principles' because they are barren and faulty. An individual lives in society and the liberals make an ideal of an individual which is faulty. Individual is nothing without a society but the liberals ignored the essence of capitalist society and the social status of an individual in the complex network of capitalist social relations. Karl Marx observed that:

> "...society does not consist of individuals: it expresses the sum of connections and relationships in which individuals find themselves. It is as though one were to say: from the standpoint of society there are neither slaves nor citizens: both are men. Rather they are so outside society. To be a slave or to be a citizen are social determinations, the relationships of Man A and Man B. Man A is not a slave as such. He is a slave within a society and because of it."[7]

Marx clearly sensitizes us that human society or individual cannot be explained without identifying the nature of social relations of human beings, which are the product of, material-economic foundations of human societies. Its implication is that individual rights have meanings only in the context of social relations, and the roots of social crisis are found in material-economic arrangements in society. Marx further alerts us: "In our view all collisions in history have their origin in the contradiction between the productive forces and the form of interaction."[8]

India is witnessing serious crisis of capital accumulation and the developing social crisis is a threat to the functioning of democratic state. This crisis of India has been intensified because the domestic exploiting classes have linked themselves with global ruling classes by surrendering the autonomy of the Indian state. While liberal democratic theorists cannot answer a basic question: Can a democratic state of peripheral developing capitalist country practice the 'first principles' enunciated by John Locke to John Rawls? Do the Liberal Theorists believe in Samuel P. Huntington's claim in "*Third Wave: Democratization in the Late Twentieth Century*?"[9]

Our analysis shows that the struggle in India is to make Indian democratic state more democratic and in this struggle, a very important agenda is opposition to capitalist-imperialist states of the developed West. Indian democratic State has to be challenged because the exploiting classes with full protection of the State have abandoned distributional agenda and have forgotten that India still has 350 million people below the poverty line. Indian nation-state is also in contradiction with crisis ridden capitalist-imperialist states, and without making the Indian state relatively autonomous of global capitalism Indian democracy cannot survive. Rights of the Indian nation-state in the context of global capitalism are linked with the rights of Indian labouring classes because the policies of structural adjustment as prescribed by capitalist-imperialist countries have hit directly the Indian poor working classes. While Indian foreign debt is nearing one trillion US Dollars the Indian State is following polices of further dependence of the country over capitalist countries. With global integration dependent states cannot practice democracy.

REFERENCES

1. Roland Axtmann, *Liberal Democracy into the twenty-first century: Globalization, integration and nation-state,* Manchester University Press, Manchester, 1996, p. 118.
2. John Plamenatz (revised by M.E. Plamenatz and Robert Wokler), *Man and Society: From Middle Ages to Locke,* Volume I, Longman, London, Second Impression, 1993, p. 339.
3. Fred O'Augustino, "Two conceptions of Autonomy", in *Economy and Society,* vol. 27, no. 1, February 1998, p. 29. See pp. 28-49.
4. John Plamenatz (Revised by M.E. Plamenatz and Robert Wokler), *Man and Society: From Montesquieu to the Early Socialists,* Volume II (1993, Second Impression), p. 270.
5. Sarap A. Kayatekin and David F. Ruceo, "Global Fragments: Subjectivity and Class Politics in Discourses of Globalization", *Economy and Society,* (1998), p. 78.
6. Etienne Balibar, "Has 'the world' changed?", in A. Calliar et al. (eds.), *Marxism in the Post-Modern Age;* Guilford Press, New York, 1995, p. 408. See pp. 405-14.
7. Karl Marx (1858), *Grundrisse,* Vintage Books, New York, 1973, p. 77.
8. Karl Marx, *German Ideology: Writings of the Young Marx on Philosophy and Society,* Anchor Books, New York, 1967, p. 454.
9. University of Oklahoma Press, Norman and London, 1991.

3

The State in Contemporary India

Any study of social institutions demands that the general laws of motion of history should be examined in interaction with living history of specific societies, and the general and the specific should be integrated to understand the whole and its relationship with parts. An analysis of specificity demands that reality has to be clearly demarcated from appearance, and the dynamic character of reality has to be comprehended in relation to its dialectics, contradictions and complexities.

Marxist formulation of the emergence and role of State has been presented in a neat model borrowed from the *Communist Manifesto*. In such a simplified model, the modern state has been presented in an 'instrumental' manner in which the state is an executive agency to subserve the interests of propertied classes. The model of the *Communist Manifesto* is correct in a limited manner. State and class relations are inextricably linked but not in a simplistic manner of the 'base' determining the "superstructure" in a deterministic manner. Because in such a model the state is a determined institution and its relation with classes is of a passive respondent.

A few statements by Marx from *The Eighteenth Brumaire of Louis Bonaparte* and together with Engels in *The German Ideology* help us in understanding the general character and role of the state, and its specific character in certain situations as in France of Louis Bonaparte.

As Frederick Engels in his introduction to *The Eighteenth Brumaire of Louis Bonaparte* draws our attention to the study of specific situations in the context of the laws of motion of history, Engels observes: ". . . Marx not only studied the past history of France with predilection, but also followed her current history in every detail, ..."

By following such a method of explanations, Marx relates Bonaparte to appropriate class context and comes to a conclusion that in certain situations the state can become *"Completely Independent"*.

Marx observes: "And yet the state power is not suspended in midair. Bonaparte represents a class and the most numerous class of French Society at that, the smallholding (Parzellen) peasants."

In the same writing, Marx observes: "Only under the second Bonaparte does the state seem to have made itself completely independent. As against civil society, the state machine has consolidated its position...."

In *The German Ideology* Marx-Discusses the essence of the state in general and of the bourgeois state in particular and he states: ".... The state is the form in which the individuals of a ruling class assert their common interests, and in which the whole civil society of an epoch is epitomized."

In the *'German Ideology,* Marx states "when modern capitalist society has developed from 'estate' to 'class' the bourgeoisie is forced to organise itself no longer locally, but nationally, and to give a general form to its average interests", and according to his judgement about such a developed bourgeois state the most perfect example of the modern state was North America.

This means that in societies where full bourgeois development has not taken place, and a stage of transition exists/the state can or may become 'a separate entity, alongside and outside civil society'.

With the above framework of Marx which is appropriate and valid for the study of a state, the specific historical development of a society, its socio-economic formations and their peculiarities and specificities at a specific stage of social development provide a proper context and methodology for the specificities of a state, Further, in a transitional stage where the old mode of production has not been completely replaced, absorbed and destroyed by the new capitalist mode of production, and where forms of ownership and relations reveal a complexity of co-existence from numerous pre-capitalist, feudal and semifeudal and monopoly capitalism, a neat and simple characterisation of the state cannot be undertaken.

If the state has to be understood in terms of classes and their relations, which it should be, transitional societies do not present the picture of developed and polarised class situations. In such a stage of social development where the co-existence and struggle of the 'old' and new has not been fully resolved, many cultural, social and political forms of authority of the old exist with the new. And if the old is showing great perseverance, stability and resilience of survival, its significance has to be grappled by analysing social institutions and their real significance.

Professor Ulyanovsky correctly says that 'multi-structuralism' is not the peculiarity of the developing countries because this was a feature, of European development also. It is 'stability' of structures and very gradual break-up of feudal relations that characterise the Third World. He observes: "The 'exclusive peculiarities' of the East do not lie in the presence of this structure, but in the variety and relative stability of structures in general and pre-capitalist (Partiarchal-subsistence and partiarchal-feudal) structures in particular."[1]

Hence in such a transitional society, optimal man "does not seek to remain something already formed, but is in the absolute movement of becoming".[2]

The capitalist mode of production in India did not emerge as a natural transformation from one stage to other but it was a product of colonial development. Colonial capitalism has specific meaning and implications for development of society, relations and institutions. The modern Indian State, like capitalism in the country was established by the British to safeguard the class interests of the metropolitan capitalism. This was the basic social goal of imperialism in India and this could not have been achieved without a powerful colonial state. Thus foreign capital and the emergence of indigenous capitalist classes looked towards the colonial state as a focal point of protection for the colonial interests. The indigenous capital found a powerful colonial state as an objective obstruction in its development. The twentieth century India was involved in struggle for transfer of state power from capitalist classes of the metropolis to the bourgeoisie of the oppressed society. This struggle for control over the Indian market waged by the indigenous bourgeoisie against the colonisers witnessed many ups and downs and conflicts and compromises not only with the imperialists but with local or indigenous feudal and semi-feudal classes. The bourgeois-led Indian nationalism fought against imperialism, mobilized the Indian masses for struggle but did not allow radicalisation of the mass struggle against internal and external oppressors and exploiters.

Thus when power was transferred and negotiated, the state power was handed over to the bourgeoisie and their political representatives with many unfinished tasks of social and economic transformations, and the state was the only instrument to achieve development of capitalism in India, and thus it could not be an inert or passive state but a very active and pre-eminent state. The Indian bourgeoisie had no one to look forward for their development except the state. The state in post-colonial situation was the repository of all basic tasks of capitalist development in this country, and these tasks were numerous which demanded a powerful state.

It is in the logic of colonial development of India that the state is an active and pre-eminent power centre for capitalist development. Thus it is not surprising that the Indian capitalist classes looked towards the state for all major economic decisions, and agreed to a situation where politics started determining economics. How far politics was successful in its crucial role of determining economics is a question worth investigating on the basis of evidence of the last three decades.

The Indian state as an engine of capitalist development is mobilizing resources, transforming productive relations by establishing conditions for the development of science *and* technology and by homogenising the multiple groups under the ideology of capitalism. Thus for serving class interests and the development of capitalism, the Indian state emerges as the chief organisation of the whole society.

A distinction should be maintained between 'state power' and 'state apparatus'. The apparatus is an instrument of power and it operates on the basis of a distinction between 'coercive instruments of the state' and 'ideological and legitimation' instruments of the state. The coercive aspects of the state apparatus become effective for the exercise of state power if ideological and legitimation instruments are strong and effective. Every state seeks legitimacy in an ideological framework, and it employs various strategies to gain legitimacy and strength.

First, the Indian state apparatus was legitimised by universal adult franchise and political parties and their leaders. The actual functioning of universal adult franchise in India has revealed many positive and negative features, but growing participation of the masses in elections helped legitimation of the state apparatuses. Every election in India helped in raising the level of mass political consciousness which was dramatized in 1977 with the defeat of the Indian Prime Minister, who was identified with the excesses of the Emergency of 1975-77. This fact reinforced that power of the political representatives to use the state apparatus depends on the mandate of the people and from the masses flows legitimacy of the political representatives.

Further, universal adult franchise and mass participation assumed that state power and state apparatus would not be used in a naked manner for the interests of 'dominant classes'. On the contrary, to win voters' legitimacy political authority would be exercised to ameliorate the living conditions of the down trodden and the oppressed classes.

The compulsions of legitimacy through electoral process demand that the dominant classes would have to share some benefits of social development with the deprived strata of society. The state had to manage the Indian society by following strategies of accommodation, adjustment, concessions and cooperation. The state could not have followed such a strategy of governance without mystifying its role of class instrument.

Secondly, colonial capitalism could not develop as a vigorous capitalism without the active role of the state apparatus in India, and the capitalist classes accepted the logic of 'state capitalism', economic planning and other regulatory mechanisms evolved by the state. Many curbs on the capitalist class imposed by the state through Reserve Bank, Companies Act 1956, Monopolies and Restrictive Trade Practices Act 1969 and Foreign Exchange Regulations Act, 1973 which were formulated in the general framework of Industrial Policy Resolutions of 1948,1956, *1977* etc. were operated by the state to 'regulate' capitalist classes and its individual members.

Not only this. The financial institutions of the state like IDBI, IFCI, ICICI, LIC, UTI, GIC and the nationalised banks provide financial resources for investment to the corporate sector in India.

As S A Pinto states: ". . . with the nationalisation of life and general insurance, there are no institutional sources of long-term finance now in the private sector. Therefore, the major part of the burden of long-term project finance is now on the financial institutions."[3] With this strategy the state and capitalists have got integrated.

Thirdly, dependence of the capitalist class on the state became crucial in India because through state legislation and intervention Indian rural relations had to be transformed to expand domestic market. In a country where 70 per cent of the people live in rural areas, the market for industrial products can be expanded only by creating purchasing power in the rural markets.

The abolition of absentee landlordism and the modernisation of agriculture around peasant-proprietor and to integrate rural market with the urban market in capitalist system could be achieved only through active state participation. The Indian capitalist development was obstructed by antiquarian land relations, and any change in complex land relations in India demanded active involvement of the State apparatus.

A capitalist class which looks towards the state apparatus for agrarian transformation, for infrastructural facilities, for financial resources for investment, and for protection against international capital has to come to terms with leading role of the state in its own long-term interests.

Without labouring the point further, it may be stated here that an underdeveloped colonial capitalism cannot become developed capitalism without active guidance, direction and control of the state, and a state which has to legitimise its authority through mass participation cannot become passive spectator to naked class rule and class exploitation. Only the state is expected to evolve multiple strategies of regulating social conduct by which the brutal pains of capitalist development are not inflicted on the working classes. In performing such a role the state evolves complex mechanisms of reconciling contradictory interests, and in the process it reveals many complex strategies for achieving growth of capitalism. Thus the major focus of study in India is that the capitalist classes are in the saddle and the capitalist state is active in safeguarding and promoting the interests of the leading classes. But in performing this basic task, the state has to undertake many other tasks for the whole society. Many a time the state evolves short-term strategies keeping in mind long-term interests of the classes. Hence while essence of the state is class but one need not abandon this "essence" by providing evidence from day-to-day policies of the state.

The process of social production is connected with a definite set of conditions of material life of society which in concrete form is based on the *forces of production and relations of production*. The production relations of a given society, that is, relations of production, exchange and distribution determine class relations in a society and their relations with the instruments of production and their ownership.

The transitional character of Indian society compels the emerging bourgeoisie to enter into coalitions and alliances with other dominant classes in the agrarian sector and this determines the essence of the Indian state.

Crisis of State Capitalism

On the positive side, the Indian state and its agencies and institutions have been able to mobilize large resources for investment.

On the negative side, there is not only high 'capital-output ratio', neither the state capitalist enterprises nor the private capitalists are able to generate enough resources through savings for reinvestment.

The Sixth Five Year Plan of the Government of India (1980-85) refers to some of the weaknesses of development of capitalism. The Plan admits: "The impact of the shortfall in the quantum of investment on the growth rate has been compounded by the fact that actual capital-output ratios have turned out to be higher than anticipated, particularly in recent years".

Table 2.1 reveals the worsening of the capitalist-output ratios.

Table 2.1: Incremental Gross Capital-Output Ratios (at 1970-71 prices)

Sl. No.	Plan	Period Cc	Capital/Output ratios
1.	First Plan	1951-52 to 55-56	3.2
2.	Second Plan	1956-57 to 60-61	4.1
3.	Third Plan	1961-62 to 65-66	5.4
4.	Annual Plans	1966-67 to 68-69	4.9
5.	Fourth Plan	1969-70 to 73-74	5.1
6.	Fifth Plan	1974-75 to 78-79	3.9

Source: Sixth Five Year Plan *(1980-85).*

Coupled with high capital-output ratio is emerging constraints on resource mobilisation because neither state capitalist enterprises nor private corporate sector is generating enough surpluses for reinvestment, as revealed by Table 2.2.

Table 2.2: Resource Mobilisation

Sl. No.	Item	Pre-Plan 1950-51	End of First Plan 55-56	End of Second Plan 60-61	End of Third Plan 65-66	End of Annual Plan 68-69	End of Plan 73-74*
	Percentage of CD at current market prices						
1.	Gross Capital formation	10.0	14.3	16.9	18.2	15.4	20.0
2.	Gross Domestic Saving	10.2	13.9	13.5	15.6	14.1	19.3
	Share in Domestic Saving						
3.	Household Saving **	10.0	15.3	19.1	31.1	20.5	28.3
4.	Public Sector Saving	18.9	10.6	23.3	23.1	17.3	12.9
5.	Private Corporate Cooperative Saving	6.8	6.2	8.8	3.9	2.6	5.7

Note: * For terminal year of the Fifth Plan.

** In financial assets other than currency and claims on the government.

Source: Sixth Five Year Plan (1980-85), p. 11.

Further, an important constraint on economic development in India is the incapability of the state apparatus and the ruling coalition of classes to eradicate rural poverty and expand domestic market for consumption of products. The Sixth Five Year Plan admits: "The land reform programme is by no means complete and has to be pursued further if we are to tackle effectively the problems of poverty and inequality."[4] The distribution of ownership of land is completely distorted in India and small and marginal farmers who constitute over 70 per cent of the landowners operate barely 24 per cent of the land.

The Plan states that the principal productive asset in rural areas in land which in 1976-77 was distributed is shown in Table 2.3.

Table 2.3: Distribution of Land (Percentage)

Sl. No.	Operational Holdings of	Number	Area Operated
1.	Less than 2 hectares	72.6	23.5
2.	2-10 hectares	24.4	50.2
3.	Over 10 hectares	3.0	26.3

Source: Sixth Five Year Plan, p. 8.

It has been repeatedly maintained that "the distribution of operational holdings thus" constitutes to be very unequal with a small number of relatively large holdings accounting for nearly 60 per cent of total land"[5]

It is further estimated that all kinds of agricultural labour households, *which are the hard core of the rural poor,* constituted 63.7 per cent of all rural households in 1974-75 compared to 55.3 per cent a decade earlier.

Distribution of property in a society determines the role state can play in regulating social relations. With the growth of urban monopoly houses with assets of Birlas and Tatas having increased to Rs. 18,00 crore each, and with a small number of relatively large holdings accounting for nearly 60 per cent of total land makes the ruling classes more powerful and they use state power to consolidate their existing status and for further growth.[6]

State, Capitalist Classes and Imperialism

The struggle for freedom from the British rule was an opportunity perceived by the capitalist classes to exercise full control over the Indian market. The negotiated transfer of power in 1947 established the control of the Indian state and the capitalist classes over the domestic market which was to be jealously protected against imperialist penetrations. But this goal could not be achieved smoothly. Hence during the first thirty-six years of independence we witnessed many struggles by India against imperialism and also many compromises had been made by Indian capitalist classes with imperialism. The Indian state and the capitalist classes have taken many steps forward against imperialism and they have also taken many steps backward in compromising with imperialism.

The Indian state has not allowed military bases to the imperialists and it has refused to be integrated in the strategic security arrangements of the imperialists. On the one hand the Indian capitalists have established their control over the national market of India, on the other, it has permitted foreign investors, transnational corporations and imperialist institutions like the World Bank and the International Monetary Fund to operate in India. It must be emphasised that India has not followed a complete open-door policy to welcome the imperialist economic interests to operate in this country. But gradually the situation has been allowed to develop in which the imperialists have gained enough foothold in India. The five-billion dollar loan from the IMF is a high watermark of such a development, and more than 7,000 technological collaborations, with or without equity participation, have opened

India to the pressures of imperialism. Under the IMF pressures, India has liberalized imports and 'deregulated' its economy for foreign investors.

To sum, up, the above discussion is focussed on the role of the Indian State in building capitalism and the complexity of tasks it has performed to achieve these goals. This path of capitalist development has created its crises and contradictions and issues which need to be examined. These are:

(a) What is the capacity of the Indian state and capitalist classes to maintain their anti-imperialist role in the context of emerging crises of capitalist development?

(b) What is the capacity of the Indian state and capitalist classes to earn their legitimacy through democratic methods in the phase of crises of capitalism?

(c) How far coercive instruments of state power especially paramilitary organisations and the army get involved in resolving emerging crises of capitalist development?

The strength and weaknesses of the Indian state and the capitalist classes would determine the path that democracy and secularism take in the country. During the struggle for freedom, the Indian capitalist class showed both its confrontationist and compromising features. This basic character of the capitalist classes has persisted during the last thirty-five years. Indian capitalism emerged under the shadow of imperialism. The history of origin of the Indian capitalist class, its ideological, political and economic struggle is different from that of the British or French bourgeoisie. The colonial setting is basic to the understanding of struggles and compromises undertaken by the Indian capitalist classes and the stages of its formation are specific to understand its strength and weaknesses. A class is formed in struggles and the level of its consciousness shows its strength. The Indian capitalist classes and the national movement were anti-imperialists but in this struggle it made compromises with caste and communal forces. A fighting and compromising class and its capacity to respond to challenges and crises poses complex questions because deductive method though helpful has serious limitations.

A tentative suggestion can be made that anti-imperialism, democracy and secularism, which are the essential features of a progressive society are all under strain and many contradictory features have emerged and the struggle between the positive and negative features of the Indian society are already being waged. Thus the future of the Indian state would be resolved in the manner in which revolutionary parties of the working classes grapple with the situation.

The process of capitalist development during the last thirty-six years has shown deceleration of industrial growth especially after 1966-67, the near-crisis of demand generation for industrial goods in the rural areas during the 70's; the emergence of inter-sectoral problems in economic development because of diversion of resources for defence expenditure; and in such a crisis in the domestic market, the role of international capitalism is increasing as dramatised by the IMF loan. The crisis of economy is the result of the correlation of class forces represented by the Indian state, but economic crisis also leads to serious crisis in the functioning of the state. Attention should be focussed on the interaction between politics and economy and its consequences for the Indian state, the capitalist class and the whole society.

REFERENCES

1. Postislav Ulyanovsky, *Present-Day Problems in Asia and Africa: Theory, Politics, Personalities* (Moscow: Progress Publishers, 1980), p. 94.
2. Marx, Engels, *Pre-Capitalist Socio-Economic Formations: A Collection* (Moscow: Progress Publishers, 1979), p. 101, quoted by Ulyanovsky, Ibid., p.136
3. S.A.A. Pinto, "Long-Term Loan Securities", *The Economic Times* (Delhi, 10 October 1981), p. iv.
4. Sixth Five Year Plan, p. 9
5. *Economic and Political Weekly* (Bombay, 26 September 1981), p. A-77.
6. See also C.P. Bhambhri, "Classes and Politics", *Patriot* (New Delhi, 14, 15, 16 July 1981).

4

Constitutional Democratic State of India: A Critique

Formal, Legal and institutional arrangements for the governance of India have been laid down in great details by the Constitution of India. The philosophy and legality underlying the Constitution establishes a democratic, federal, secular and welfare State in India. Carl J. Friedrich, in his classic *Constitutional Government and Democracy*, observes:

> Constitutionalism by dividing power provides a system of effective restraints upon governmental action. For studying it, one has to explore the methods and techniques by which such restraints are established and maintained. Putting it in another, more familiar, but less exact way, it is a body of rules ensuring fairplay, thus rendering the government 'responsible'.[1]

The constitutional democratic State of India is the best example of Friedrich's picture of constitutionalism. The Indian Constitution has provided for complex web of checks and balances to ensure 'accountability' and 'responsibility' of every public institution and public functionary. Parliamentary democratic State ensures accountability of the political executive and competitive politics and periodical elections, on the basis of universal adult franchise, are meant to ensure *popular* control over the political executive. The political executive is dependent on the verdict of the voters and it has to abide by the decisions of the independent Supreme Court which is the *Guarantor* of the Constitution and the Rule of Law.

R.M. MacIver, in his classic, *The Modern State*, observes that "Representative government distinguishes the modern State from all others".[2]

The Indian Constitution makers established a 'modern State' by evolving a scheme of representative government at the Centre, the State and the local levels in a federal country and MacIver's essential principle, like Friedrich's, is fully contained in the Indian Constitution.

Further, modern Marxist and Liberal Democratic Theories demand a few new things from the modern States at the close of the twentieth century. The liberal theorists evaluate a Constitutional Democratic State on the basis of the effectiveness of the institutions of the State to protect and promote *individual rights and justice.* The State is a means to an end. The development of a liberated individual is the goal of all social institutions, including the State and autonomous civil society is an essential condition for promotion of individual personality and potentialities. Edward Shils elaborates on this theme of homogenisation of the individual and local communities by the power of the Centre which is a threat to the peripheries. Shils observes:

> The growth of national societies, of national and international intellectual and professional communities, of ethnic communities—all of these have grown at the cost of local communities. The primacy of kinship, as a criterion on the basis of which solidarity was formed, has receded. The attachment to locality has been attenuated by the extension of attachment to larger territories, to provincial or national territories. There are even instances where attachment to national territories has become very ineffectual and attachment to transnational territories and to humanity beyond kinship, ethnicity and nationality.[3]

The constitutional democratic State of India operates under the limitations of Part III of the Constitution which provides for Fundamental Rights for individuals which protect not only the political rights but also cultural rights of every citizen of India, including the minorities. The Supreme Court of India, as a guardian of the constitutional democracy, is a watchdog of Fundamental Rights the Indian citizens. The concept of individual rights has expanded in the Western Liberal Democratic theory where good governance depends on deference to Human Rights of the citizens. Durga Das Basu observes: The ambit of the freedom of religion guaranteed by Articles 25 and 26 has been widened by the judicial interpretation that what is guaranteed by Articles 25 and 26 is the right of the *individual* to practise and propagate not only matters of faith or belief but also those rituals and observances which are regarded as integral parts of religion by the followers of its doctrine."[4]

Thus, the greatest human right of Indians, in a highly religious society, which also happens to be home of all major religions and belief systems of the world, has been fully guaranteed by the constitutional democratic State of India and Durga Das Basu observes: "The sum total of the above provisions make our State more secular than even the United States of America."[5]

Secularism in India is a necessary but not a sufficient condition for the modern liberal theorists to accept that individual citizen in India has enough freedom to develop his own potential.

Stephen Macedo in *Capitalism, Citizenship and Community* states that "The authors of *Habits of the Heart* (Robert N. Bellah, Richard Madsen, William M. Sullivan, Ann Swindler, and Steven M. Tripton) charge that America is losing the institutions that help to create the kind of person who could sustain a connection to a wider political community and thus ultimately support the maintenance of free institutions.[6] If the home of liberal democracy is castigated for crippling individual rights, liberal democrats cannot fully accept that the Indian State protects preserves and promotes Human Rights. Stephen Macedo's own position is "Liberals who take Tocqueville seriously should be concerned about people's connections with larger wholes than sustain their allegiance while supporting their individuality, their liberty, and their capacity for self-government. It is not enough to hold out a vision of selfless social harmony that is incapable of attracting the energetic support of people as we know them".[7]

The yardstick of the Western democratic liberals is freedom for the individuals and the nature of the State. Every democratic and constitutional State will be scrutinised on the basis of its Human Rights record and India cannot be an exception to this rule. The critique of Indian State by the Indian liberals is on the basis of the actual practice of the institutions of the State in dealing with the issues of individual rights and justice.

The European Marxist writers, like Ralph Miliband and N. Poulantzas from 1970s and early 1980s, drew their inspiration from Italian communist philosopher Gramsci and they have maintained that the capitalist State has ideological apparatuses and administrative coercive apparatuses to govern for the extraction of surplus value. Every capitalist State hegemonises on the basis of its ideology and the citizens are conditioned to view the capitalist State as 'legitimate'. "A critique of State emerges only when we concentrate on the issues of State hegemony, legitimacy and the role of the apparatuses of the State[8]."

The sum and substance of the discussion in the preceding paras is that the formal, legal and institutional structure of the democratic, pluralist, federal and welfare constitutional State of India is a framework which is based on normative and many ethical principles with emphasis on legality which takes care of political and social morality. But the actual practice of the constitutional State of India cannot be understood without focusing attention on some real processes of politics which seem to be contrary to the images of the Constitution makers.

It was the explicit and the implicit premise of the Constitution makers that universal adult franchise with regular elections will make a highly apathetic and apolitical society quite politicised and socially assertive. Constitutional democratic State of India has ten elections to the Lower House of the Indian Parliament and regular elections for the State Assemblies and by 73rd Amendment of the Constitution, regular elections for the local self-governing institutions have been made legally compulsory. A democratic State gains in legitimacy where people participate in governance through regular elections and hold the political executive accountable and 'responsible' to use the concept of Friedrich and Maciver. For Marxists, if a State has strong legitimacy, its capacities to hegemonise its citizens increased and the coercive apparatuses of the State are not employed in a ruthless manner to deal with people's protests and struggles. Similarly, the Western liberal democrats concede that States with strong democratic and electoral legitimacy are relatively better in protecting Human Rights than the States which have weak democrats legitimacy. The democratic legitimacy of the Indian State has been seriously questioned by the liberals and the Marxists. The liberals in India have maintained that the election process is completely vitiated and rigged. The glowing corruption of the electoral process has eroded the legitimacy of the democratic and constitutional State of India. The Indian political class is manufacturing electoral legitimacy through completely unfair electoral practices. The constitutional democratic State of India has lost its moral foundations because it is based on manipulated and rigged electoral process. The pillar of democratic and constitutional State of India is people's vote and this pillar lies in shambles. If elections have become illegitimate, if Indian democratic, federal and constitutional State is also illegitimate, the philosophy of the Constitution makers has met with its Waterloo because of the actual practice of Indian electoral process.

The Marxists and many socially 'marginal' groups who are at the 'periphery' of the society maintain that the democratic State of India has been derailed because instead of 'negotiation' with the deprived groups on demands, it has become confrontational State. The Constitution makers laid down the legal framework for 'accommodation' of demands of the labouring classes and cultural minority groups. It was expected that during the last 47 years this process of political accommodation will get strengthened. Unfortunately failure to accommodate has led to a situation where politics of coercion as concretised by the bureaucratic and police apparatuses of the Indian State has emerged more significant than the politics of accommodation. This trend of suppression of emerging social assertions has been growing and the Indian State had to enact the Terrorist and Disruptive Activities (Prevention) Act (TADA) of 1985. Not only this, the traditional police and paramilitary forces, like the Border Security Force, the Central Reserve Police Force and Armed Police Force of every State Government has expanded in numbers and their budgetary allocations have increased astronomically. Further, new forces like the Rapid Action Force and 30 battalions of the Rashtriya Rifles, a new para-military arm under the Army Command, has been created in 1994. The reason for the establishment of new Rashtriya Rifles is that the army in India is over-stretched in maintaining domestic civil law and order. An Army Officer makes a telling comment on the creation of the Rashtriya Rifles as follows: "At present some of our boys on internal security duties are not even managing one night's rest in a week."[9] India is *witnessing growing politicisation along with policisation of the society.*

Explanations for the Weakening of Constitutional Democratic State

Rajni Kothari, who has combined positions of superstructural analysis in *Politics in India*[10] with philosophical anarchist perspective in *State Against Democracy: In Search of Human Governance*,[11] has explained that the crisis of the constitutional State in India is post-Nehruvian because the institutions for governance have been delegitimised and destroyed. If this is the explanation, then institutions for governance should be reformed and restored back to their strength. Political executive, bureaucracy, judiciary, Indian federalism and all democratic institutions have been completely weakened, and in Kothari's analysis "restoration of democratic institutions is the need of the hour. In his philosophical-anarchist mould, Rajni Kothari observes that the model of Indian economic and political development has led to the disenfranchisement of the tribals and the cultural minority groups of India and it has led to peripheralisation of the majority of the people. The Indian State has lost its legitimacy because the peripheral social groups have not been *empowered* to use Amartya Sen's concept of Empowerment. Amartya Sen has suggested that if India can spend more resources on education, health and implement land reforms, democratic strength of India can be restored.

Marxist critique of the constitutional democratic State of India is based on historical materialism and political economy approach. Many streams of Marxist critique have emerged during the last 47 years. First, India has a very 'skewed[7] market and the absolute majority of the people do not have purchasing power. This is a serious constraint on the political economy of the Indian State and unless purchasing power is created by involving the labour classes in the productive process of India, the Indian State will remain externally and internally vulnerable. It is a vulnerable State because it has a very narrow social base because of the type of capitalist path of development followed by it.[12]

India can resolve its multi-dimensional crises if it can tackle 'demand constraint' by deepening and broadening the Indian market. The Indian State is in the danger of losing its sovereignty to global capitalism if it does not address itself to the problems of rural India and the deprivations of the working classes. Second, a Marxist critique is rooted in the history of State formation in India. The democratic and constitutional State of India has emerged out of a very powerful anti-colonial Third World nationalism, but it is a State in the process of formation and it is a *weak State,* The essence of this State is weaker ideological hegemony, weak political legitimacy and fragmented and fractionalised State institutions for governance. This phenomenon needs explanation.[13]

India is a multi-structural society where the Indian State is building modern capitalism and modern institutions for governance on the basis of social relations and values which belong to the past. The present India is haunted by the legacies of the past, like caste, community, territoriality and social exclusivity of superior-subordinate cultural hierarchies. The Indian State does not have ideological hegemony because India is involved in a basic struggle to fight against the hangovers of the traditional identities with the values of egalitarianism, secularism and democracy of the modern State system. This social and cultural struggle is fundamental and it has complex political manifestations. If on the one hand, the modern Indian State is crippled by the hangovers of the appeals of the historical past, on the other, economic development of India is based on class differentials, regional differentials, rural-urban disparities, rich States and backward States conflicts and the global pressures of the New World Political and Economic Order. The leader of the New World Order sees India as a 'market' and it demands from the Indian State maintenance of standards of Western values of governance. This aspect of external dimensions of the Indian State cannot be ignored because in the present inter-dependent and highly stratified global power relations, the Indian State will have to respond to subtle and sometimes open pressures of the aid-giving countries. It is not only the ideological hegemony of the Indian State which is weak because of the conflicts between the continuing power of the past historical consciousness and the emerging trends of modernisation. Such a conflict between the inherited loyalties of the past and the weak rising forces of modernisation leads to weakening of the democratic legitimacy of the State. The political class has defamed and derailed the electoral process, and the fractions and fragments of the political class have intensified caste, and community, region and religious divisions to create a political constituency for winning elections. In the process, every political party has become weak and sectionalised.[14]

How can Indian political executive and bureaucratic institutions gain democratic strength when elections have become contest of sectarianism? Political leaders have intensified sectarian violent conflicts and it requires regular intervention and involvement of the para-military forces in the routine governance of India. Facts speak for themselves. The Indian Lower House of the Parliament was informed on August 25, 1994 that the expenditure on the Border Security Force has been increasing every successive year since 1991 and it has reached a high level of Rs. 949.13 crore of 1993-94. The annual expenditure on the BSF for 1991-92 was Rs. 719.24 crore and for 1992-93 it was Rs. 80.52 crore.[15]

Conclusion

It may be mentioned that if politics and elections are reformed along with the reform of bureaucracy and judiciary governance of India will be according to the *spirit* and not to the *letter* of the Indian Constitution. While 'reforming the institutions' is a necessary condition for governance of the country, it is not a sufficient condition to deal with the multidimensional crises of the Constitutional democratic State of India. If politicisation of India is a positive sign of democratization of Indian society the growing policisation is a sign of growing social discontent in the country. India is involved in a dialectical process of conflict between the positive and the negative as reflected in the demoralisation of society as well as policisation of the country.[16] Many post-Marxists, who believe in class politics, and liberal democrats have drawn our attention to *the autonomy of the political.* Without going into the details of the relative autonomy of the State, it will suffice to say that if sectarianism of politics is continued unchecked the State apparatus will become captive for, by and of the dominant sectarian groups. Such a process is at work in India which is reflected in caste *versus* caste, community *versus* community, region *versus* region and tribe *versus* tribe politics.[17] In such a situation, relative autonomy of the State becomes a distant dream.

REFERENCES

1. Carl J. Friedrich, *Constitutional Government and Democracy,* New Delhi, Oxford and IBH, (Revised Edn.), 1966 p. 26.
2. R.M. MacIver, *The Modern State,* London, Oxford University Press, (reprint) 1966, p. 141.
3. Edward Shils, "The Cultural of Local Communities", in *Regional Diversity in Europe: Role of Different Cultures in the Construction of the European Union,* Toronto, October 1, 1993, p. 133.
4. Durga Das Basu, *Introduction to the Constitution of India,* New Delhi, Prentice Hall of India, (15th ed.), 1993, p. 112.
5. *Ibid.,* p. 115.
6. Stephen Macedo, *Capitalism, Citizenship and Community,* London 1993.
7. Ellen Frankel Paul *et al.* (eds.), *Capitalism,* Oxford, Basil Blackwell, 1989, pp. 138-39.
8. A. Gramsci, *Selections from the Prison Notebooks,* London, Lawrence and Wishart, 1971; also see N. Poulantzas, *State, Power, Socialism,* London, Verso (Translated P. Camiller), 1980.
9. Manoj Joshi, "Rashtriya Rifles Battalions to Ease Army's Burden", New Delhi, *The Times of India,* August 11, 1994, p. 5
10. Rajni Kothari, *Politics in India,* New Delhi, Orient Longman, 1970.
11. Rajni Kothari, *State Against Democracy: In Search of Human Governance,* Delhi, Ajanta, 1988.
12. For different interpretation, see Deepak Nayyar (ed.), *Industrial Growth and Strength: The Debate in India,* Bombay, Sameeksha Trust, 1993.
13. See C.P. Bhambhri, *Politics in India: 1947-1987,* New Delhi, Vikas, 1988; *Political Process in India: 1947-1991,* Delhi, Vikas, 1992; *Politics in India: 1991-1992,* Delhi, Shipra, 1992; *Politics in India: 1992-1993,* Delhi, Shipra, 1993; and *Indian Politics Since Independence,* Delhi, Shipra, 1994.
14. See C.P. Bhambhri, *Elections 1991: An Analysis,* Delhi, D.K. Publishers, 1991.
15. "Answer to the Lok Sabha", *The Times of India,* Delhi, August 26, 1994, p. 5.
16. T.V. Sathya Murthy (ed.), *State and Nation in the Context of Social Change,* Vol. I, Oxford, Oxford University Press, 1994.
17. See for Marxist complex discussion on politics, Etienne Balibar, *Masses, Classes, Ideas: Studies on Politics and Philosophy Before and After Marx* (translated by James Swenson), New York and London, Routledge, 1993.

5

Indian State, Social Classes and Secularism

The demolition of the Babri Masjid at Ayodhya on December 6, 1992 has again revealed the serious weaknesses and vulnerabilities of the Indian State to protect and promote its own values and commitments to democracy and secularism. A deeper analysis is required to understand and explain the emergence of militant and violent communalism of the Hindus, Muslims and Sikhs during the 1980s in India. A secular State in a multi-religious society is confronted by militant religious assertions and identities by all the major religious communities in the country. A secular State becomes very vulnerable if the major religious communities asserting their separate religious identities and social order faces militant religious confrontations. The events of the 1980s have clearly established that India has a weak secular State and the State is involved in a basic struggle to defend secularism in the face of emerging militant religious assertions in society. Further, the developments of the 1980s clearly establish a need for an examination of the relationships between the Indian State and complex and contradictory social forces and processes which have generated social conflicts on the basis of competing identities. Indian society and State are a product of a long historical process and it is imperative to focus attention on the historical forces which are at work in India. Marx had observed about the mid-nineteenth century that:

> We, like all the rest of Continental Europe, suffer not only from the development of capitalist production, but also from the incompleteness of that development. Alongside of modern evils, a whole series of inherited evils oppress us, arising from the passive survival of antiquated modes of production, with their inevitable train of social and political anachronism. We suffer not only from the living, but from the dead.[1]

Every significant social explanation about Indian society and State emerges from the above-mentioned observation of Karl Marx. First, India has a long history and the settled society witnessed many State systems and the contemporary State of India is the inheritor of all preceding major State systems especially the Hindu imperial States, the Mughal State and the British Colonial

State. Every successor State system in India inherited and continued with some significant features and elements of the preceding State systems and the Indian State system is built on *continuity and change.* Thus the history of India is an integral part of Indian society and State. Second, this long evolution of Indian history is closely linked with the emergence of the different modes of production from tribal to feudal, to capitalism. The crises and contradictions of the various modes of production were resolved under specific historical developments of India. The feudal and capitalist modes of production have very significant Indian specificities because of the specific epochs of Indian history. Third, social relations, cultural values, belief systems and superstructural arrangements for managing the Indian society are also a product of long evolution of Indian history and many belief systems and social values have persisted for a long period in Indian society. Many essential value systems of Indian society were consolidated and strengthened and some other values were weakened and destroyed in the process of long historical evolution of India. But the values which have persisted are an integral part of the making of the contemporary Indian society. And these inherited social values, institutions and arrangements which determine social relations are in serious conflict with the modern values of democracy, secularism, social equality, scientific rationality and humanistic tolerance. Since history is an integral part of Indian political process, a brief discussion of Indian historical development may be mentioned here to properly understand the crisis of modern secular and democratic State of India.

D.D. Kosambi maintains that when India developed from 'tribe' to 'society', it was 'bogged down in the filthy swamp of superstition'. And 'superstition reduced the need for violence'.[2]

The pillars of Vedic-Brahman caste society were (a) superstition, (b) self-sustaining and close-knit village community, (c) caste system, and (d) religion, ritual and superstition According to Kosambi, "The cause of evolution has left its clear, indelible mark upon the complex Indian society of today".[3] An uninterrupted feature of Indian society is the persistence of religiously sanctioned rituals and norms of behaviour and social conduct.[4]

This long persistence of caste, ritualised and superstition-based religion in India was facilitated by a system of 'feudalism from above' which later on became 'feudalism from below' and this process helped in the evolution of the feudal State where 'feudalism from above' means a State wherein an emperor or powerful king levied tribute from subordinates who still ruled in their own right and did what they liked within their own territories—as long as they paid the paramount ruler. What is meant by feudalism 'from below' follows . . . where a class of land-owners developed within the village, between the State and the peasantry, regularly to wield armed power over the local population.[5]

Thus the Hindu feudal system of the Gupta and Harsha Imperial State systems, when shaken by the Muslim invasions and mediaeval Muslim State systems shook the Indian society, neither the Hindu belief systems were completely weakened and destroyed by the Mughal State nor the Hindu and Mughal rulers could stand against the powerful attack of the British over India. The gradual expansion of the British rule over India with a decisive battle of Plassey in 1757 and the decisive defeat of the Indian opposition to the British rule in 1857 established complete control of the colonial State over India. The meaning of British conquest of India is quite significant for understanding the problems of contemporary Indian State.

It is not only that the declining and decaying Mughal State could not stand against the onslaughts of the British military power, the British rulers also brought an advanced 'mode of production' for the Indian society. Karl Marx observes that:

> In all cases of conquest, three things are possible. The conquering people subjugates the conquered under its own mode of production (*e.g.* the English in Ireland in this century, and partly in India); or it leaves the old mode intact and contents itself with a tribute (*e.g.* Turks and Romans); or a reciprocal interaction takes place whereby something new, a synthesis, arises (the Germanic conquests, in part). In all cases, the mode of production, whether that of the conquering people, that of the conquered, or that emerging from the fusion of both, is decisive for the new distribution which arises.[6]

The above observation of Karl Marx suggests an important approach to situate the impact of the British rule over India. Since the bourgeois civilization is the most advanced form of civilization till the emergence of the socialist civilization, India was brought under the control of the most advanced form of civilization of the whole nineteenth century and till the middle of the twentieth century. Since the basic goal of the colonial rule over India was to exploit the whole Indian society, the British established a very powerful 'rent-seeking' colonial State and bureaucracy in India. The colonial State in India established many mechanisms of extracting social surplus from India and for this purpose, the British created a very complex system of *'landlordism'* in the country. If, on the one hand, the British created a system of land revenue collection on the basis of 'landlordism', on the other, the colonial capital controlled plantation, mines and industry in India. The colonial State followed industrial, fiscal, monetary and regulatory policies which were preferential for the British capital and discriminatory against the emerging indigenous Indian capitalist class. The Indian capitalist class emerged during the last decades of the nineteenth century and during the twentieth century but the emerging indigenous capitalist class was always involved in contest and struggle against the British colonial State which always protected, promoted and showed preferential treatment to the British capital in India. This contest between the 'protected' British capital and the 'discriminated' Indian capital was revealed many a time. If the British planters founded the Indian Tea Association in 1881, the Indians founded the 'Indian Tea Planters' Association. If the British Associated Chambers of Commerce and Industry was founded in

1920, the nationalist Indian capitalist class established the Federation of Indian Chamber of Commerce and Industry in 1927. Walchand Hirachand observed in the 1930s that:

> It is hardly possible to write with restraint on the treatment which Indian shipping has received from its own government.[7]

J.R.D. Tata, while addressing an audience in London in May 1945, observed that:

> There might have been isolated cases of expansion, but on the whole, when armament factories and other specialised industries connected with the war have been excluded, there has been none.[8]

G.D. Birla writing in 1953 *In the Shadow of the Mahatma* observes that:

> When I was sixteen, I started an independent business of mine as a broker, and thus began my contact with Englishmen, who were my patrons and clients. During my association with them, I began to see their superiority in business methods, their organising capacity and their many other virtues. But their racial arrogance could not be concealed. I was not allowed to use the lift to go upto their office, nor their benches while waiting to see them. I smarted under these insults, and this created within me a political interest which, from 1912 until today, I have fully maintained".[9]

The process of class formation is historically conditioned and the British colonial rule played a crucial role in determining the levels of class consciousness of the emerging bourgeoisie of India. Further, the British rulers followed complex social, political and administrative policies to rule over India for achieving their basic goal of exploitation of the whole Indian society. The British established a very powerful colonial bureaucracy and a uniform Indian Penal Code, the Criminal Procedure Code and the Indian Evidence Act for the governance of India. Since Indian social relationships were very complex, the British showed an immense cleverness and caution in dealing with established social norms and traditions of the heterogeneous and complex Indian society. Moreover, the Ghost of 1857 War always haunted the British in India and they did not want a Repetition of such a large scale revolt against their rule. The cautious social policies of the British rulers resulted in the continuation of religion, superstition, rituals and caste system in Modern India, and the cleverness of British politics was reflected in Divide and Rule especially with reference to Hindus and Muslims. The British rulers in India feared the Muslims because of the events of 1857 and because of the *'Wahabi'* frontier wars and conspiracies of the 1860s and its anti-British approach of the 1870s. The British rulers also feared the pan-Islamic sentiments of the Indian Muslims and thus till the end of the nineteenth century, the British followed policies of hostility towards the Muslims. Further, two religious communities in India were also acquiring confrontational approaches and attitude. Sumit further observes that: "But 'Communalism' proper was also acquiring, for the first time in the 1880s and 90s something like an all India dimension".[10]

The twentieth century India began its political journey with the emergence of Hindu and Muslim communalism, on the one hand, and all-India 'non-sectarian' nationalism, on the other. Sumit Sarkar asserts that:

> Yet British responsibility for the encouragement of communal separatism remains an undeniable fact.[11]

Sumit Sarkar mentions that Agha Khan while organizing the Muslim league assured Dunlop Smith on behalf of the Muslim leaders in October 1906 that the Muslim leadership will not move 'in any matter before first finding out if the step to be taken has the full approval of Government privately....'[12]

Similarly, the Hindu communalists through the Maharaja of Darbhanga had declared that 'with the Hindus loyalty or *Rajbhakti* is an element of religion'.[13]

Thus Hindu and Muslim communalism continued to remain pro-British till the Transfer of Power on August 15, 1947, the Indian National Congress remained the major platform of anti-colonial nationalism. The anti-colonial struggle was broad-based under Gandhian leadership and a multi-religious, multi-lingual, multi-class and multiethnic democratic platform was consolidated to confront the British colonial rulers.

Gandhian leadership of anti-colonial national movement brought peasantry in a big way to strengthen and broaden the social base of Indian nationalism. India witnessed national radicalisation during the Quit India Movement of 1942 and national and social radicalisation during *Tebhaga* peasant struggle in Bengal, the Telengana peasant struggle in Hyderabad State, the mutiny of R.I.N, ratings in 1946 and the INA Trials. India during 1945 to 1947 was qualitatively different. While on the one hand, nationalist and social forces had launched their offensive against the British rule, on the other, India was plunged in 'communal holocaust' and the worst riots took place in Calcutta, Noakhali, Bihar and Punjab. The Direct Action Day of the Muslim League started riots in Calcutta, and they spread like wild fire in other parts of India. Every major community was infected by aggressive communal feelings and the policy of *'Divide and Rule'* ended with the policy of *'Divide and Quit'*. India was partitioned on communal consideration and the new State of India emerged on August 15, 1947 as a result of *'non-sectarian'* anti-colonial nationalism.

The essence of Indian independence lies in many historical continuities and changes of a fundamental nature. First, the Independence of India is a qualitative break with the past because the British colonial rule ended due to the anti-colonial struggle of the Indians. Freedom of India was not a gift of the retreating and declining British imperialist power, it was won by the struggle and sacrifices made by the Indians. Second, the bourgeois democratic revolution of India consisted of nationalist and anti-colonial bourgeoisie, patriotic and anti-feudal and anti-landlord peasantry, and modern, democratic, secular and patriotic nationalist leadership of India. Since social dialectics always reveals contradictory features revealing the unity of opposites, a few other specific features of *'continuity'* of India may be mentioned to understand and appreciate the *'inherited'* social situation on the eve of Indian independence. First, like all anti-colonial Third World nationalisms, India inherited an 'underdeveloped' and highly distorted economy because of colonial exploitation. Every indicator of agricultural and industrial underdevelopment and backwardness of economy was prevalent in India on August 15, 1947. Along with low growth levels of the economy, India inherited an archaic and highly complex agrarian arrangements created by the colonial rulers to exploit Indian agriculture. Peasantry had to be liberated from the feudal and absentee landlords and the tenants and the share-croppers had to be provided tenurial security and legal protections against exploitation by the vested interests. Second, India also inherited archaic pre-capitalist and pre-modern social belief systems based on caste, superstition, ritualism and religion. Third, the levels of social and class consciousness of Indians were conditioned by a differentiated process where some of the modern belief systems and values were very thinly distributed among the classes and strata of society and the dominant belief system was traditional and linked with the past.

The social classes and the Indian State emerged on the eve of Independence with this baggage of history of nationalism, modernism, underdevelopment and social hegemony of traditionalism. The bourgeois democratic revolution in India clearly reveals its positive and negative features and the Indian State and the social classes have been involved during the last forty-seven years to grapple with the problems of *transition* in which lot of inherited baggage of history has to be gradually weakened and destroyed and the foundations of a modern, secular democratic and federal State have to be strengthened and consolidated. A very important task of the Indian State and the social classes during this phase of transition is to transform the material foundations of society for changing not only the social relations of production but also for changing the social values of society on the basis of democratic equality and secularism.

It has been mentioned earlier that the British colonial rule over India laid down the foundations of the capitalist mode of production with all its limitations and deformities because of the specific colonial setting of India, in the process of the development of Indian variant of capitalism, emerged the Indian capitalist class during the colonial rule. The dominant tendency of this class was *'nationalist* and it actively supported the anti-colonial national movement of India. The Indian capitalist class also recognised its limitations and in the Bombay Plan of 1944, the leaders of Indian industry, clearly recognised that the Indian State will play an *active* role in the economic development of post-independence India. Thus the Indian State and the leading classes had convergence of opinion in the *activist* role of the State in transforming the economy and social relations in India. The State launched many programmes for the capitalist development of India. India witnessed the launching of the system of economic planning and the programme of land reforms to break the structures of inherited underdevelopment of the country. The emphasis of the Indian State was on building a relatively self-reliant capitalism on the basis of economic planning, and commanding heights for the State sector. This mode of State-capitalist development also strengthened the relative autonomy of the Indian State in global matters and this model provided strength to the Indian State to follow the policy of 'non-alignment' in world affairs.[14]

The foreign policy of 'non-alignment' was an assertion of Indian nationalism in world affairs but its domestic strength was provided by the model of economic planning which was based on relatively self-reliant State capitalism. The Laws of Motion of capitalist development of India were energised by the institutional arrangements created by the State in the field of science, technology and public financial institutions. India established a whole network of public financial institutions to mobilise savings and resources for capitalist development. The Industrial Finance Corporation of India, the Industrial Development Bank of India, the Unit Trust of India, the General Insurance Corporation of India, the Life Insurance Corporation of India, the Industrial Credit and Investment Corporation of India, the National Bank for Agricultural and Rural Development, the Export-Import Bank of India, the Securities and Exchange Board of India, the nationalized banks like the State Bank of India are all controlled by the Indian State to support the development of State capitalism in the country. The Indian State has established scientific and research laboratories, institutes of technology and agricultural universities to undertake research and development activities and also train highly skilled scientific personnel for the requirements of modern industrial and agricultural economy of the country. The Indian State is the prime mover in the development of the material forces of production for capitalistic development.

In a primarily agrarian country, agrarian reforms are a pre-requisite for economic development and social change. The State governments in India legislated various land reforms measures after independence and the absentee landlords were abolished. The contents and implementation of Land Reform legislations varied from State to State depending on the local power of the rural landlords. After forty years of independence, India's agrarian structure shows following major characteristics. First, according to the census of 1992, 545.93 million people are engaged in agricultural operations. Second, during the 1990s 150 million are agricultural workers in India and the absolute majority of them are still in debt from *'womb to tomb'*.

The National Commission on Rural Labour and the sub-committee of the Parliamentary Committee of the Labour Ministry in 1987 observed that:

> The State enforcement machinery, instead of being sympathetic towards the agricultural workers for the realization of minimum wages, is generally unfriendly.[15]

Third, the landless agricultural workers and the marginal farmers are involved either in a struggle for the payment of minimum wages or for the implementation of land reforms or for both the goals in different parts of the country. Next, in the Green Revolution area the 'rich capitalist farmer' has emerged in India and has marketable surpluses because he is involved in commodity production. The land reforms have replaced the traditional landlords by the intermediate castes who are the beneficiaries of the land reforms. These 'Other Backward Caste' peasants have economic power and they are also influenced by the 'feudal ethos' of caste domination and discrimination against the *Sudras* who are landless agricultural workers.

The agrarian power structure has its own dialectics and domination and exploitation is the social reality of agrariarn India. Indian agriculture has been linked with modern industry, the national market and the 'surplus producing peasantry' has emerged as a very powerful mainstay of the institution of private property in rural India. In spite of changes in rural economy, rural tyranny on he basis of castes or gender differences has not come to an end. The Indian peasantry is an integral part of capitalist market economy of the country, its social orientations and values are authoritarian, undemocratic and backward looking. The rural oligrachy uses modern inputs of production, but it is a thousand miles away from the modern values of democratic equality and Secularism.

A few significant questions about the *class orientations* of the Indian capitalist class and the surplus producing peasantry need to be probed to explain the nature of Indian crisis and the role of the Indian State.

The Indian State: Challenges and Tasks

A democratic, secular, modernising capitalist, pluralist and federal State is operating in a specific historical social context of India and the World capitalist system. It must be clearly stated that 'every form of production creates its own legal relations, form of government etc....' All the bourgeois economists are aware of is that production can be carried on better under the modern police than *e.g.*, on the principle of might makes right. They forget only that this principle is also a legal relation, and that the right of the stronger prevails in their 'constitutional republics' as well, only in another form.[16] The State never hangs in the air, it is solidly linked with and founded on property relations and classes in society. Marx recognises the relationship between material foundations of society and legal superstructure of the State, he also recognises that the *State is essential for civil society*. Marx observes that:

> Civil society embraces the whole material intercourse of individuals within a definite stage of the development of productive forces. It embraces the whole commercial and industrial life of a given State and, insofar, transcends the State and the, nation, though, on the other hand again, it must assert itself in its foreign relations as nationality and inwardly must organise itself as State.[17]

Marx also maintains that 'civil society, as such only develops with the bourgeoisie and hence it emerges only in eighteenth century Europe. Marx clearly mentions that the real contradiction is of the bourgeoisie and the proletariat and he clearly observes that:

> Of class the classes that stand face to face with the bourgeoisie today, the proletariat alone is a really revolutionary class. The other classes decay and finally disappear in the face of modern industry; the proletariat is its special and essential product.[18]

While Mao-Ze-Dong's *On Contradiction* and *On Practice* remains Marxist classics, Mao's peasant revolution is a product of historical specificity of China and the revolutionary role of peasantry in India requires a specific analysis on the basis of Marx's own writings and historical specificities of Indian society.

A few specific features of Indian society may be mentioned to analyse the challenges and the tasks before the Indian State.

(1) Sacred and supernatural elements dominate and determine the value system and daily existence of the absolute majority of the Indian society. A democratic and secular State has to deal with a highly religious society where traditions and cultural values are integrally linked with sacred religious texts and scriptures. Holy men and Holy places evolve spontaneous and voluntary respect and regard from the absolute majority of the Indians. The places of the worship, the priestly classes and the supernatural play a vital role in determining levels of human consciousness in India. A minority of the modern and secular segments of society exist and interact with the majority of the religious believers with a view to secularise society and polity to achieve the goals of democratic revolution in India.

It is extremely simplistic to say that religion and its aggressive form of communalism is a 'ruling ideology of the ruling classes in India'. If religion is a ruling class ideology, the democratic forces can use religion for social and democratic struggles. A secular and democratic State of India provides enough space (with all its limitations and distortions) to the advanced forces of the oppressed masses to use the road of religion against the oppressors and the exploiting classes. Why can't a poor Hindu believer be organized against a rich Hindu believer through the idiom of religion by democratic political forces? Temples, Gurudwaras and Mosques are operating as 'State within the State' because the millions of common people hold them sacred places of worship, and the State functionaries earn illegitimacy if they enter the places of worship even for legitimate reasons. A democratic and secular State has to exercise great restraint and constraint while dealing with the religious sentiments of the people and the places of religious worship.

India is a weak democratic and secular State because 'sacred and supernatural' are very powerful factors in Indian society. The 1980s witnessed the emergence of militant religious assertions of a section of Hindus, Muslims and Sikhs. The Blue Star Operation of 1984 made political representatives of the Indian State very cautious in dealing with the religious sentiments and places of worship in the country. During the 1980s and the 1990s, the Indian Government adopted a legal approach to deal with places of worship. The Religious Institutions (Prevention of Misuse) Act, 1988 remains a formal law and the Temples, Mosques like Jama Masjid of Delhi and Hazratabal shrine at Srinagar, the Golden Temple at Amritsar and other Gurudwaras' are openly used by the clergy for political purposes. The Place of Worship Act, 1991 provides a legal guarantee to maintain the religious identity of all historical places of worship but it will not be able to stand against popular and spontaneous religious movement against any place of worship. Political executives in India have adopted many manipulative strategies to deal with the power of clergy. It has adopted the strategy of dividing the clergy. It has allowed the All-India Muslim Personal Law Board to mobilize the traditional *'Qazis'* or religious adjudicators by assuring that the State will not intervene in Muslim Personal Law. The modernising and reformative State of India has adopted an extremely cautious and gradual approach towards social traditions which have religious sanction. The Shah Bano case proves the weakness of the modernising State to push a reform which would alienate a religious community because the clergy enjoy more legitimacy than the democratic, secular and reformist State of India. Hindu, Muslim and Sikh communalists are successful in bringing religion into politics because the ugly side of democratic politics is observable and apparent to every one, but religion does not offer any solution for social problems is not clearly understood by the religious believers who are guided by the teaching of the priests.

(2) The social contradictions of Indian society are also mediated by the historical specificities of India. The dominant mode of production in India is capitalism and the power of the exploiting classes can be challenged only by the united efforts of the exploited working masses of India. Are the Indian exploiting classes and the State confronted with a serious and powerful challenge from the exploited classes? This issue can be analysed by focussing attention on the role of the capitalist classes, the peasantry, the proletariat and the potentialities or limitations of the accommodative capacities of the Indian State.

Mao-Ze-Dong's Peasant Revolution in China inspired many Indian revolutionary struggles beginning with the Telengana Peasant Uprising of the Communist Party of India and many Marxist-Leninist-Maoist groups who discovered revolutionary potential in the Indian peasantry. The armed struggles of the People's War Group in Andhra or Maoist Groups in Bihar or in the tribal areas of Madhya Pradesh and their strategies of 'liberated areas' brings into sharp focus the role of peasantry in India. A few important questions regarding peasantry may be examined for understanding their role in India. It is correct to maintain that the Indian peasantry is internally differentiated but it is premature to conclude from this that the rural oppressors and oppressed are involved in a polarized class struggle. Caste and Community feelings mediate in a very powerful manner in peasant consciousness in India. It is also wrong to maintain that the Indian peasant understands the nature of national contradictions and has evolved a proper class perspective of revolutionary development. The Maoists have a romanticised view of peasant virtues and peasant consciousness. Peasantry in India is not only internally differentiated, it is fragmented on the basis of religion, caste, language, region and sect. The contradictory trends of Indian peasantry have been always observed in their politics and movements. Further, the uneven level of economic development of India has also facilitated the fragmentation of the peasantry. If on the one hand, the struggle in Bihar is for the payment of 'minimum wages and the implementation of Land Reforms and Ceiling Act', on the other, the Bharatiya Kisan Sangh in Gujarat has launched a violent struggle against the high power tariffs levied by the Gujarat Electricity Board. If the Maoist and the People War Group administer 'justice' to the class enemy, the Bharatiya Kisan Sangh launches 'village bandh' and uses force and violence against the State functionaries for protecting its interests.[19] The contradictory approaches of the peasantry have been observed on every crucial national issue. M.D. Nanjundaswamy of the Karnataka Rajya Ryota Sangh is involved in a struggle to *drive out'* the multinationals like Cargill Seeds Limited in Bellary and W.R. Grace Company at Tumkur in Karnataka, Sharad Joshi of the Setkari Sangathan of Maharashtra is involved in an active struggle for the defence of the GATT proposals of Arthur Dunkel.[20]

The Bharatiya Kisan Union and the peasant leaders like Charan Singh, Mahendra Singh Tikait, Sharad Joshi etc. have successfully used their mobilising power to achieve higher prices for agricultural produce, subsidised supply of fertilisers, power and irrigation facilities and rich peasants have mobilised electoral and political support for all-India and regional parties which would primarily protect the interests of the rich peasants. The peasant movements in India have proved that the peasantry wants all the advantages of the capitalist market, but it has no perspective of either national problems or contradictions between India and global capitalism. Since the peasantry in India is parochialised and fragmented, it cannot be the vanguard of secularisation and democratisation of the Indian society. Peasant consciousness is determined by the caste system of the 'twice born' and the *'Sudra'*. In spite of the upward mobility of the intermediate castes who are the beneficiaries of land reforms and the modernisation of agriculture, caste remains a major reference point of the Indian rural society. Can caste struggles be converted into struggles for the democratisation of the Indian society? The popular democratic base of Indian State will be broadened and strengthened if caste consciousness can become a force for the liberation of the oppressed castes. The policy of reservations in public services announced by V.P. Singh on August 9, 1990, does not give much hope for the development of secular potential of caste system. Caste versus caste has encouraged casteism and the casteisation of society has emerged as a powerful reality of India.[21]

If peasantry has limited potential of becoming an agent of modernisation, secularisation and transformation of Indian society, the other leading capitalist class also requires a close scrutiny. The capitalist class and the Indian State is the major transformer of Indian society but a few doubts have arisen about the current role of the Indian capitalist class and the State in relation to the world capitalist system and also around its transformational role in Indian society.

It is essential to state that the Indian capitalist class gained in power because of economic planning and active role of the State in Indian economy, the Indian capitalist class is dependent on the Indian State for its development. Since the liberalisation and globalisation of the Indian economy during the 1990s, a very important question has arisen about the nationalist character of the Indian bourgeoisie. Indian bourgeoisie had contested against the colonial rule for the independence of the Indian market, and after the independence of India, the Indian State and the Indian capitalist classes remained anti-imperialist and the Indian national interests were safeguarded from imperialist penetration and assault. Has the Indian bourgeoisie capitulated before western capitalist countries in the 1990s? Was the balance of payments crisis of 1991 sufficient to make the Indian State and the Indian capitalist class succumb before the pressures of the world capitalist countries?

It may be pointed out that the Indian State has to operate in a qualitatively different global milieu in the 1990s. India is a very small player and the western capitalist countries are very powerful. The collapse of the erstwhile socialist system has been disastrous for 'relatively autonomous' and non-aligned Third World State systems. In spite of extremely adverse global circumstances, the Indian State has no reason to capitulate before the western industrialised countries. First, the Indian capitalist class has emerged out of the balance of payments shock of 1991 and it has asserted its relative autonomy in relation to world capitalism. In a pre-budget meeting between the Minister of Finance, Dr. Man Mohan Singh and the leaders of Indian private corporate sector, some industrialists accused the Government of India for treating Indian industry as *'second-class citizens'* and one industrialist put in a memorandum that:

> In no other country of the world is discriminatory liberalisation more evident than in our case, with foreigners being clearly invited, incited, encouraged and colluded with to take over our industries, to destroy our manufacturing base and in the long run shamelessly mortage our economic sovereignty.[22]

The Indian State and the Indian capitalist classes are a product of historical struggle against colonialism and this historical consciousness may have weakened but it has not been replaced by neo-colonial and compradorism of the bourgeoisie and the Indian State.

Second, Indian economic development can be made relatively self-reliant if the Indian State implements land reforms legislations and deepens and expands the Indian market. The schemes for the generation of the purchasing power of 850 million people of India can make India stand against western capitalist countries. Sukhamoy Chakravarty refers to this fact while observing that:

> Looking back, it seems to me that while our achievements during the last thirty years of planning have by no means been insignificant in the area-of agricultural production, industrial diversification and technological acquisition, we have not been able to make a major impact on the lives of the vast mass of our people.[23]

The Growth Model of Development requires some important shifts to generate rural employment, income distribution and amelioration of the deprived masses so that they actively participate in the process of economic development. This shift in the strategies of development model will ensure relative autonomy of the Indian State in the post-cold war phase of western capitalist hegemonism.

Accommodative Potentialities of the Indian State

A democratic, representational, secular, capitalist, federal, reformist, modernist and anti-imperialist State of India is confronted with multi-dimensional challenges based on caste, community, language, region and politics of the bullet has emerged as an important factor in different parts of the country. Inter-religious, inter-ethnic, inter-caste, inter-tribe, intra-ethnic, intra-caste and intra-tribe conflicts have taken violent forms and some parts of India have witnessed ethnic cleansing. The North-East India is involved in inter-tribal and intra-tribal violent confrontations, Punjab and Kashmir have witnessed violent inter-religious and secessionist movements and it has led to the migration of populations. The Indian State has created more battalions of para-military forces and it has modernised its police forces to deal with emerging social conflicts in different parts of the country.

A study conducted by the Government of India observes that:

> With the ever increasing threats to internal security, the job of the policeman has become highly stressful and hazardous. Consequently, the number of police personnel losing their lives on duty has considerably increased since the Hot Springs incident of 1959.[24]

The study reveals that during 1961-62 to 1970-71,1,543 policemen died while on duty, in 1971-72 to 1980-81, the number of such deaths went up to 3,352 and in 1981-82 to 1990-91, it increased to 7,714. During just five years i.e., 1987-1992, 5,283 police personnel lost their lives while on duty.[25]

If on the one hand, *policisation* of the Indian society has rapidly increased, on the other, democratic elections have been regularly held in India. This is the social dialectics of India.

The democratic State of India has witnessed caste, class, inter-religious, ethnic and regional challenges, and it has also accommodated many legitimate aspirations and demands of many social groups. The most important illustration of democratic accommodation by the Indian State is North-East India. Arunachal Pradesh does not have a common language because according to the Census of 1991, the 26 major and 120 sub-tribes speak many dialects and they do not accept one language. The political journey of Arunachal Pradesh has been on the basis of 'gradualism'. Arunachal Pradesh still comes under restricted area and it operates under the Bengal Frontier Act 1873. The domestic visitors of India require an 'inner line permit to enter the State'. It was administratively a part of North East Frontier Agency, and became a Union Territory on January 20, 1972 and then it graduated to a full-fledged State on February 20, 1987.[26]

Mizoram was annexed by the British in 1887 and throughout the British period it was treated as an *"excluded political area"*. It was administered 'directly' by the Provincial Governor and outside the jurisdiction of Assam Legislative Assembly. The Mizos voted for the first time in 1952 and Mizoram became a Union Territory in 1972 and elections to the Mizoram Legislative Assembly were held on April 18,1972. Mizoram witnessed insurgency for twenty years and Rajiv-Laldenga Accord of 1986 brought Mizoram back to democracy. Mizoram became a full-fledged State in 1987 and democratic elections and cultural autonomy have become the foundations of Mizoram politics after Rajiv-Laldenga Accord.[27]

The North-East India has witnessed insurgency, inter-tribal and intra-tribal conflicts during the last forty-seven years. The National Socialist Council of Nagaland and the Indo-Burma Revolutionary Front are involved in Naga versus Naga and Naga versus Kuki armed conflicts.[28]

The democratic State of India has many a time successfully accommodated conflicting and competing pluralities because the central State authority of India enjoyed democratic legitimacy and it possessed political capabilities to accommodate specifics from North-East India to Kashmir. It will be involved in ethnic cleansing, river water disputes, and inter-religious holocausts if the authority of the Central State collapses in India.[29] India is a country of thousands of minorities and the collapse of the democratic Central State authority will lead to Hobbesian war of *all against all*. Similarly, any *homogenisation* of Indian cultural diversities in the name of Hindutva will also lead to the disintegration of India. Eric Hobsbawn's warning to the territorial national States of Eastern Europe is applicable to India. Hobsbawm noted that 'the attempt to form homogeneous nation-States in Europe would be based on 'mass expulsion or extermination of minorities. In the case of India, strong secular, democratic, federal Central State authority can be the real defender of pluralities of India. A lesson from Yugoslavia may also be learnt. The Constitution of 1974 provided that 'all citizens to coexist peacefully, without fear of domination by any single ethnic or cultural group'. The six *'nations'* of South Slavs were the Serbs, Croats, Montenegrins, Slovenes, Muslims and Macedonians, and their languages—Serbians, Croatian, Slovene and Macedonian—were the *official'* languages of Yugoslavia. Yugoslavia had no minority and the central State became weak and collapsed after the death of Tito leading to the tragedy of erstwhile Yugoslavia.

The Indian State, social classes and all important strata of society are involved in a basic struggle to build a strong democratic and secular State to avoid the tragedies of Yugoslavia and civil war situations of Afghanistan after the withdrawal of the Soviet Russia and the United States of America. Marx had clearly stated that 'civil society' needs an organized 'State', and without the State, civil society simply ceases to exist. The social and economic transformation of India is linked with the development of science and technology. Modernisation of society is linked with the modernisation of the means of production and changes in material foundations of society lead to changes in the whole superstructure of society. These things do not happen in a deterministic way or in a sequential manner. Indian society has to go through a zig zag process of ups and downs but the positive trends of the last forty-seven years should not be allowed to be weakened by the forces of either homogenisation or by the forces of philosophico-anarchism who believe in the power of 'voluntarism' and consider the State as an 'unnecessary evil'. The State systems of the Third World are under attack by the world capitalist system and voluntarism, non-governmental actions and freedom for the markets are the solutions offered by global capitalism to weaken the State system of the Third World. Julius Nyerere of Tanzania, Kwame Nkrumah of Ghana, Leopold Senghor of Senegal wanted to create Pan-Africanism, Nasser of Egypt wanted to establish pan-Arab unity and Nehru of India dreamt of Asian identity but the imperialists, after *'squeezing Africa'* have abandoned it to fight tribal divisions, the Arab unity lies in a shambles and the Asian countries have fought more wars among themselves than against any outside power. After destroying pan-Arab, pan-African and pan-Asian unity, the western capitalist countries in 1990s are delegitimising the role of the State in nation-building and the local collaborating classes of western imperialism are selling the ideology of the superiority of Non-Governmental Action against the State. The Third World is involved in a fundamental *'ideological'* struggle of the role of the State in nation-building and its opponents are western capitalist countries and infantile romanticists, who prefer 'group voluntarism' over collective action through democratic, representative and accountable State. The Indian State is a product of anti-colonial struggle for freedom, and the present struggle is concerned with the task of the deepening and broadening of the democratic, secular and federal context and substance of the Indian State. The agenda is to reform the Indian State with a view to strengthen its secular and accommodative capacities.

REFERENCES

1. Karl Marx, *Capital,* Vol. 1, Donna Torr, ed., George Allen and Unwin, London, 1949, author's preface pp. xvii-xviii.
2. D.D. Kosambi, *The Culture and Civilisation of India: A Historical Outline,* Vikas, Delhi, 1972 (reprint), pp. 22-23
3. *Ibid.,* p. 40.
4. Also see Declan Quingley, *The Interpretation of Caste,* Clarendon Press, Oxford, p. 19.

5. D.D. Kosambi, *An Introduction to the Study of Indian History*, Popular Book Depot, Bombay, 1956, p. 275.
6. Karl Marx, *Grundtoddr: Foundations of the Critique of Political Economy*, Translated with Foreword by Martin Nicolaus, Vintage Books, New York, 1973, p. 97.
7. Arjun Sen, 'FICCI's Lingering Colonial Hangover', *The Economic Times* (Delhi), December 19, 1993 p. 5.
8. Sen, *Ibid.*, p. 5.
9. G.D. Birla, *In the Shadow of the Mahatma*, Bombay, 1953. Also see Bipin Chandra, *Nationalism and Colonialism in Modern India*, Delhi, 1979.
10. Sumit Sarkar, *Modern India: 1885-1947*, Macmillan, Delhi, 1983, p. 79.
11. Sarkar, *Ibid.*, p. 141.
12. *Ibid.*
13. *Ibid.*, p. 142.
14. For Planning Experiment see, Sukhamoy Chakravarty, *Selected Economic Writings*, Oxford University Press, Delhi, 1993.
15. Editorial under the Caption: 'Too Poor to Matter', *The Statesman* (New Delhi), October 11, 1993, p. 8.
16. Karl Marx, *Grundrisse, op. cit.*, p. 88.
17. Karl Marx, 'Theses on Fauerback', in Karl Marx and Frederick Engels, *Selected Works*, Volume One, Progress Publishers, Moscow, 1976 (Third Reprint), p. 76.
18. Karl Marx, *Manifesto of the Communist Party: Collected Works*, Vol. 1, *op. cit.*, p. 117.
19. See *The Times of India* (Delhi), December 20, 1993. See also *The Statesman* (Delhi), December 20, 1993.
20. See *The Times of India* (Delhi), December 20, 1993. Also see CO., 'Farmer's Movement: Fighting for Liberalisation', *Economic and Political Weekly*, Vol. XXVIII, no. 50, December 11, 1993, pp. 2708-2710.
21. See Lars Rudeback, ed., *When Democracy Makes Sense*. Upsala, 1992. Also see Barrington Moore Jr., *Social Origins of Dictatorship and Democracy*, (Beacon Press, Boston, 1966).
22. 'Liberalisation Discriminatory, Accuses Industry', *The Times of India* (Delhi), December 14, 1993, p. 15.
23. Sukhamoy Chakravarty, *Selected Economic Writings*, Oxford University Press, Delhi, 1993, p. 406.
24. *The Times of India* (Delhi), October 24, 1993.
25. *Ibid.*
26. *The Statesman*, (Delhi), October 22, 1993, p. 4.
27. See Animesh Ray, *Mizoram*, National Book Trust, Delhi, 1993. Also see Debasnish Munshi, 'Mizoram Goes to Polls Today', *The Times of India* (Delhi), November 30, 1993, p. 4.
28. See Manoj Joshi, 'Need for Imaginative Nagaland Leadership', *The Times of India* (Delhi), December 23, 1993, p. 7; also see Ashis K. Biswan, *'NSCN-IBRE* Confrontation: Fresh Violence Likely', *The Hindustan Times* (Delhi), December 23, 1993, p. 7.
29. See 'Eric Hobsbawm, *Nations and Nationalism Since 1780*, Cambridge University Press, Cambridge, 1990.

6

Culture and Democracy: Will India Become a Hindu State?

The problematization of social phenomena in modern terms was conditioned by the universalist theories of Karl Marx, classical political economy, and Max Weber inspired modernisation theorists. These big or totalizing theories or schools of thought occupied a central-stage in intellectual inquiry and analysis of human societies because it was maintained that causal explanations of the social problematic could not be identified without attempting interconnections between the social whole and its various parts and elements. It was in the logic of this intellectual discourse that it attracted big critiques which challenged Marx, classical political economy philosophers and Weberian modernisation theorists and neo-liberals. Two different kinds of intellectual developments occurred in the post-World War II advanced industrial societies and the newly emerging decolonised societies of Asia, Africa and Latin America. Since large issues confronting the Western developed societies seem to have been settled by the 1990s, modernisation, rationalism, and universalism were rejected and replaced by an intellectual perspective based on the 'relativization of truth' and post-Modernist 'uncertainties' and ambiguities. In the newly emerging decolonised societies the received wisdom of modernization theorists was closely scrutinized, and it was either adapted to local situations or rejected on the plea that the *Old Societies* of Asia, Africa and Latin America have a specific historical cultural context and this makes our societies an exception and unique. In opposition to 'Universalist[7] intellectual theories of the West, emerged a Historicist approach which *emphasized the values of cultural relativism* and offered a powerful critique of European Enlightenment, science, reason and especially the universalist theories of modernization. It was maintained that *'we are different'* and we have to situate our institutions for governance on the basis of our specific historical and cultural context. H. Barth made a distinction between histoncism as a "method which seeks to understand man, his culture, and society in their historical uniqueness" and philosophical historicism (a product of the former): "the conception of man as the historic being par excellence began to invalidate ideas that assumed human reason to be essentially unchangeable. Truth became relativized "every epoch, every unified social group, every nation or culture was said to have its own truth".[1]

Two aspects of this 'uniqueness' or 'historical exceptionalism' of Third World societies deserve a notice. First, it is a reaction to the *'Europeanization of the Earth'* by the historically victimized societies of Asia, Africa and Latin America.[2] Second, many important theoreticians of the West have maintained that the institutional arrangements for the governance of a society cannot be transplanted or exported exogenously, there have to be specific cultural conditions which provide a fertile and hospitable ground for the functioning of the State institutions. Ernest Gellner maintains, along with many other Western scholars, that a strong 'civil society' is essential to counterbalance the power of the State, and such civil society according to Gellner has to be pluralist. Gellner does not stop here. A 'certain kind' of pluralist civil society which is secular, individualistic, built on capitalist economic relations of scientifically minded rather than superstition is pre-requisite for libertarian democratic arrangements for governance. Such a pluralist civil society of Gellner is naturally an inevitable gift of 'capitalism'.[3] If the logic of Gellner is followed then none of Third World societies have pre-requisites for participatory democratic governance because these societies have to go through the long historical phase of industrial development and free market economy. In the same tone, Raymond Williams maintains that the New in history began with the Industrial Revolution. He observes:

> "The Industrial Revolution, which eventually swept or impinged on most of the world, began in England. The fundamentally new social and cultural relationships and issues which are part of that historically decisive transition were therefore, first felt, in their intense and unprecedented immediacy, within this culture .... Thus though it is true that comparable changes happened in other societies, and new forms of thought and art were created to respond to them, often in equally or more penetrating and interesting ways than in these English writers, it is nevertheless of some permanent general importance to see what happened where it happened first."[4]

While elaborating his perspective, Williams maintains that the modern industrialism contains "alternative ideas of the nature of social relations" and that the modern capitalist social relations are based on "Individualism" to "protect individuals in this basic right to set their own course".[5]

The colonisers, the liberal scholars, the Orientalists and the Western racists have contributed in various degrees to divide human societies between We and Others and within our societies glorifiers of the past also asserted that the Eastern Societies are distinct and historically unique.[6]

This longish discussion needs a close scrutiny. First, to use a phrase of French social theorist, Pierre Bourdieu, that in history "The dead seizes the living". Globalisation is the essence of modern capitalism and without going into the detailed critique of Wellerstein's 'World-System Theory', it must be accepted that capitalism brought a kind of economic global integration. A polarized world emerged under global capitalism which can be characterised as the 'centre' of capitalism and the 'periphery' of global system. The colonised periphery became a backward, underdeveloped rural economy and the capitalist centre assumed the commanding heights of governance in the era of capitalism. Colonial history in the various phases of global capitalism had far-reaching impact on the economic social and cultural texture of the colonised societies. It is wrong to maintain that the so-called West and East are separate, on the other, they were linked together in a historically determined relationship of dominance and subordination, of rulers and ruled and this relationship exercised a great impact on the making and unmaking of the Third World. How can this common shared global history be wished away? The capitalist globalisation left a deep impact on the economy, social structures and the systems of governance of the exploited and dominated colonised societies. The modern globalisation had serious cultural consequences for the peoples under 'bondage' and the historical logic of this long phase of global linkages had contradictory implications for the dominated societies. If on the one hand, the Western capitalism projected new world view and cultural values for the whole humanity, on the other, the Eastern societies were compelled to look seriously at their heritage and find meanings for various historical and cultural continuities and discontinuities. Every important society of Asia, Africa and Latin America had a long history which preceded the colonial historical experience. It deserves an emphasis that neither the Eastern societies are 'unique'[7] nor they are replica or a carbon copy of the other Europeanized Earth. If on the one hand, global linkages are a reality, on the other, general and specific socio-historical and politico-cultural context of Third World countries has to be taken into consideration while analysing the nature of modern state institutions in these countries. The exogenous and endogenous social realities are interpenetrating and social or cultural exclusivism is an unreal assertion. Talking about his conviction, Pierre Bourdieu observed:

> ". . .that one cannot grasp the most profound logic of the social world unless one becomes immersed in the specificity of an empirical reality, historically situated and dated, but only in order to construct it as an instance *(Cas de figure)* in a finite universe of public configurations."[7]

While problematizing the Indian social phenomena, a few special facts about India deserve mentioning. First, contemporary India is a product of very powerful anti-colonial Third World nationalism. In this long anti-colonial struggle, Indians were involved in multiple tasks of constructing of a national ideology on the basis of which powerful colonial rule could be confronted and opposed. A rediscovery and reinterpretation of the Indian long historical heritage was a contentious intellectual and political exercise. While Sri Aurobindo Ghosh and Swatantrayaveer V.D. Savarkar were talking of Hindu Nation based on *Sanatana Dharrna,* Mohan Das Karamchand Gandhi and Jawaharlal Nehru challenged such an interpretation of India. Gandhi and Nehru emphasized that India consists of multiple socio-cultural and religious belief systems and this co-existence of rich cultural pluralist traditions is the essence of Indian religious ethos. India has many little traditions and this cultural and social mosaic of India has survived through multiple cultural interactions and interpretations. Jawaharlal Nehru in his seminal work entitled *"The Discovery of India"* strongly contested and refuted all ideological constructions towards homogenization under any rigid structure of Hinduism. Indian nationalist leaders were not only contesting the right of British colonisers to rule over India, they also struggled in defence of nationalism based on the values of democracy, secularism, fundamental rights to all religious and cultural communities and socio-cultural pluralism. The point to be noted is that during the modern period of Indian history, cultural and political issues have been interlinked and it will be non-historical to ignore the cultural context of Indian democratic experiment. Not only this is our inheritance, it is also a powerful contemporary reality because the inter-connections between culture and politics have to be clearly established to safeguard the future of secular democracy of India.

Second, while colonial capitalism integrated India in the world capitalist system, the cultural enterprise of the British colonizers failed to penetrate the inner socio-cultural and religious fabric of Indian society. The colonizers had a cultural agenda of *'civilize'* the Indian *'brutes'* but the ancient, evolving and resilient Indian civilization absorbed many modernising aspects of the colonial project, and the Indian cultural journey continued in its own way. The response of Indians to the powerful cultural project of the colonial State was quite constructive because the Indians were compelled to search for their own cultural roots and identity.

Contemporary Hinduism as a Cultural and Political Project

India is involved in a fundamental struggle about the meanings of Hinduism and its relationship with State power. Since culture and politics in India overlap and interpenetrate, it has become a multi-dimensional struggle. Indian social and moral order is closely linked with broad religious world view and belief systems. Religiously sanctioned rituals are practised by the absolute majority of Indians. Since a very fragile boundary separates culture from religious belief Systems, it facilitates the task of homogenizers to integrate cultural diversities under a rigid religious scheme.

What is Hinduism? Is it reconciliable with modern democratic institutional arrangements for the governance of India? Is Hinduism definable like Christianity or Islam? These questions are occupying the centre-stage of politics in India and society is getting polarized on the issue of the place of religion in Indian politics. An attempt is being made by the believers of homogenizing and hegemonozing Hinduism to displace in politics who believe that there is no coherent inner structure of Hinduism and India is a multi-cultural, multi-religious, multi-national and multi-lingual country in which different socio-cultural communities exist as a matter of their right and enjoy equal freedoms.

Is unity in diversity or homogeneity the essence of India? Since India is a civilization of millenia, many migrants came and occupied regions and in the process these regions have emerged as cultural entities. Bridget and Raymond observe:

> "Since the end of the Pleistocene there have been repeated arrivals of new elements, from both East and West; and this continuing process has through the years built upon the indigenous foundation the complicated structure and hierarchy of Indian society. Many of these arrivals constituted new groups within the total body, all more or less self-contained, and many encapsulating features of the culture they had brought with them, together with much that they absorbed from their surroundings. Thus, throughout her pre-history, India has presented an increasingly rich and varied fabric, wooven of many strands".[8]

Bridget and Raymond further assert that:

> "One of the distinctive features of South Asian culture in historic and recent times is the way in which it has encapsulated communities at many different cultural and technological levels, allowing them to a large extent, to retain their identity and establish intercommunity relationships".[9]

The past and the present 'hegemonizers' of Hinduism maintain that the Hindu's self-definition is based on the *Sacred* Books and these determine the whole way of life of a Hindu. Even this view is contested. J.N Mohanty unambiguously states that Indian philosophy and religion is neither based on the authority of the sacred *Vedas* nor it has any fixed numbers or clearly delimited "Schools".[10] Mohanty further affirms that:

> "What distinguishes Indian philosophy is rather its concerns, questions, goals, style, rhetoric. Consistently with this, we should strive after hitherto unexplored possibilities, new *darsanas.*"[11]

Similarly, Suvira Jaiswal emphasises that religion and rituals are always socially contextualized and as Indian society evolved from tribal society to settled agricultural society, the Brahmanical view of Hinduism emerged and in a long process of development the ruling classes 'laid down precepts of social and moral conduct' to be followed by the Hindus.[12]

This Brahmanical Hinduism was contested by the subordinate castes and many important religious movements like *Bhakti,* or spiritual inspirers like Kabir, Nanak and many others influenced large number of people who did not accept Brahmanical way of imposed Hinduism.

Monotheism, Polytheism, Theism, Atheism have all been part of Hindu cultural ethos. *The cultural essence of India has been cross-cutting ties and overlapping identities* and this achievement of Indian society has seen its own dialectics of conflicts, opposition and accommodation. Since Indian cultural traditions are multiple, the relations between *Self* and *Other,* and between identities and differences have gone through a zig zag process of ups and downs. Homogeneity and heterogeinity has been the hallmark of Indian struggle for self-definition and the contest has been around 'homogeneity' versus 'heterogeneity'.[13]

It has been mentioned that cultural conflicts in India are fully reflected in the political area of democratic politics. Competitive, multi-party parliamentary democracy, federalism and secularism are the basic institutional arrangements for the governance of India. Political legitimacy in India is based on electoral verdict and Independent India has held eleven elections for the national Parliament. Every election in India is issue-based and political contests are growingly assuming great significance because a party which believes in Hegemonizing Project of Hinduism in a multi-religious and multi-cultural society wants a democratic national political sanction for its agenda of Hinduism. While the party of Hinduism has been growing in strength, its secular and democratic political opponents have successfully challenged its Hindu Agenda.

The following table clearly shows that the Bharatiya Janata Party (earlier named as Bharatiya Jana Sangh) has a very limited electoral legitimacy even in a country where the so-called Hindus are in an absolute majority. The latest national elections which were held in April- May 1996, the Party of the Hindus (BJP) got only 20 per cent of the national votes polled, and all opposition parties which believe in secular democracy received 80 per cent of the polled votes.

Table 5.1: Electoral Performance of Hindu Religious Party

Year	*Total Seats*	*Seats contested*	*Seats Won*	*Electorate (lakhs)*	*Turnout (%)*
1952	489	94	3	1059.4	45.7
1957	494	30	4	1205.1	47.7
1962	494	96	14	1151.7	55.4
1967	520	251	35	1458.7	61.3
1971	518	160	22	1466.0	55.3
1977	542	405	295	1889.2	60.5
1980	542	–	–	1978.2	57.0
1984	542	229	2	2496.3	64.1
1989	543	226	86	3007.8	62.0
1991	543	468	120	2751.1	56.7

Note: Lakhs: Ten lakhs is equal to one million.

Will India Become a Hindu State?

The above discussion shows that there are various weighty cultural and political reasons to show that the Constitutional Democratic State of India will remain secular and it will not become a formal or informal Hindu Theocratic State. Indian multi-culturalism is a reality and homo-geneizing project of Brahmanical Hinduism has been always contested by cultural regions and large segments of people who by birth happen to be Hindus. The absolute majority of Hindus live a way of life where coexistence with pluralities and diversities, complimentarities and competition, cooperation and conflict, tolerance and intolerance are daily existential experiences. The forces of Hegemony are confronted by powerful social and cultural forces of anti-Hegemony and a 'large number of low castes' think differently from the high castes.[14] Further, this cultural pluralism and competitive democratic politics reinforce one another in dealing with the challenge of Hindu homogenizers.

A question which cannot be ignored is that the growing mass appeal of the homogeneizers must have some reasons in the material arrangements of Indian society which attract poor Indians to the ideology of the ruling segment of Hindu society. Indian democratic experiment has to reckon with the issue of social inequality. The Hindu homogenizers cannot be opposed effectively by the democratic forces of multi-culturalism without bringing the issue of social equality at the centre-stage of democratic agenda. It has been witnessed in recent times that empty slogans of modernisers have conceded social spaces to religious fundamentalists because poor, socially insecure and exploited sections of society get attracted by the promises of priestly class which represents the past by painting a dark picture of the present. If the vast majority of struggling masses actually experience that the present offers no 'hope' they look towards the priests for promise of prosperity. In summation, it may be mentioned that the Indian democracy has to handle the issue of culture along with the issue social equality for dealing with the challenge of the cultural and political forces representing *Hindutva*. Politics is *reflective* of social reality and politics *intervenes* to alter such a reality. Politics never hangs in the air. As a mirror reflection of Indian reality, democracy cannot ignore the issue of culture and social inequality and as an 'autonomous' activity, politics has to change social relations. This is the task of politics in India as in other developing societies.

REFERENCES

1. See: H. Barth, *Truth and Ideology*, Berkeley: University of California Press, 1976, p. 81,) quoted by Jorge Larrain: *Ideology of Cultural Identity Modernity and the Third World Presence* (Cambridge, U.K. Polity Press, 1994, p. 167).
2. See Hussel, quoted by J.N. Mohanty: *Essays on Indian Philosophy: Traditional and Modern* (ed. by Purushottama Bilimoria) (Delhi: Oxford University Press, 1993, p. 333).
3. For details see: Ernest Gellner, *Conditions of Liberty: Civil Society and its Rivals:* London, Hamish Hamilton, 1995.
4. Raymond Williams: *Culture and Society: Coleridge to Orwell* (London, U.K., The Hogarth Press, 1993 in Foreword to 1987 Edition).
5. Raymond Williams, *op. cit.*, p. 325.
6. See Gabriel A. Almond and Sidney Verba: *The Civic Culture*, Princeton: Princeton University Press, 1963. In the book, participatory, active, passive, civic and political culture was elaborated to evaluate growing institution in the Western and non-Western societies.

7. Pierre Bourdieu, *"Concluding Remarks: For a Sociogentic Understanding of Intellectual Works"* in Craig Calhoun, Edward Li Puma and Moishe Postone (eds), *Bourdieu: Critical Perspectives,* Cambridge, U.K. Polity Press, 1995 (Reprint), pp. 271-272.
8. Bridget and Raymond Allchin, *The Rise of Civilization in India and Pakistan,* Cambridge, U.K, Cambridge University Press (New Delhi: South Asia Edition, Foundation Books), 1996, p. 348.
9. Bridget and Raymond, *op. cit.,* p. 11; also see D.D. Kosambi, *The Culture and Civilization of Ancient India in Historical Outline* (London: Asia, 1965); A.L. Basham, *The Origins and Development of Classical Hinduism* (edited and Annotated by Kenneth G. Zyshn (Delhi: Oxford University Press, 1990); D.D. Kosambi, *An Introduction to the Study of Indian History* (Bombay, Asia: 1956); Romila Thapar, *Interpreting Early India* (New Delhi: Oxford University Press, 1992).
10. See J. N. Mohanty, *Essays on Indian Philosophy: Traditional and Modern,* Edited by Purushottam Bilimoria (Delhi: Oxford University Press, 1993, pp. 330-339).
11. Mohanty, *op. cit.,* pp. 334-35
12. See Suvira Jaiswal, *The Origin and Development of Vaisnavism: Vaisnavism from 200 B.C. to A.D. 500* (Benaras: Munshi Ram Manohar Lal Publishers Pvt. Ltd., second edition, 1981).
13. Also see David Theo Goldberg, *Multi-culturalism: A Critical Reader,* Oxford: U.K., Blackwell, 1994.
14. See Mary Searle Chatterjee and Ursula Sharma (eds), *Contextualising Cost: Post Dumontian Approaches* (Oxford, U.K., Blackwell Publishers, 1994).

7

The Indian State: Conflicts and Contradictions

Many a time appearance is confused with reality and constant development of society is explained in a neat manner either by an abstract theory or with the help of concrete observable social facts. Many complexities and contradictions of social development can be grappled with only if proper inter-connections are established among the seemingly contradictory social facts and by going behind and beyond the observable social reality. Social dialectics can be comprehended only if the abstract and the concrete are related in a manner that the general and the specific convey meanings in an inter-connected manner. This is the only approach to understand the unity of opposites in the actual processes of social dialectics.[1]

Any ascent from the abstract to the concrete is possible if historical specificities of a society are properly related with general laws of human social development. The starting point of human social development is that human beings are continuously involved in creating new and complex productive forces in society. The ongoing process of emerging productive forces determines productive relations in society. The emerging productive forces and relations of production move from a stage of harmony to disharmony and contradiction. When productive forces and production relations get disjointed, crises and contradictions emerge in society and the resolution of these contradictions is a process of ups and downs, upheavals, struggles, defeats and successes. The process of resolution of social contradictions is a long process and every institution in society has to cope with the challenges posed by social forces in defence of the social order and the forces which are struggling to change the social order. The most important institution in society which defends the social order[2] and which has to be opposed for transforming the social order is the State.

The State is the central social institution responsible for the maintenance of society, and its specific role in any historical epoch is determined by its role and its legitimacy. The exercise of power by the State in society has to be concretely identified and its biases and tilts have to be related to the existing productive forces and production relations of a specific society. To sum up, the essence of the State, *i.e.*, its coercive power does not exhaust the totality of its functions in society. Further the essence of the State cannot be properly comprehended without relating it to the totality of cultural, ideological and philosophical mainstreams of a society. Thus we are grappling with the complexity of the State and its essence, by establishing a dynamic interaction and inter-relationship between the material foundations of society and its cultural, ideological and philosophical worldview of which human beings of that society live and may wish to live.

The Colonial Phase

During the last forty years, the Indian State has been actively involved in the building of capitalism in a specific global context and on a social soil which had been completely distorted by colonial exploitation and plunder. The history of capitalist development in India being different from the history of capitalists development in the West European countries the role of the Indian State is fundamentally different from the role of the State in a comparable stage in Western capitalist countries.

During colonial phase, the agrarian structure of India was shackled by social and economic chains. The burden of land revenue imposed by the colonial State, and the exploitation of the peasantry by the feudal, semi-feudal and landlord classes created a situation where productive forces and production relations in agriculture remained primitive based on manual labour and acute exploitation of the toiling masses. India was structurally linked with the world capitalist system; the impact of this linkage was economic and social disaster for the peasantry, for it was involved in an international system on the basis of unequal terms of trade and an imposed international division of labour. Except in tea plantation and sugar and cotton cultivation, which were linked with emerging factory production in the middle of the nineteenth and twentieth centuries, the level of productive forces in agrarian society remained low because manual labour was the law of economic activity. In urban India, along with dominant colonial capital, the indigenous capitalist class gradually emerged on the shoulders and under the shadow of colonialism. It underwent a process of recruitment and formation under colonial rule which was different from the processes of formation of the capitalist classes of West European capitalist countries, making it a specific capitalist class of a colony. Many opportunities to start capitalist enterprises opened up before traders, contractors, speculators and entrepreneurial families in the late nineteenth and twentieth centuries, but every such opportunity was constrained by the presence of colonial capital and the role of the colonial State.

Colonial development in India was marked by three important features. First, the whole of Indian society was linked with the world capitalist system and the whole of India was subjected to exploitation because of structural linkages of the metropolis and the periphery. Second, within India the linkage between the capitalist factory system and society was extremely weak. Manual labour was employed in agriculture, which produced no surpluses. Thus, while they were subjected to the emerging laws of the capitalist market on the one hand, on the other, millions of manual labourers in rural India gained nothing in terms of development of the productive forces from the development of the market. Third, the development of the indigenous bourgeoisie was constrained because of the presence of colonial capital and the colonial State. This was our inheritance on the eve of independence and the Indian State has since been actively involved in building capitalism on the basis of such an inheritance.

Integrally linked with colonial economic development was a very powerful social process, based on social antagonism in Indian society, *i.e.,* the anti-colonial national movement. The social contradictions under the colonial phase were concretised on the basis of a multi-class platform for national liberation. Two features of the national liberation platform need emphasis here. First, the national liberation movement was a broad-based democratic movement involving many strata of society. Since it was a multi-class movement, many contending, competing and contradictory social outlooks found expression, but there was fundamental agreement that the British should be thrown out of India and only after the British quit would the economic and social transformation of the country be possible. Second, in spite of its multi-class character, a bloc of exploiting classes, led by the Indian National Congress, asserted itself very clearly when power was transferred to the Indians by the British. In the making and unmaking of India during British rule there were both negative and positive social tendencies, and the social dialectics of pre-independence India left a direct mark on the post-independence phase of development of the Indian State and society. The bloc of exploiting classes which had crystallised during the struggle for independence and the political leadership of the Indian National Congress waged their anti-imperialist struggle by large-scale mass mobilisation. In this process commitment to democracy, economic development and social transformation emerged as pillars of post-independence State power.

Building Capitalism

After independence State power was exercised by the bloc of exploiting classes to build capitalism, and for the last four decades the Indian State has been a vehicle of capitalist development. At least two reasons may be cited to explain the active role of the Indian State in the building of capitalism. First, the bloc of exploiting classes found itself in a central position in the State which emerged after the transfer of power. Second, the colonial distortion in the economy could be set right only by large-scale intervention by the State for economic and social reconstruction. Only the State could perform the multiple and complex tasks involved in the capitalist modernisation of an underdeveloped economy which had been distorted by colonial intervention.[3]

The framework of capitalist modernisation, agrarian transformation and social development was provided by the five-year plans, the concrete policies and institutions of the State and the dynamics generated by the democratic process in the country. The specific strategies for capitalist development evolved by the Indian State over the last forty years are as follows. First, it has set up a

State sector which is of crucial importance in the development of the economy. The State sector is involved not only in providing the infrastructure for development, but also in the production of machines and industrial equipment for industrial development. Second, it has established scientific and specialised institutions for the development of modern and technologically-based productive forces. Third, it has established institutions for the development of technical manpower skills for development of modern industries. Fourth, State-owned institutions like the Life Insurance Corporation, commercial banks and the Unit Trust of India have been set up, which are involved in the mobilisation of resources and savings. Fifth, it has formulated monetary and fiscal policies which regulate and direct investments. Sixth, there are State-established institutions like the Industrial Development Bank of India, the Finance Corporation of India and the Export-Import Bank of India, which provide credit and policy guidelines for economic development.

The Indian State follows a mix of regulatory and facilitating policies for the development of the private corporate sector in the country. It is regulated through licensing and promoted through financing.[4]

Capitalist development required a restructuring of agrarian social relations so that a national capitalist market could develop in unity between agriculture and industry. The State intervened in the restructuring of agrarian society after independence, with a view to changing the land ownership pattern and developing new productive forces for raising agricultural output. The strategy of agrarian transformation was based on gradual and step-by-step implementation of land reforms. Productive forces were also developed in stages, especially beginning from 1966-67. The main components of land reform were abolition of absentee landlordism, imposition of ceilings over land ownership, distribution of surplus land to the tiller and security of tenants. The legal power of the State was used to change the ownership pattern, but special factors linked to land ownership, like caste, ethnicity and religiosity, remained out of reach of State intervention.

The most significant of the agrarian reforms was the abolition of absentee landlordism, which was achieved by paying handsome compensations, amounting to Rs. 1,500 crore, to the exploiting classes. However, the reform did not lead to the transfer of land to the tillers; marginal, small and medium farmers, share-croppers, tenants-at-will and landlords continued to constitute the agrarian power hierarchy. Thus, property relations remained unchanged and agrarian exploitation continued.

The landowners exercised their social and political power to retard and sabotage the implementation of land reforms; and distribution of surplus land to the landless could not succeed because the rural oligarchy, which was part of the bloc of exploiting classes, used State power to protect its property interests. The goal of the land reforms was to ensure the continuation of the hold of property owners in rural India; and that of the development of productive forces in agriculture was to expand and deepen the national capitalist market of India. Charan Singh has clearly stated how 'rural stability' was the goal of land reforms:

> Much thought was given to the political aspect of the land reform, since the drafters of the legislation were cognisant of the need to ensure political stability in the countryside. But by strengthening the principle of private property where it was the weakest, that is, at the base of the social pyramid, the reforms created a huge class of strong opponents of the class war ideology. By multiplying the number of independent land owning peasants there have come into being a middle-of-the road stable rural society and a barrier against political extremism. It is fair to conclude that the agrarian reform has taken the wind out of the political sails of the disrupters of peace and opponents of ordered progress.[5]

Development of the national capitalist market through land reforms and development of productive forces for modernisation of agriculture was uppermost in the consciousness of the leaders of the State as well. Jawaharlal Nehru remarked:

> The whole policy of land reforms, apart from removing the burden on the actual tiller, was to spread the income from land more evenly among the peasantry and thus giving them more purchasing power. In this way, the internal market would expand and the productive forces of the country would grow. We cannot go on increasing our production unless we increase our consumption. We cannot increase our consumption unless there is the wherewithal to buy among large numbers of people.[6]

The class character of the Indian State becomes clear from the perspective on land reforms clearly expressed by political representatives of the exploiting classes in terms of stability of property owners and expansion of the market.

Contradictions in the Political Economy of India

How far has the Indian State been able to achieve its goals of capitalist development? How far has the strategy of gradual and step-by-step capitalist development been successful? What are the conflicts and contradictions that have emerged in following the path of capitalist development? What are the intra-class and inter-class conflicts that have emerged within the bloc of exploiting classes because of the social dialectics of development over the last forty years? How has the Indian State tackled the democratic pressure of 'society from below'?

The consequences of the capitalist path of development have been contradictory. On the one hand, the social base of Indian capitalism had expanded by bringing numerous social groups into the capitalist process. On the other hand, in spite of the Monopoly and Restrictive Trade Practices Act, indigenous monopoly capitalism has been strengthened as a leading group of the capitalist classes. A few facts make the situation clear. Of more than 2,500 public limited companies which are registered in the various stock exchanges of the country, 500 account for 98 per cent of the trading activity. In 1985, their market capitalisation was of the order of Rs. 16,300 crore. One-fifth of these 500 companies are subsidiaries of multinationals and four-fifths are Indian companies. Small and medium capitalists have also emerged in substantial numbers. The number of small-scale units increased from 4.16 lakh in 1973-74 to 10.48 lakh in 1983-84 and their production in value terms increased from Rs. 7,200 crore to over Rs. 40,000 crore. Of a total of 230 lakh workers employed in the organised sector, 79 lakh are in the small-scale sector. Capitalist development during the last forty years has also witnessed a change from manufactories to highly sophisticated machine manufacturing industries, and in certain sectors, machines for the production of machines have emerged on the scene, facilitating re-equipment of the emerging manufacturing sector of the factory production system.

From the mid-sixties, onwards agriculture has been linked with industry both as a producer of raw material and as a consumer of machine-produced inputs like tractors, tubewells and fertilisers. Hence the conflict within the bloc of exploiting classes is not between rural interests and supporters of industry along the lines that the countryside is ignored in the capitalist path of development, for both the landlords and emerging capitalist farmers have increased their economic power in this process. The conflict is between the rural rich and the urban rich, both classes trying for more control over State power for controlling the resources of the State. It is a conflict for the control of political power among the coalitional partners of the exploiting classes, with the rural rich feeling discriminated against because more resources are cornered by the urban capitalists.

It has been suggested that the peasants' real income from crops like wheat and rice have gone down and that this has adversely affected the peasant which leads to conflict situations between rural and urban India.

To sum up, the political superstructure in India is marked by inter-class and intra-class conflicts within the exploiting classes, in terms of a desire to increase their share of economic and political power in the country. These conflicts are reflected in all institutions of the State.

The developments in India clearly reveal both unity and a level of polarisation in the capitalist market. This is the contradiction in the political economy of capitalism in India, based on the fact that while millions of people are involved in manual labour in economic activity with primitive productive forces, highly developed productive forces have emerged in the advanced capitalist sector. When highly advanced productive forces coexist with a low level of economic activity there is a limitation on the quantum of accumulation and surpluses for investment. In this kind of political economy, the demand constraint and resource constraint are a product of the structure of the economy where though millions of manual workers are victims of the laws of the market, their economic contribution and involvement in the market are marginal. This situation of a polarised economy of demand and resource constraint leads to deceleration of industrial development. Shirokov observes:

> In peasant economies possessing limited resources, an absolute and relative increase in rural population should result in a further partitioning of land holdings. Since under constant technologies this would result in a parcellisation of holdings and a decline in incomes of direct producers, while a growing overpopulation would encourage a search for auxiliary forms of income, the outcome would be a reduction in the market surplus, on the one hand, and a preservation of semi-natural or else natural reproduction in peasant farms. This would make it impossible to provide for the reproduction of variable capital in industry on a national basis and would gradually reduce the size of industrial market.[7]

A few important implications of the demand and resource constraint in the Indian political economy may be mentioned here. First, the labouring classes, because of their low economic status, have to survive on the basis of 'non-economic' authority structures based on caste, ethnicity, religion and so on. Second, such a polarised economy cannot fulfil system-forming and integrating functions in a society. Because of these characteristic weaknesses of the developing capitalist economy, the State is still struggling to integrate the society. A situation of states within a State still exists in India due to social challenges to the legitimate authority of the State in the form of organised religions, castes and communities. The Indian State is still in the process of formation because the economy is still in the process of capitalist development. Such a State has many challenges to face before it can socially integrate the country. In a process where capitalism has yet to complete the tasks of 'system formation', the State may develop all the formal apparatuses for ensuring social stability, and yet the challenges faced by it are so formidable that real stability is not possible.

Three factors act a challenge to the process of State formation in India. First, capitalist development being very slow, and capitalist production relations and advanced productive forces having yet to establish their dominance in the economy, various social contradictions have emerged. These lead to situations of conflict where non-economic categories of caste, religion and ethnicity become mobilising factors of the socially discontented people against the authority of the State.

Second, in the process of establishing hegemony, the exploiting classes are challenging each other for control over State power. This challenge comes mainly from the rich peasantry/rural oligarchy which uses caste, religion and region to fight its battle against monopoly capitalism. This struggle has also shown that democratically elected governments have not been able to deliver the goods, for they have to be dismissed under the pressure of mass movements led by the rich peasantry. For instance, the Akali Dal, which represents the landlords and rich peasantry of Punjab, created conditions where the elected majority of the Congress Party could no longer administer the State. The central government had to intervene to meet the challenge of the Akali Dal and the Army had to be deployed. The Indian State is apparently very stable but in actual practice has suffered serious assaults on its stability; in the process its State apparatus has emerged fractured and divided on caste, communal and regional bases. During the last six years, the movements in Assam, Punjab and Gujarat have clearly revealed the regionalisation, communalisation and casteism of the State apparatus and have led to social violence, bloodshed and deaths which the State could counter only by using its reserve power, the Army. The movements in Assam, Punjab and Gujarat reflect the vulnerability of the Indian State in a context where capitalism has yet to achieve a system-forming and integrating role. The capitalist classes as the leading social group are themselves linked with the traditional social and cultural base of society and are unable to accelerate the processes of capitalist modernisation. Thus the State, which is the chief instrument of modernisation, reveals serious weaknesses because its important class components are carrying the baggage of the past.

Third, in a situation of building capitalism with the labouring classes making limited or no contribution to capitalist accumulation and social surpluses for investment, the capitalist classes look towards imperialism for aid and private capital for investments. The Indian capitalist classes and the Indian State are opening their markets to multinationals and liberalising the terms of investment for foreign capital because that is an alternative open to them for raising resources and encouraging investment. India has invited private foreign investment in many key sectors of the manufacturing and petroleum industries, and the outstanding foreign loans liability of India is Rs. 24,004.39 crore, excluding earlier repayment of the principal. The Seventh Five-Year Plan has encouraged the Indian private corporate sector to develop the economy, and the government is consciously evolving polices to welcome foreign capital and technology, so that capitalist development may take a quantum jump. The internal crisis is attempted to be resolved by external intervention.

Social Conflicts and Contradictions

The role of the State in contemporary India revolves around its capacity to resolve social conflicts and contradictions. During the early phases of development, the Indian State dealt with social challenges through coercion and accommodation. Of late, however, new situations of conflict have emerged and the State is revealing serious weaknesses in dealing with them. Two significant social conflicts have emerged during the last few years and the sources of these conflicts require discussion.

First, in agrarian India, the class struggle is fought on a caste basis. The State has evolved many programmes and policies—like fixing of minimum wages for landless agricultural workers, the Integrated Rural Development

Programme and rural employment guarantee schemes, the food-for-work programme and rural credit through nationalised banks — to generate employment in the rural areas and to create purchasing power among the rural poor. But these strategies have not succeeded because the rural power structure comes in the way of implementation of the programmes; the result is that rural conflicts have become violent. The emerging middle peasant castes, with their control over land and public resources, fight against the oppressed classes and castes if they demand their legitimate share of wages and returns for hard work. R.K. Hazari observes:

> The tensions in the south which marked the anti-Brahmin movement have almost disappeared there now, because while the Brahmin might still be part of the non-Brahmin consciousness, he is not that material or important there any more. The tensions and conflicts that matter are those on the ground between different sections of the farming community, and between the farm owning communities and those who work without owning the land. At this level, the tensions are violent with no holds barred. This phenomenon can be seen, for instance, in the northwest between the Jat and the Chamar, in the south between the Nadars, Mudaliars and the Pulayas, in the east between the Bhumihar/Yadav and the Chamar. Within the fold of the green revolution in Haryana, it can be between the Jat, the Ahir and the Bishnoi. Accompanying there is the tension between the small and large farmers, the dry and the wet farmers, and between those with rival claims to water. Participation in the green revolution has become one of the instruments of acquiring power. There is rivalry in politics, in administration and in cooperative and educational institutions.[8]

The conflicts have reached a stage where landlords have established their own private armies for social oppression, having lost faith in the capacity of the State, which represents their own class interests, to punish the poor. All through the year 1985, the state of Gujarat was rife with social violence unleashed by the dominant classes and castes against Muslims and the poor; the state government was paralysed and the Army had to be deployed for months to maintain law and order. Through these caste conflicts the ruling classes and castes drove home the message that, though the Congress party could win elections with the support of the poor, it could not govern without the support, approval and sanction of the former. Such developments make it clear to the Indian State that if it hampers the privileges of the dominant classes and castes, it will not be allowed to govern or maintain law and order. The rich have enough private resources and guns to challenge the power of the State if it goes against them.

In all societies, the State enjoys relative autonomy in managing the conflicting and competing social interests of the bloc of ruling classes and their opponents. Such relative autonomy of the State cannot be accepted as a positive factor because in order to promote the interests of the ruling classes it can unleash repression against the exploited classes. Alexei Levkovsky draws attention to this aspect of the State. 'In transitional society, the superstructure, primarily the State, has a great impact on the economic basis, on the course of the class struggle, and on the direction of changes in society as a whole.' But, in this case, the relative independence of the State apparatus in transitional society is a negative factor that inhibits progressive changes, and one that not infrequently becomes an instrument of counter-revolution and neo-colonialism.[9] In the Indian context, the State has shown authoritarian tendencies in meeting the economic crises and their manifestations in social and political crises.

Second, institutionalised religion has shown its capacity to challenge the authority of the Indian State, as the events of the last five years in Punjab clearly reveal. A situation of a state within a State has developed there, using the priests, the Golden Temple and the resources of the gurudwaras and exposing serious weaknesses in the so-called democratic and secular State of India. The response of the Indian State to the challenge of those who controlled the Golden Temple at Amritsar was wrong because it underrated the power of religion in Indian society. In the clash between religion and the State, the victory went to the believers, not to the secularists. With the entry of the Army into the Golden Temple, all acts of omission and commission of the armed group in the temple were forgotten and forgiven by Sikh believers. The Indian State emerged the loser vis-a-vis the religious believers of the Sikh community.

The basic issues that the State has to grapple with in contemporary India, namely, traditional culture, philosophy and religion, can be met only through an alternative ideology of materialism, science and secularism. During the last four decades the Indian State has been changing the material foundations of Indian society, but at the ideological level the hold of ancient India and its belief systems is strong and persisting. It would be mechanical to suggest that material transformations in society bring about ideological and superstructural transformations. The Indian State and the strata of the bourgeoisie committed to capitalist modernisation have clearly failed in propagating the ideology of secularism, in shaking off the shackles of religion, caste and community loyalties which are binding on all classes in India; the bourgeoisie, the middle classes, the peasantry and the working classes.

Conclusion

The discussion on the role of the Indian State can be concluded by emphasising some of its salient features. First, the process of capitalist modernisation of India has to go through many stages of transition before capitalism becomes mature as a dominant mode of production in society. The stages of transition have revealed many serious conflicts and contradictions and the State has to deal with multiple levels of social conflicts. Second, many responses of the State in the past in facing conflict situations have revealed authoritarian trends and in the future too such authoritarian responses are possible. Third, in the process of transition, all classes are in the process of formation and a clear crystallisation of class relations has yet to emerge. There are serious internal cleavages and conflicts among classes, and the formation of class coalitions reveals many internal weaknesses which are reflected in the weakness of the State in dealing with the complex and contradictory demands and pressures of society. The soft option for a weak State which is subjected to contradictory pressures is to respond in an authoritarian manner. This is the authoritarianism of a weak State. Fourth, the internal weakness of the Indian State is and will be exploited by the imperialists who have an important social base in a State which is following the path of capitalist modernisation. Finally, the modern Indian State has to grapple with the challenges posed by socially traditional structures either by accommodating some parts of the tradition or by confronting some aspects of traditional challenge. The real challenge to the modern Indian State is from organised religious groups which threaten its democratic and secular character. To sum up, the State in India has to grapple with challenges from classes, castes and religious social groups internally, and imperialism externally.

REFERENCES

1. E. V. Ilyenkov. *The Dialectics of the Abstract and the Concrete in Marx's Capital,* Moscow, 1982, pp. 137-38. 'The ascent from the abstract to the concrete without its opposite, without the ascent from the concrete to the abstract, would become a purely scholastic linking up of readymade abstractions borrowed uncritically. Contrariwise, a reduction of the concrete to the abstract performed at random, without a clearly realised general idea of research, without hypothesis, cannot and will not yield a theory either. It will only yield a disjointed heap of meagre abstractions/
2. V.I. Lenin, *'The Economic Content of Nardoism and the Criticism of It,' Collected Works,* Vol. 1, Moscow, 1977, p. 355' . . . .The State can on no account be something inert, it always acts and acts very energetically. It is always active and never passive.'
3. O.D. Ulrikh, *The Third World: Problems in the Development of the State Sector,* Moscow, 1975, p. 20. Also see Fyodor Burlatsky, *The Modern State and Politics,* Moscow, 1978. 'The essence of the State's economic function in the process of social reproduction is its direct and indirect participation in the formation of new production relations and in changing the character of productive forces in "Third World" countries.'
4. R.K. Hazari, *Essays on Industrial Policy,* New Delhi, 1986, p. 51. 'Contemporary industrial policy has aimed at rapid growth of industry as a spearhead of all-round economic development through a vigorous and strategic expansion of public sector enterprises, strong inducements for private investment and simultaneous efforts to bring about institutional changes and social reforms which would ultimately facilitate sustained industrial growth.'
5. Charan Singh, *Land Reforms in UP and the Kulaks,* Delhi, 1986, p. 40.
6. Jawaharlal Nehru, *Fortnightly Note to the Chief Ministers,* 5 August 1954.
7. Glery Shirokov, *The Industrial Revolution in the East,* Moscow, 1981, p. 42.
8. R. K. Hazari, 'National Unit, 1. Some Socio-Economic Aspects.' *Economic Times,* Bombay, 2 January 1986, pp. 5-9.
9. For this idea see Alexei Levkovsky, *Capitalism in India,* New Delhi, and Glery Shirokov, *op. cit.*

8

Political System: Nature of Contradictions

Politics and society are involved in a dynamic relationship of change and stability. In this complex relationship between politics and society, politics reflects social forces and processes, and it intervenes in changing, controlling and managing the social forces. It is simplistic to maintain that politics is an instrument in the hands of social forces. On the contrary, delinking of politics from its social milieu reduces politics to the level of passivity. Politics is an active force in the shaping of a society and in this task politics and society make many adjustments with each other and they also come into conflict because powerful social forces may challenge the controlling power of politics. Harmony and disharmony between politics and society is an on-going process in all societies especially in those societies which are passing through a period of extended transition.

Concretely, in a class-divided society which is characterized by contradictions, politics has to manage social contradictions and resolve social conflicts, and in performing this task politics gets its legitimacy through universal adult franchise in a liberal, competitive, open political system. Organized political parties project themselves as competitors of legitimacy and harmonizers of conflicting interests and demands on the basis of market mechanisms of bargaining, competition, mutual accommodation and give and take. Many serious doubts exist about the capacity of politics in class-divided societies to reconcile contradictory social forces. In spite of institutionalized accommodation based on the legitimacy of universal franchise, politics uses coercion to suppress basic social conflicts but even this coercion is legitimized and mystified by the politics of democratic participation. Historically when social contradictions are not manageable, liberal democracies have allowed themselves to be replaced by fascist regimes or formally elected leaders have exercised powers in a fascistic manner. It is not without reason that all liberal democratic regimes in the western countries are highly centralized and bureaucratized because electoral legitimacy is not enough to manage social contradictions. Presidential or prime ministerial systems in the western liberal democracies are a response to specific situations of class-divided societies where centralization of governmental authority is an inevitable development to contain social contradictions.

The theory of politics of developed capitalist countries is relevant to appreciate the role of politics in a society, its linkages with social forces, its real tasks of contradiction-management, and its processes of centralization of political power in all advanced capitalist countries. Since India is building capitalism, and the essential role of politics in India is the management of social contradictions, some of the historical and theoretical insights of advanced capitalist democracies would be helpful in explaining some aspects of the functioning of Indian political system. The theoretical question for all capitalist countries, developed and developing, is the capacity of politics and its institutional network to reconcile popular participation with capitalist system or the contradictions which exist between equality provided by adult franchise and socio-economic inequality of the capitalist system.

I

The historical specificity of India is based on its ancient cultural heritage and its arrested growth brought by the British colonial rule. The persistence of ancient social beliefs, religiosity, caste structure and many other feudal and semi-feudal social structures and belief systems have made Indian society fragmented and complex. The British colonial system structurally integrated India with the world capitalist system and as a colony India was linked with the world capitalist system as a market for exploitation. An international division of labour was imposed on India by the colonizers where India was to produce and export primary products and import finished and manufactured products and since this international division of labour based on unequal terms of trade persisted for centuries, India's economic development was completely distorted and its economic vitality was destroyed. To achieve the goals of colonialism, the British adopted following major policies for the exploitation of India.

1. The Indian agrarian structure was brought under diverse kind of land relations based on *Zamindari, Rayotwari* and *Mahalwari* systems, which created class of absentee landlords, *Jagirdars,* etc. in some regions but irrespective of the systems the peasantry was subjected to maximum exploitation for colonial benefits. Since cottage industries and other allied small scale enterprises linked with village self-sufficient economy were destroyed, rural India was reeling under poverty and under-development to fulfil the greed of the colonizers and their indigenous local collaborating and exploiting classes.
2. Since colonial exploitation was the major goal of the British, the colonial state in India undertook some public works for development and the colonial state also introduced a legal system based on the sanctity of the institution of private property in India.
3. While the British capital was active and dominant in plantation and industry, slowly and gradually indigenous capitalist class also developed in the field of textile, jute, sugar, etc. The indigenous capitalist class of India developed on the shoulders and under the shadow of British imperialism. The indigenous capitalist class got an opportunity in the inter-war period but it

also experienced difficulties of development because the British colonizers were in control of the Indian market. Because of inter-war spurt, on the eve of independence 121 identifiable large economic interests, including 69 Indian groups (now known as Big Business groups) controlled Rs. 350 crores of paid up capital, amounting to about 73 per cent of the total paid up capital in India in 1947.[1] Two important facts emerge from the development of Indian capitalism under the shadow of colonialism. First, Indian capitalist class, unlike capitalist classes of the developed European capitalist countries, did not emerge after a sustained and successful struggle against feudalism. Second, Indian capitalism became monopolistic without going through the long process of competitive capitalism. Hence it was capitalism in a colonial setting with its historical distinctiveness and specificity. Further, Indian capitalism with its monopolistic character emerged in a country on the basis of a retarded and underdeveloped industrialization. It would not be wrong to say that India had a capitalist class without industrialization of the country. It was a peripheral capitalist class of a colony with limited industrial economy.

Malenbaum comments:

> After allowing for the expansion in service facilities and in coal output needed for the railway system, there was little evidence of industrial diversification, while each large textile factory was soon surrounded by a large number of machine repair shops; they remained small scale make shift enterprises. (And again) Nor did the advent of steel give rise to modern machine building machinery.[2]

Analysing the pre-colonial development of India, Malyaroy rightly observes:

> The investment barrier put up by foreign competition had an especially adverse effect on the development of capital-intensive branches of heavy industry. As a result, industrial capital was unable to create a complex of branches which would provide for its material reproduction, and the latter was conditioned by internal economic ties because of its dependence on a foreign industrial base.[3]

In such a situation, the Indian State undertook the task of building capitalism after independence of the country.

This was the context in which the mighty British empire was challenged by the Indian National Movement. The Indian capitalist class had a clear convergence of interests with struggle for India's freedom. The Indian capitalist class objectively experienced obstructions in development because the colonizers had a control over the Indian market. The freedom of India was objectively freedom for the Indian market and the capitalist class identified itself with the anti-imperialist national movement. The Indian national movement was democratic, its mobilization appeals especially from 1920s were to broad masses of the people and its organizational structure was flexible and accommodative of different strata of the society. Heterogeneous social groups rubbed their shoulders in the struggle for freedom, and dominant exploiting groups identified themselves with the cause for freedom. On the eve of independence, we inherited a national movement and leadership which was committed to participatory democracy and the capitalist path of development. The Indian National Congress wanted to perform a historic task of reconciling equality based on participatory democracy and inequality of the capitalist social order. The proclaimed goals of Indian political system were democratic freedoms, periodical elections, competitive politics, secular state with separation of religion from politics, and division of powers among various states of India in a federal arrangement. It was also stated in the constitutional arrangement for governance that a democratic, secular and federal political system would actively promote and initiate goals of economic transformation of the country. The role of Indian political system was not that of a night watchman, but of an active motive force for economic development.

All political systems proclaim their goals but their validity has to be examined empirically and a different set of questions have to be raised to examine the relevance of formal goals of political system and the real activities and achievements of the system.

II

A profile of thirty-eight years of the functioning of democratic, secular, federal and activist political system reveals its positive and negative features, its achievements and failures, and on the basis of such a dialectical understanding of the last thirty-eight years emerging tendencies and trends can be emphasized.

The most important achievement of Indian political system is the holding of periodical elections on the basis of universal adult franchise and at regular intervals. The impact of elections on Indian society has been qualitative, the percentage of voters' turnout has been extremely satisfactory, gradually the voters have started evaluating governmental performance, the distance between government and the voters has been narrowed down, competition in politics has been legitimized and gradually the secular source of power, *i.e.* the voter has emerged as a new factor in Indian society where traditionally power is based on caste hierarchy or property or religious and scriptural superiority. Participatory politics has raised the level of political awareness of the masses and government has become a critical factor in voter's life. It must be stated that the process is slow, and it has also revealed many negative features, but by all standards adult franchise has been a revolutionary social factor in India. Politicization of an indifferent and apathetic community is the first step towards democratic advancement of a society and elections have achieved this in India.

Table 7.1 on voters' turn-out clearly reveals a trend where we start from 45.7% in 1952 and in five elections, it is above 55.0% and in two watershed years of 1967 and 1977 the turnout is 61.3% and 60.5% respectively. In the 1984 Lok Sabha elections voters' turnout was about 60%.

Another significant achievement of the last thirty-eight years has been party alternation and peaceful transition from a defeated party to an electorally

Table 7.1: Lok Sabha Elections

Year of Election	*Votes Polled in Lok Sabha %*
1952	45.7
1957	47.7
1962	55.4
1967	61.3
1971	55.3
1977	60.5
1980	54.0

successful groups of a party. People's verdict in 1977 was accepted without any resistance.

While these two achievements of the democratic process in India are significant, they would get eroded or reduced to a formal position if the negative forces which are intervening in the political process are not eliminated. The appearance of democracy is different from the reality of democracy. Politics operates at many levels and electoral level and succession and alternation of parties is only one level in the dynamics of power in society. Elections legitimize the wielders of political power but this does not determine the totality of politics. All political systems have parts and elements, and one element in democratic political system is elections but many other social forces intervene in the process of politics and the exercise of political power in society. An identification of power coalition in society is essential to determine the real nature of political power and such a power coalition in India consists of the exploiting classes, *i.e.* the capitalist classes, landlords and rich peasants and their power goals have to be analysed because they determine crucial and basic decisions in society.

Since independence India has been involved in building a capitalist society and in this basic task the political system is actively involved. The following tasks have been undertaken by the Indian political system for building capitalism:

(a) The Industrial Policy of the Government of India recognizes the supportive role of public policy for the development of private corporate sector. All important infrastructure industries are owned and managed by the government and through infrastructural support government has facilitated the growth of private corporate sector during the last thirty-eight years.

(b) The government mobilizes national resources for industrial development and these resources are shared by the state capitalist sector and the private corporate sector. The LIC, the nationalized banks, the IDBI, ICICI, and other financial institutions owned by the government provide financial resources for private capitalist enterprises.

(c) The government controls the setting up of industries, products and lays down capacities for production by the private corporate sector. The government has facilitated the development of private capitalism by regulatory, supportive and subsidy mechanisms and during the last thirty-eight years the expansion and diversification of private capitalism has taken place under the protective umbrella provided by the Indian government. The government legislation to check monopolies under the MRTP Act is just a formal intention than a reality. The government controlled financial institutions extend financial support to the Big Business because a close liaison exists between politico-bureaucratic apparatus of decision making and organized private corporate sector.

In spite of the efforts of last thirty-eight years, crisis of capitalist development is quite visible in India. It is correct to maintain that gradual structural transformation has taken place in the Indian economy but the rate of industrial growth has been quite slow. Many factors have been identified for the slow rate of industrial growth in India and deceleration of industrial development has been recognized. The *Economic Times* in an editorial on "Outlook for Industry", commented; "In sum, stray data on production or industrial licensing may give a misleading optimistic picture of industrial growth. It needs to be recognized that organized industry has been overtaken by diffidence in the wake of shortcomings in policy and implementation."[4]

The Planning Commission appraisals and FICCI documents have found infrastructural constraints and adverse input-output ratios as the villain of the piece for industrial deceleration in India. The Reserve Bank of India Report (1983-84) has characterized India as "a high cost and low productivity industrial system", and thus deceleration has been explained in spite of the fact that investment in the economy has risen from 18.2% in 1965-66 to 23.3% in 1983-84. But inefficiency of capitalist development has not affected profit accumulation and growth in assets of the Big Business. In spite of the recognized inefficiency of the capitalist system, private corporate sector has thrived on the basis of subsidies and protection provided by the government.

Our contention is that "high cost and low productivity industrial system" is not the only valid explanation of deceleration and in spite of the fact that private capitalists are accumulating rates of profit even under this industrial environment, they would like to accumulate more profits if they can achieve it. Some other explanation has to be found to understand the crisis of capitalism in India and for this, a look at the agrarian structure would be essential.

Two tendencies of capitalist development in India may be mentioned here. They are: (a) the social base of Indian capitalism has expanded, and (b) the manufacturing sector has not emerged as dominating factor in India in spite of capitalist development of the last thirty-eight years.

During the last thirty-eight years, India has developed big, medium and small-scale private enterprises which have expanded the social basis of capitalism in the country. Quantitative expansion brings qualitative social transformations. The growth of small scale sector is expanding the base of capitalism.

Irrespective of large scale sickness in small scale sector, more people are getting involved in the capitalist system of production. The capitalist development of last thirty-eight years is reflected not only in the expansion of the big, medium and small scale capitalist expansion, many new social groups like the politicians, bureaucrats, middle and lower middle class salaried groups are involved in making investment of their savings in capitalist enterprises in India. The present buoyancy in the stock market is because of investments of the household savings in the country.

In spite of expansion in the social base of Indian capitalism, the capitalist mode of production has not become dominant in the country. Not only this, capitalist development is slow and distorted and the tertiary sector has grown with a faster speed than the manufacturing sector.

Table 7.2: Estimates of Production and Employment in Small Scale Sector

Year	*Production (Rs. Crores)*	*Employment (Number in lakhs)*
1973-74	7,200	39.7
1974-75	9,200	40.0
1975-76	11,000	45.9
1976-77	12,400	39.8
1977-78	14,300	54.0
1978-79	15,790	63.8
1979-80	21,635	67.0
1980-81	28,060	71.0
1981-82	32,600	75.0
1982-83	35,000	79.0
1983-84	41,300	84.51
1985-85	50,520[b]	90.0

(a) See G. Ramachandran "Small Scale Units: How Phenomenal their Growth?" *Economic Times* (Bombay), 19 December 1985, p. 5.

(b) RBI, *Annual Report*, 1984-85.

Table 7.3 clearly shows that development of Industry has not shown any "dynamism". The pattern of capitalist development in the advanced capitalist countries was based on the emergence of manufacturing sector as central and later on it was followed by the tertiary sector but in India the reverse of it is happening. Its implication is that structural transformation brought by capitalist development is slow and even distorted. Further, Indian capitalism is developing on the social soil of feudal, semi-feudal, landlord, rich peasant, medium, and marginal farmer who is involved in sharecropping and insecure tenancy right. The absolute majority of the landless agricultural workers are still involved in struggles to get minimum wages from the landlords.

The Indian capitalist class had joined the Indian national movement actively to liberate the Indian market from the colonial control and during the last thirty-eight years the main interest of the capitalist class is to expand and deepen the development of the national market of India and the first step in this direction was to abolish absentee landlordism and princely feudal order after independence of the country because these social forces were an obstruction in the way of agrarian regeneration of India. While the abolition of absentee

Table 7.3: Net Domestic Product Originating form Commodity Producing and Tertiary Sectors

(Rs. crores at current prices)

Year	*Net domestic Production sector*	*Primary sector*	*Secondary sector*	*Commodity producing sector*	*Tertiary sector*	*Per cent share Commodity producing sector*	*N D P Tertiary sector*
1	2	3	4	5	6	7	8
1970-71	34,519	17,307	6,790	24,097	10,422	69.8	30.2
1975-76	62,324	27,732	13,179	40,911	21,413	65.6	34.4
1976-77	66,987	28,395	15,029	43,424	23,563	64.8	35.2
1977-78	75,712	32,527	16,917	49,444	26,268	66.3	34.7
1978-79	81,351	3,428	18,943	52,371	28,980	64.4	35.6
1979-80	88,353	34,493	21,097	55,590	32,763	63.9	37.1
1980-81	105,536	42,022	24,314	66,336	39,200	62.9	37.1
1981-82	120,813	47,646	27,023	74,669	46,144	61.8	38,2
1982-83	133,151	51,125	30,130	81,225	51,896	61.0	39.0
1983-84	160,279	65,174	35,119	100,293	59,986	62.6	37.4

landlordism and princely feudal order by paying proper compensation was considered essential for capitalist development of India, restructuring of property relations in the agrarian society was not on the agenda of state capitalist reformist policies. After the abolition of absentee landlordism and other intermediaries the distribution of landownership and agrarian assets was skewed in favour of a minority.

Landownership is the crux of social power in rural India and the landless agricultural workers, small and marginal peasants, medium and large farmers constitute agrarian hierarchy where landlords and rich farmers sit like a cobra with large ownership of assets. The policies of the Government of India and the state governments during the last three decades brought qualitative growth in the power of the powerful social groups in rural India. For increasing agricultural productivity and for expanding the market for industrial products, the governments at the Centre and the states have subsidized agricultural development. The strategy of HYV, irrigation development, subsidy for consumption of fertilizers, loans for tractors and pumpsets, subsidized rates of power, fixing of procurement prices have raised the production of foodgrains from 50 million tonnes to about 145 million tonnes. The logic of government sponsored and supported programmes and subsidies for agricultural development is that those strata of rural society who own assets are the real and direct beneficiaries of such programmes. The strategy of Green Revolution has revealed class and regional or social and spatial conflicts and contradictions.

It is not maintained that the government has not given its attention to rural poverty eradication programme. The government has fixed minimum wages for landless agricultural workers, it has started Rural Employment Guarantee Scheme, Food for Work programme, Integrated Rural Development Programme and many other reformist programmes. When these government sponsored rural poverty eradication programmes come into direct contact with rural property structure, the limitations of such programmes become obvious. According to Dantwala between 1964-65 and 1974-75, the number of rural households has increased from 70.4 million to 82.1 million or by 17 per cent. The number may go to 100 million by 1985, and thus the number of poor households would be about 40 to 50 million. During the same period (1964-65 to 1974-75) the number of agricultural labour households increased from 15.3 million to 20.8 million. Not only the number of landless agricultural workers has increased, the number of marginal holdings has also increased.[5] Thus, observed over a long time, the number of rural poor has increased and actual constraint over capitalist development in India is 48 per cent of people living below the poverty line who are not part of Indian market mechanism. The growth in the sale of industrial products is not possible because of structural arrangements of property relations in India. This is the fountain source of contradiction and crisis in society and politics in India. The landlords and rich peasants want control over resources of the Indian State and during the decades of Green Revolution they have experienced that the more public resources they can corner, the greater would be their prosperity. The transformation from colonial to post-colonial State in India is that while agriculture was over-taxed in colonial India, in post-Independence phase not only the landlords and rich peasants pay marginal or no taxes, but they also get substantial support from the State exchequer. Hence control over the Indian State apparatus is their basic goal for their own advancement and containment of class struggle in the rural areas. Similarly, the capitalist classes want to control the Indian political system for their economic prosperity and containment of challenge to their property. Reasons for active involvement of the exploiting classes in politics are quite clear and they have to come to terms with the politico-bureaucratic State apparatus and the logic of adult franchise. The power of landlords in politics is clearly revealed in the manner in which they have successfully sabotaged implementation of land reform ceiling over landholdings and distribution of the surplus land to the landless agricultural workers. According to the Seventh Five Year Plan, "7.2 million acres of land have been declared surplus, and 4.4 million acres distributed. Of this 1.6 million acres are involved in litigation and 0.82 million acres have been reserved for specific public purposes." The Plan document observes:

> The full potential of land redistribution has not been realized both in terms of covering the entire surplus that may be available and taking

possession of and distribution of the already identified legal and administrative bottlenecks have led to large gaps between declaration of surplus land, taking actual possession of land and its distribution.[6]

The social context of Indian politics is provided not only by the role of capitalist classes or landlords and rich peasants, but also by the role and interest of the politico-bureaucratic class in India. This is a specific social phenomenon in all Third World countries which led Kalecki to describe them as "Intermediate Regimes". India is not an "Intermediate Regime" but the power, interests and stakes of political and bureaucratic actors in the political system in conjunction with property owners and sometimes in disconjunction with property owners deserve attention.

The politico-bureaucratic stratum of society plays a pre-eminent role in managing public affairs by regulating the productive system and by intervening in the conflictual social processes. Politico-bureaucratic stratum exercises power to manage society and also to maximize individual advantages for personal benefits. Politics as an activity has general societal concerns and at the same time individual interests of the decision-makers in politics have to be satisfied and promoted. Since government is the chief regulator of the Indian economy, politico-bureaucratic decision-makers exercise their power for protecting and promoting the interests of various competing classes in society and they also exercise this power for self-advancement. The Government of India is not only building capitalism as an abstraction, the politico-bureaucratic decision-makers are beneficiaries of capitalist development. The government functionaries support capitalists and in the process they also appropriate huge benefits for themselves. During the last thirty years, politico-bureacratic strata of society have appropriated huge resources through their power of decision-making. It is not without reason that all important political leaders and members of public bureaucracy have financial interests in industry, trade, commerce and modern farms. The concept of private property has been strengthened during the last thirty-eight years and politico-bureaucratic decision-makers are an integral part of private property structure in Indian society. Politico-bureaucratic stratum safeguards private property system and uses its power to accumulate private property for itself. Political and administrative power is a resource to accumulate private property.

The relationship among the capitalist classes, agrarian power groups and politico-bureaucratic stratum is quite complex. The profits of the Indian capitalist classes are not earned only through their entrepreneurial skills. The capitalist classes are extracting surplus value by manipulating family, community and political linkages and in this process the capitalist classes have recognized that they have to make accommodation with politico-bureaucratic decision-makers. The political leaders can accumulate resources and defend their interests and interests of other exploiting classes on the basis of electoral legitimacy. If a politician does not win an election his power comes to an end. The winning of an election is crucial for a politician and this being the sole source of his power, the role of parties, elections and coalition-making assumes critical factor in a democratic set up. To sum up, major classes and groups in society compete and collaborate, but the exercise of power is dependent on parties and electoral successes.

III

The central focus of the above description is that India is in the process of building capitalism in a society which is predominantly agrarian and with many pre-capitalistic structures. In this historical process of grand transition, class contradictions, regional imbalances, pre-capitalist loyalties like caste, religion and community are involved in conflicts and politics has to mediate in these conflicts and contradictions. Such a mediation of politics in complex and contradictory social situation is done through political parties. The central role of political parties has been recognized both by liberal political theorists and Marxist political theory. While the perspectives of politics of Western liberal theorists and Marxists have fundamental differences, they recognize the role of party system while assigning different goals to parties. The twentieth century Western political theorists like Robert Michaels, Max Weber, M. Duverger, Sartori and Lipset have maintained that inequality of society and equality of adult franchise can be reconciled by the intervention of organized party system. The Marxists believe that capitalism and democracy are irreconcilable and party as a vanguard of class struggles can usher in socialism and fight against capitalism. In spite of these fundamental differences, organized parties are crucial in the modern nation-state and India is no exception to this. The Congress Party established a coalition of the exploiting classes and such a Congress coalition operated the State apparatus. While the Congress Party fought many internal struggles, many individuals and groups walked out of it, and whenever walkouts took place, it tried to co-opt some sections of dissatisfied classes within the Congress system. During the last thirty-eight years, except for the BJP and the Communist parties, all other political groups and their leaders with the exception of a small socialist group are erstwhile Congressmen, At the national level, Congress after many splits, and erstwhile Congressmen with new party labels, are competing for political power; the BJP, the two Communist Parties, and regional formations like the Akali Dal, the DMK/AIADMK, etc., are involved actively in political competition. Since every political party including the Congress has to fight and win the elections, it would be essential to analyse the nature of political and social groups which walked out of the Congress and formed parties like the Lok Dal or the Janata. It would also be essential to understand the social goals of major contenders for political power in India.

The middle of the 1960s is objectively the beginning of emerging challenge to the Congress coalition and its main source is the Green Revolution. During the last twenty years, the Green Revolution has brought benefits and economic power to the landlords and rich peasant in the countryside. The Congress was protecting their interest, but many leaders of landlords and rich peasantry felt that they could achieve political power on their own and the electoral debacle of the Congress in 1967 is a watershed in this process. The Congress and the powerful agrarian classes had no contradiction because the sabotaging of land reforms which was in the interest of powerful agrarian classes, was achieved by the presence of these classes in the Congress Party and state governments formed by the Congress. From the mid-1960s leaders of the rich peasantry wanted power directly through their own parties so that they could control governmental power and resources directly for their benefit. Charan Singh, Kumbha Ram Arya, Devi Lai, Nathu Ram Mirdha and many others who are in either Lok Dal, or in the Janata or in the Congress (S) are erstwhile Congressmen who walked out of the Congress to maximize their share in the government resources by forming political parties which should compete against the Congress. At least three reasons can be identified to explain the phenomenon of a large chunk of peasantry walking out of the Congress. First, some of the leaders of peasantry have a feeling that they have vote banks and they win elections in the rural areas because of their patron position over the clients. Since they have an independent election winning capacity why should they remain part of an umbrella coalition of the Congress. Second, these leaders of the peasantry experienced that control over the government provides them control over public resources. After successfully sabotaging the land reform as part of the Congress calition, leaders of the peasantry want to control government resources for further advancement of their personal and class power. Third, during the last two decades the phenomenon of middle peasant and middle or backward castes has emerged in the rural India and they are questioning the domination of the so-called "forward castes" and their traditional power in the rural India. Writing about Bihar, Das observed:

> The Jat-Yadav-Ahir conglomerate (is involved) . . .in a common process of economic transition caused by changing production relations, come together *politically* and take pride in calling themselves by the otherwise odd 'Backwards'. Ironically also, many members of this grouping are hardly backward in terms of their productive activities or even economic position. Hardly peasants as they are, they have benefited in a marked manner from the 'small-peasant policies' introduced by the government and have taken advantage of the technological, biological and chemical innovations that go by the name of 'Green Revolution' to improve and consolidate their economic position and political influence. They are also in the forefront of the popular Bihari sport of *harijan* burning which translated into its basis is nothing other than exploitation and oppression of agricultural labourers and share-croppers.[7]

Every class or a segment of class in rural India is tempted to form its own party with a view to control governmental power and public resources. The middle peasants and backward castes and their parties are agitated over reservation in bureaucracy and are pressurizing the acceptance of Mandal Commission report on Backward Caste Reservations which is resisted by entrenched social groups. Parties and leaders of the Lok Dal or Janata or Akali Dal are playing class politics through the idiom of caste or religion. In response to challenge posed by the Lok Dal or Janata or Congress (S), the Congress is also shifting components of its electoral alliance and bringing in traditional forward castes and giving them a preeminent position in the governments of Uttar Pradesh, Bihar, Madhya Pradesh, Gujarat, etc. The Congress Party in Maharashtra has recovered its ground by placating the Maratha castes. An important scenario of party competition in India is shifts away and shifts to the Congress in rural areas where powerful rural rich are either forming their own parties or supporting the Congress. The process of capitalist development has benefited the rich peasants but now they want to assert their separateness by raising the issue of rural versus urban, and agriculture versus industry. In spite of ideological rhetoric of Charan Singh, or Devi Lal or other Jat, Yadav, Ahir, Kurmi leaders, their real goal is to control levers of power not as a junior partner in the capitalist-peasant coalition of the Congress but as a separate and distinct identity.

It may be stated here that in rural India there is no contradiction between the landless agricultural worker, marginal and medium farmer but caste is used to divide these natural allies and this not only has increased violence in rural India, it has also paid rich dividends in the elections. Our analysis shows that party competition in India between the Congress and non-Communist and non-BJP parties is because of the breakdown of the Congress coalition and it is competition among the various segments of the exploiting classes for control over government and public resources for sectional and group purposes.

The BJP is a party of the high caste Hindus and it is supported by urban trading and commercial classes. The BJP also gets support from lower and middle classes in urban India whose economic status is unsatisfactory and they consider members of various non-Hindu communities as a threat because of secular policies of the Indian government. The BJP believes in the ideology of one Nation which means Hindu nation and as a party of traders and businessmen it is objectively pro-imperialist. It is a party with cadre, organization, well-built leadership and a long-term perspective of capturing State power to rule over Hindu India. As various parties have made *Jati* as *Jativad,* i.e. casteism, the BJP has made religion as communalism and in spite of its protestations it is a full-blooded communal party which mixes religion with politics. Such a mixture leads to reactions by other communities and instead of integrating the multi-religious and multi-lingual Indian nation, the BJP is a disintegrating factor. During the last thirty-eight years, major democratic parties including the Congress exploited caste and religion for electoral purposes and in the process they politicized caste and religion and solidified these divisive tendencies. All leading classes and major democratic parties in India have strengthened caste and religious divisions and they have fought their political and power battles through caste and religion. It is not without reason that the Hindu caste parties and Hindu communal parties like the BJP came to an understanding with the Janata party in spite of contradictions between the peasantry and commercial and trading communities.

It was argued by some social scientists that old castes are playing a new role in politics and involvement of religion in politics would secularize religion and caste. The functionalist and status quo approach towards caste, religion and politics has been disproved by reality of last thirty-eighty years where casteism and communalism has increased and has led to serious violent conflicts in the Indian society. The capitalist classes and their major political parties like the Congress or the Swatantra Party also employed caste and religion to win elections and divide the communities and groups in caste and religious identities. It has been stated above that the Indian capitalist class had not emerged fighting and destroying the feudal and semi-feudal structures. The capitalist classes in India have used pre-capitalist relations for political power because the Indian capitalists themselves believe in religion, caste and community loyalties. It must be clearly understood that neither the capitalist classes nor their political representatives were insulated from traditional religious beliefs and world view and they employed precapitalist loyalties for gaining legitimacy in democratic politics.

1. Politics in India has become an instrument to exercise power and use public resources for class, group and personal advancement. The road to political legitimacy is through ballot and electoral alliances have been formed on caste and community basis. After winning the elections, the capitalist classes, landlords and rich peasants, politico-bureaucratic decision-makers use their political power or political linkages for cornering public resources for their advancement.

2. Political parties in India are confronted with a situation of shifting and transitory alliances because gradually the Congress coalition is breaking down and the emergent social groups in rural India are walking out of the Congress by forming their parties or walking into the Congress. Competition to control political power is confined primarily to various components of the Congress coalition.

3. Caste and religion have become a powerful divisive force in politics because all major democratic parties and leading social classes have fought their political battle of legitimacy on caste and religious basis. Secular politics in India was always weak and now its foundations are being challenged. The prospects of democratic and secular Indian political system are in doubt because of the new strength shown by caste and religion in politics, and the incapacity of democratic parties to fight against these divisive and disintegrating forces in the country. The Janata and the Lok Dal are comfortable in the company of the BJP, while Congress is comfortable in the company of the Shiva Sena and other communal elements. This is a challenge to the democratic and secular Indian political system.

4. Social violence in the rural and urban areas is increasing because the crisis of capitalist development is felt by the vulnerable and deprived strata of the society. The Indian political system is not able to protect the life of the poor because the State apparatus is controlled by the representatives of the exploiting classes. The private armies of landlords, the lumpen youth of the democratic parties, the communal and caste groups financed by smugglers are always able to inflict heavy physical injuries on the poor in rural and urban areas and State functionaries find themselves helpless to intervene because they cannot act against their financiers and political mentors.

5. The Indian political system is facing challenges from social groups and classes which are anti-democratic, anti-secular and anti-unity and diversity of a federal system. Since the deprived and vulnerable strata of society and their political parties are not a threat to the existing property relations, various segments of property owners are fighting their own battles for supremacy over the political system. It has been seen in history that the exploiting classes compete against one another in politics when threat of revolutionary change is not present. This is the historical situation in India. Various segments of the exploiting classes are involved in political competition in which a segment of the exploiting class is able to corner maximum public resources. The capitalist classes, the rich peasants and the politico-bureaucratic decision-makers are major competitors in politics, and while competing against one another, they also collaborate because they are interested in the present political system which is giving dividends. The big business houses, the medium level capitalists, the landlords and rich peasants, the politico-bureaucratic decision-makers have all enhanced their assets and capacity to manipulate public resources through the existing political system and the victims of real crisis can be managed by brutalities of the State apparatus, the lumpen youth, and the communal and caste warfare. Democratic legitimacy insulates ruling classes from public accountability and 48% of the population living below the poverty line can be subjected to tyranny of the landlord and the high caste and communal mafias. The issue that the ruling classes know that gradually democratic consciousness is developing in India and it would be difficult to terrorize the poor and for this conscious efforts are being made by ruling classes to manipulate the masses on religious and caste basis.

The dialectics of the Indian political system is that gradually masses are gaining the democratic consciousness through election and economic struggle. The ruling classes are responding to the growing consciousness of the masses by manipulating caste and religion and also by use of brute force. Political parties which play a critical role in the body politic of a nation-state are making shifting alliances and transitory adjustments. In a situation like this, democratic political systems capacity to harmonize the conflicting demands of various coalition partners of the exploiting classes is on test. To sum-up, Indian politics has entered a phase of conflict between the exploiting and exploited classes but the challenge from the exploited classes is not a serious threat to the ruling coalitions The consequence of the absence of threat from the exploited classes is responsible for intra-exploiting classes competition in India for control over political power and public resources. The central explanation for the above mentioned tendencies in Indian politics flows from the type of capitalism which is being built in the country. Since the capitalist classes are not ready to assault feudal and semi-feudal social attitudes and the coalition of capitalists and landlords has proved politically viable by the exploiting classes, the tyrannical effect of such an arrangement is felt everyday by the exploited poor in India.

REFERENCES

1. G.K. Shirokov, *Industrialisation of India* (Moscow: Progress Publishers, 1973). p. 49. The paid up capital of all joint stock companies in India was Rs. 479.5 crores (number 2=.853) on 31 March 1947. See R.K. Nigam and N.C. Chaudhuri, *The Corporate Sector in India: A Factual Presentation of Long and Short-Term Trends* (New Delhi: Government of India, 1961).
2. W. Malenbaum, *Prospects for Indian Development* (London: George Allen & Unwin, 1962), pp. 153-4.
3. Oleg Malyarov, "The Formation of Industrial Capital in India", in *India: Problems of Development* (Moscow: USSR Academy of Sciences, 1981), p. 9.
4. *The Economic Times* (Bombay), 3 October 1984, p. 5.
5. M.L. Dantwala, "Agrarian Structure: Bumper Harvests and Rural Poverty", *Economic Times* (Bombay), 23 July 1984.
6. *Seventh Five Year Plan:* 1985-90 (New Delhi: Government of India 1985) vol. 2, p. 63. Also see Francine R. Frankel, *India's Political Economy 1947-1977: The Gradual Revolution* (Delhi: Oxford University Press, 1978).
7. Arvind N. Das, "Class in Itself, Caste for Itself: Social Articulation in Bihar", *Economic and Political Weekly* (Bombay), vol. 19, no. 37, 15 September 1984, p. 161.

9

Political Economy of the Indian State: 1991-1996

The colonial exploitation of India had led to under-development of the economy and after the transfer of power on August 15, 1947, the Indian State took upon itself the responsibility of reconstruction and development of the country. India consciously chose the path of State capitalism based on import-substitution, industrialization and relative self-reliant development. A social consensus existed within the country that the Indian State has to be the engine of growth because the challenges of an underdeveloped economy were quite formidable and there was no other social institution which could play the role of accelerating economic growth with social justice. This State-led model of economic development experienced strains and stresses and the crisis burst in 1991 when India was on the verge of defaulting its foreign exchange obligations and the international community was not ready to bail out crisis-ridden India without a commitment that the Indian State would vacate its over-occupied space in the economy and allow market forces to manage economic problems of the country. India broke with the past which was based on the path of State-led planned capitalism, and globalization, liberalization, deregulation and privatization came to replace the old path of self-reliant regulated economy. It was a basic shift and the former Finance Minister of India, Dr. Man Mohan Singh (1991-1996) always claimed that the New Economic Policy was irreversible and it was proved by the Economic Programme of the new United Front Government established in June 1996. Since a basic shift has occurred in the Indian path of development, it deserves explanations. Conscious public policy decisions are neither *ad hoc* nor they are abandoned unless some fundamental change has taken place in the correlationship of social forces of a society and India cannot be an exception to this general rule.

Two different sets of explanations have been offered to understand the genesis of the birth of New Economic Policy in India. If one looks at India from the global perspective, it can be suggested that India has to adapt itself with the New World Order of the 1990s. Globalization of the Indian economy and its integration with the world capitalist system had become imperative because of the collapse of the European socialist countries and the end of Cold

War. India would have been left behind if it had not adjusted itself with the new global political and economic situations.

The other set of explanations have emerged by emphasizing that the State-led capitalist development of India arrived at a dead end because neither the rate of growth was commensurate with the needs of the country nor the macro-economic and fiscal policies were in proper shape because the market forces were suppressed to resolve serious macro-economic and fiscal issues of the country. It has been maintained that the path of State capitalism followed by India from 1947 to 1991 deserved to be abandoned because State regulated economy had become completely dysfunctional and the State sector instead of acting as an engine of growth had become primarily responsible for the deep crisis of the economy. Jagdish Bhagwati in his *"India in Transition: Freeing the Economy" (1994)* is quite emphatic that India is *"The Model That Couldn't Work"* Jagdish Bhagwati observes:

> "History has its unforeseen ironies. The post-war period, now spanning four decades through the 1980s, began with both a strong economic performance and western empathy and approbation of India's developmental efforts and ideas. It ended with an economy in serious difficulty and, worse, the perception that India had not merely chosen the wrong economic path but had also marginalized herself in world economic affairs in consequence".[1]

Bhagwati also maintains that the attempts of Mrs. Indira Gandhi and Mr. Rajiv Gandhi in the 1980s to loosen the State control over the economy were half-hearted and the New Economic Policy of the P.V. Naramsimha Rao Government from 1991 was a real break with the past.

Pranab Bardhan while analysing the political economy of India on the basis of pressure and interest group theory of American social science, argues that India has three "proprietary classes", *i.e.,* the industrial capitalist class, the rich farmers and the professionals in the public sector. While these three "proprietary classes" compete for State resources, they also compete against one another for the promotion of their specific group interests. Thus the nature of Indian State and social power relations is responsible for the crisis of Indian economy.[2]

Sukhamoy Chakravarty in his *"Development Planning: The Indian Experience"* evaluates the thirty-five years (1950-85) of Indian economic development. Chakravarty catalogues the achievements of these thirty-five years. First, compared to the past of India (1900-50), the economic growth (1950-85) was impressive and it is reflected in the growth of domestic saving rate 'from around 10 per cent of GDP in the early fifties to around 23 per cent' in the 1980s. Second, India's average rate of inflation 'has been a very modest by international standards'. Third, India's inward looking strategy of industrial development provided resilience and stability to the country's development and considerable 'capital formation in human terms' emerged because of this strategy of development. Chakravarty is conscious of the large scale 'poverty' prevailing in the country, and suggests that 'India should make small farms viable for accelerating growth and removal of poverty.'[3]

Sukhamoy Chakravarty's evaluation as compared with either Jagdish Bhagwati or Pranab Bardhan's suggests that the State-led path of development can deliver the goods if distributional crisis is tackled and growing "Social dualism" is prevented.

Unlike Chakravarty's emphasis on 'distribution, and structural problems', Bardhan is stuck with the role of interest groups in India. Bardhan observes, "The Indian public economy has thus become an elaborate net work of patronage and subsidies. The heterogeneous interest groups fight and bargain for their share in the spoils of the system and often strike compromises in the form of 'log-rolling' in the usual fashion of pressure-group politics".[4]

What is New Economic Policy (1991-1996)

The basic shift in India has been from the State-centred and State-led development to export-led industrialization with great encouragement to foreign investment and technology. Linked with this shift is the structural adjustment model of the IMF and the World Bank where "fiscal deficit" in India has to be curbed, limited and eliminated. Its implication is that the public institutions and public investments have to be displaced by market determined investment and production decisions. Since the Indian State is suffering from "fiscal crisis", the foreign borrowings will act as substitute for domestic savings but its prerequisite is macro-economic stabilization, structural adjustment and fiscal reform. The Indian economy internally will deregulate itself and allow free play of 'market-forces' to determine economic decisions, and externally, international trade, international finance and international investment will act as new engines of growth for the country. Thus liberalization and globalization are two interrelated pillars of the new journey in India.

Multiple exogeneous and endogeneous factors have played their role in bringing this shift and a few of them may be highlighted. While the domestic factors leading to the fiscal crisis of 1991 have been already mentioned, a few important external motivating factors need be emphasized. The world has entered a new phase of capitalism in which the transnational corporations have brought *"globalization of production and capital"* and every nation-State has to adjust with this new reality of the 1990s. An American scholar castigates that the US did not understand the implications of 'an inter-dependent world'. Peter B. Kenen observes that:

> "The problems of economic inter-dependence have long been familiar to policy-makers in most countries; their national economies are very open compared to the US economy. But the problems are becoming familiar to Americans too. The American economy has become more

open. Furthermore, US economic policies affect the health of the world economy, and controversies about economic policies tend to migrate into the political arena, affecting the quality of international cooperation in diplomatic and strategic matters".[5]

It is essential to expose the myth of 'interdependent' world and identify the main features of global capitalism in the 1990s. Barbara Stallings in her article "*The New International Context of Development*" mentions that major international changes in the 1990s are "the end of Cold War, increasing competition among capitalist powers, globalization of production and trade, shifting patterns of finance, and new ideological currents".[6]

These five changes identified by Barbara Stallings expose the theory of interdependent world, and emphasise the domination by the capitalist countries over the whole world in spite of Barbara Stallings and Wolfgang Streech's description of "Capitalism in Conflict", *i.e.,* the United States, Europe, and Japan in the post-Cold War world are competent and the loss, of 'Hegemony' of the United States' capitalism over global operations has happened. Amit Bhaduri and Deepak Nayyar further highlight two important features of the new transnational corporation-led global political economy. First, global daily transactions in foreign exchange are around one trillion US dollars, and Bhaduri and Nayyar observe that:

"Indeed, most of the foreign exchange transactions (over 90 per cent) in international markets are not related to international trade. They are speculative movements of financing in the ownership of various forms of existing paper assets, somewhat similar to what we see in stock markets".[7]

The second feature of the multinational corporations is that the maximum trade is 'among different branches of the same multinational' situated in different countries of the world. Thus neither 'speculative' finance capital nor 'infra-firm trade' among the different affiliates of the global branches can lead to development of the Third World including India. D.H. Pai Panandikar in his article "*How vulnerable are we to FIIs?*" refers to the experience of March to May 1996 when the Indian rupee had weakened and exchanged for 37 to a US dollar. This dominance of the US dollar affects our stock and other financial markets. Pai Panandikar observes that:

"A bull phase in the ASEAN can start a bull phase on our stock exchanges. A crisis in Mexico and our stock market is depressed. A rise in the interest rate in the US can mean a fall in share prices on the BSE.... Our financial policies, therefore can no longer be framed in the domestic context alone".[8]

A pertinent question is: Is the Indian State and its institutional arrangement 'capable' of dealing with powerful global capitalism which is characterised by 'speculations' and 'intra-firm trade' and global financial fluctuations and crises?[9]

India has to grapple with the ideological package of global capitalism and the new Western fundamentalism of Free Market Economy. India built its powerful State sector from 1950 to 1985 in spite of the hostility of the International Financial Institutions and the Western Aid givers.[10]

S. Guhan in his paper written for the World Bank observes:

> "In the late 1960s, when the Bank overcame its unwillingness to lend to public sector enterprises, the breakthrough had particularly beneficial results in South Asia by enabling substantial investments in oil, gas, and coal throughout most of the region; in fertilizer manufacture in India, Pakistan and Bangladesh; and in the tree crop sector in Sri Lanka. These major exceptions apart, the Bank has not been able to shed its inhibition toward public ownership at the ideological or at the practical level.... In India, although a Bank study of the steel sector identified opportunities for lending for rehabilitation and improvement, the Bank finally decided not to proceed."[11]

This new globalization is based on a powerful ideology which is directed against State enterprises and State's role in the productive system of India. John P. Lewis in his important book *"Governance and Reform: Essays in Indian Political Economy"*, provides an inside story of the interaction between the Government of India, the United States and USAID establishment in Delhi during the 1960s and early 1970s and it clearly brings out that in this interaction a lot of bargaining took place between the Indians and the policy-makers in the United States.[12] Thus India has to grapple with transnational corporations not only for capital or technology or production collaborations, but also with their ideology which is based on the theory of the retreat of the State and sovereignty of the market forces. This is the new meaning for India with the global capitalism of the 1990s. If the State-centred and State-led development is not the agenda of the Indian policy-makers, and if market forces have to resolve the issues of investment and production, then: What is the relevance of nation-state? If a nation-State is not responsible for the basic decisions for the economy and society of a country, why should citizens owe it any loyalty? The Indian democratic State is bound to face a serious crisis because globalization and liberalization are bound to erode the popular legitimacy of the State. If the State is not perceived as an active promoter of the interests of 335 million Indians who are living below poverty line, and if the Indian State cannot effectively deal with growing rural-urban social and economic divide, the democratic sanction from such a State will be either withdrawn or it will be lukewarm. What are the chances of democratization of a country in the global reality of transnational division of labour? According to a study:

> ". . . . We will adopt an 'agnostic' position on any generalizable overall relationship between democracy and political/economic dependence

in transnational relations. This does not mean, however, that the position of a country in the transnational division of labour and inter-state relations is irrelevant for its chances of democratization. It does mean that these chances are dependent on power relations among groups and institutions whose interests stand to benefit or suffer by democratization. Transnational power relations are an integrated part of these constellations that interact with the other forces and developments".[13]

In a class-divided society like India, the majority of the oppressed, exploited and vulnerable social groups support the State for a better future. A retreating State in India cannot remain democratic because serious social cleavages and crises cannot be resolved by accepting the new methodology of market forces.

Indian Experience of 1991 to 1996

The *Economic Survey* of the Government of India is an official document of the policies, performance and trends of the future economic development of the country. The *Economic Survey* of 1995-96 clearly states:

(a) "Greater access and use of foreign investment is necessary for promoting higher growth of output, exports and employment". (p. 15)

(b) "FDI has proved to be the most effective and rapid method of technology transfer (in the from of knowledge, technical and marketing skills, organization and management systems, new material and products) and effective promotion of cooperative advantage through exports. Even when it forms a small fraction of the total domestic investment, its catalytic role is out of proportion to its size". (p. 15)

(c) "The response of foreign investment flows to the liberalization measures has been very encouraging. Over the last three years they have grown at an average of 100 per cent per year. From US$ 620 million in 1993-94, foreign direct investment (FDI) more than doubled to US$ 1.31 billion in 1994-95. During April-November 1995, FDI flows were US$ 1.27 billion, showing a growth of 110 per cent over the corresponding period of 1994-95". (p. 15)

(d) The liberalizers were also not worried about the foreign debt of India. "India's external debt rose from US$ 92.70 billion at the end of March 1994 to US$ 99.04 billion at the end of March 1995. Of the US$ 6.34 billion increase in external debt during 1994-95 as much as US$ 5.61 billion or 88 per cent of the increase was due to changes in the exchange rate of the US$ dollar versus other major currencies in which India's debt is denominated". (p. 12)[14]

The Indian State functionaries are neither worried about the increase in foreign debt of US$ 5.61 billion only because of the US Government's decision on exchange rate nor they are worried about the net out-flow.

The Graph 1 clearly reveals that the so-called foreign aid is a utopia, India is involved in reverse flow of resources to the Western capitalist countries. Closely linked with the issue of foreign debt and foreign aid is the hierarchy of foreign investors in India.

Graph 1
External Aid Transactions

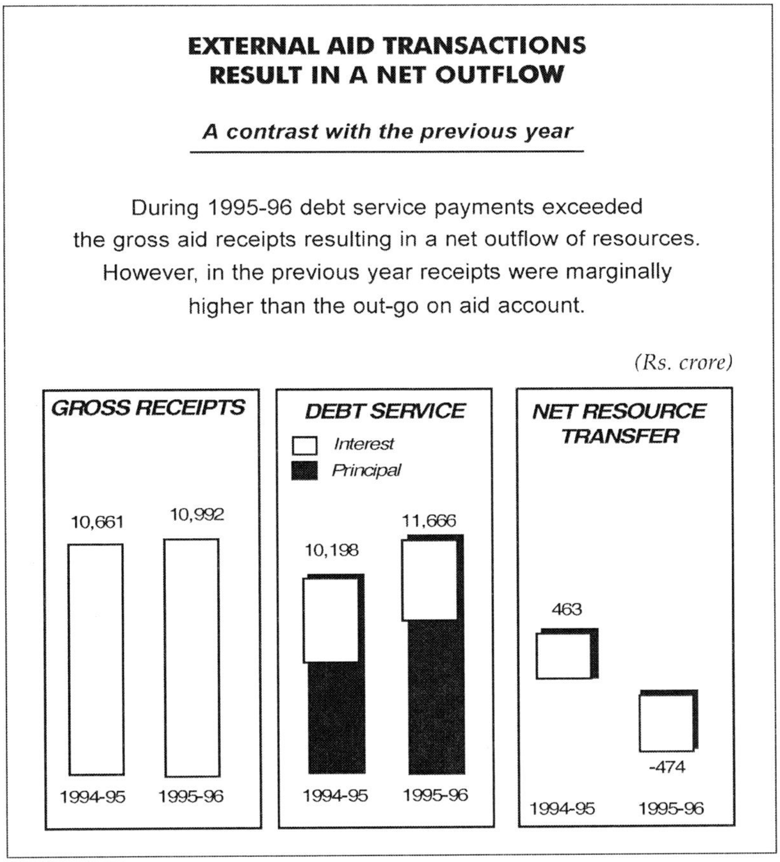

Source: *Monthly Economic Report*, May, 1996.

Graph 2 of foreign investors even on the basis of two months of 1996 shows that the United States is emerging as an important actor in Indian political economy with serious consequences for the sovereignty of the Indian State.

Graph 2
Top Ten Foreign Investors in India

(Foreign direct investment approved during Jan. and Feb. 1996)

(Rs. million)

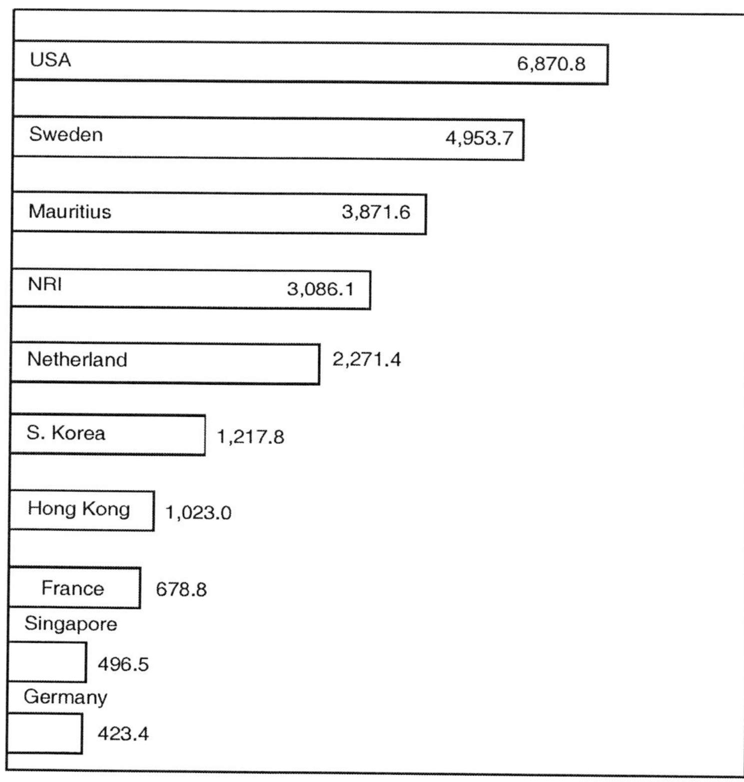

Source: *The Times of India*, New Delhi, Friday May 31, 1996.

Graph 3 further comprises the finding based on Graph 2 that the US role in Indian public affairs is increasing because of its growing economic clout in the Indian economy.

This sector-wise break up is quite important because, besides telecommunications in which transnational corporations are playing a big role, Indians are happy to receive foreign investment in the promotion of Tourism and Hotel Industry. The distinction between priority and non-priority areas has got blurred in attracting the foreign investors. Not only this, multinationals are leading in filing patent applications in India. The *Economic Survey* claimed that foreign capital brings the advantages of technology transfer to India. This claim has been belied by facts.

Graph 3
Foreign Direct Investment

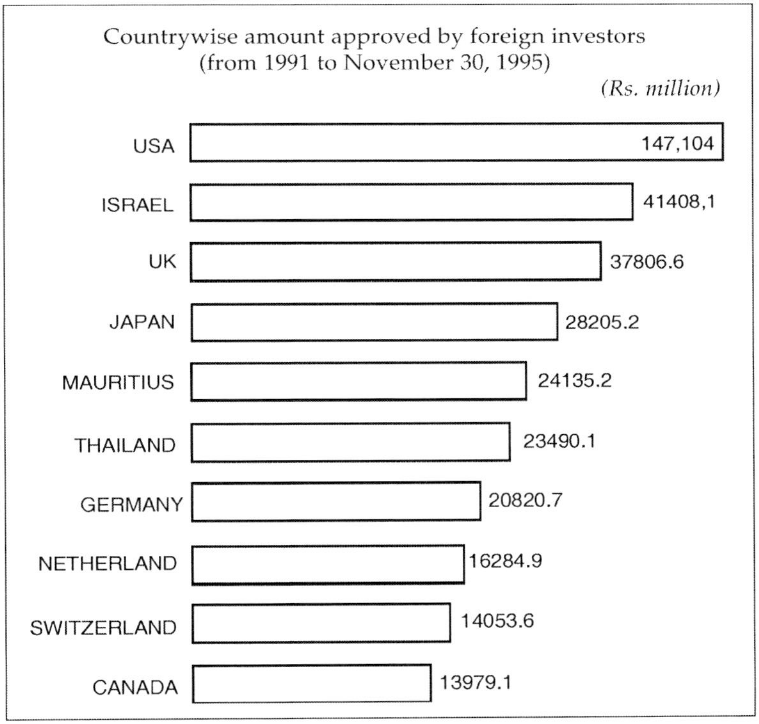

Source: The Pioneer.

It is worth mentioning that out of 255 electronics patent applications filed 226 are from multinationals like Motorola, Daewoo Electronics, IBM and Sony. And these are in the information technology related areas. Globalization, liberalization and the actual working of the New Economic Policy has created foreign debt burden, and the myth of technology transfer has been exposed by the patent registered by the multinational corporations. The New Economic Policy has not only aggravated social cleavages and disparities, it has also encouraged and institutionalized regional disparities and imbalances in India. The demand pattern of the exploiting urban and rural classes has determined the priorities of foreign investors. The telling example is the automobile sector in India, all multinationals are active in India in producing expensive and luxury cars for the exploiting classes. Similarly, advanced regions in India have attracted more foreign funds than the relatively backward regions.

Graph 5 clearly reveals that developed states like Maharashtra, Gujarat and Karnataka are attractive places for foreign investors. If this Graph is seen with inter-state income disparity, the gravity of growing disparities across the classes and regions becomes sharp. The most backward states and the most

Graph 4
Sectorwise Foreign Direct Investment Approved

(August 1991 to January 1996)

(Rs. million)

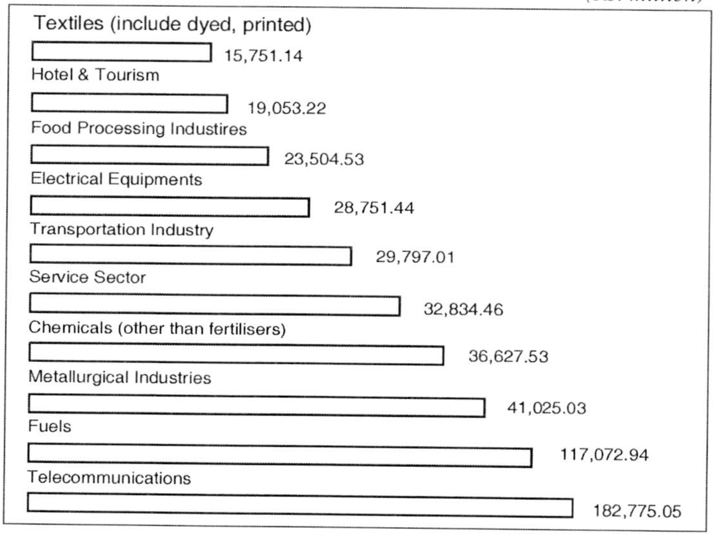

Source: *SIA Newsletter*, February 1996.

Table 8.1: Major MNCs Who have Filed for Patents in Electronics

Applicant	*No. of Applications*
Motorola Inc	33
Daewoo Electronics	31
Siemens Akteingesellschaft	19
Ionica International	11
Qualcomm Inc	11
IBM Corporation	6
Thomson Consumer Elec	6
Discovision Associates	6
General Electric Co	5
Phillips Electronics NV	5
Sony Corporation	5

Source: *The Economic Times*, New Delhi, May 23, 1996.

developed states in terms of income are competing for free for all foreign investments.

Explanations for the Changes in the Policies of the Indian State in 1991-96

While State has a class essence, in late industrializing peripheral countries like India, Ministers and bureaucrats along with other managerial groups have

Graph 5
Foreign Direct Investment

Statewise amount approved and invested by foreign investors from August '91 to December '95

(Rs. million)

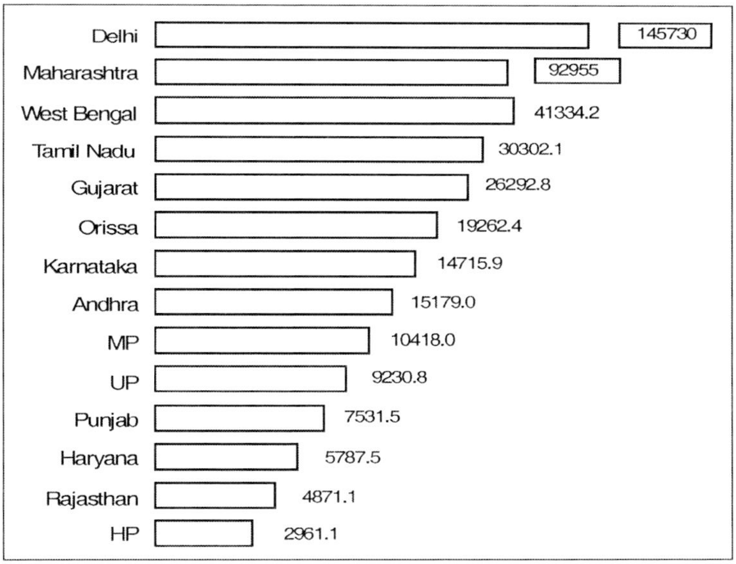

Source: Ministry of Industry.

their autonomous interests. While the Balance of Exchange crisis of 1991 was used as an excuse for changing the economic path of development, the reasons for this basic change are not linked with the 1991 crisis.

Since 1991 is a break with the past, an important feature of the Indian State during the 1950s to early 1980s may be mentioned. The Indian State was relatively autonomous of the local dominant classes and fractions of the classes, and externally it operated in an international milieu on the basis of bargaining.

Only one illustration will prove the point. The late J.R.D. Tata, the leader of Big Business in India, had social and family relations with Jawaharlal Nehru and Mrs. Indira Gandhi. A biographer of Tata informs us that J.R.D. Tata did not get any 'encouragement' from Nehru and Indira Gandhi when he expressed his ideas on 'economy' to them.[15] John P. Lewis informs us that President Lyndon Johnson created a lot of difficult problems for the USAID establishment in Delhi by stopping food supply to India because he was very annoyed with Mrs. Indira Gandhi on her attitude and policy towards US war in Vietnam.[16] Sinco the Green Revolution in India, capitalist farmer or Landlord capitalism, characterised by Utsa Patnaik as an important factor, has emerged along with the other fractions of the industrial and merchant bourgeoisies in India. These social classes and fractions have conflicts among themselves, and they are also united in pursuing

Graph 6
Inter-State Income Disparity

Per capite net state domestic product in rupee at current prices. Punjab tops the list of major indian states in terms of per-capita income closely followed by Maharashtra and Haryana. Bihar is at the foot of the ladder with a per-capita income as low as Rs. 10.00 per day.

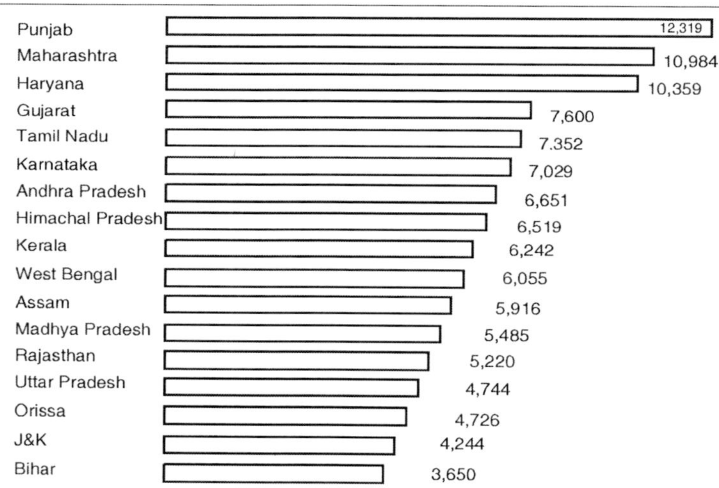

Note: Data pertain to the major Indian states with population over five million each as per 1991 census.

the path of private appropriation and these divided fractions are represented in different political parties and groups like the Congress Party, the Janata Dal, the Bhartiya Janata Party and the regional parties. The centre-stage of politics has been occupied by these parties which are reflecting the social goals of different fractions of the exploiting classes. This political development has few consequences for the Indian State. First, since these political groups keep on alternating in the corridors of power, along with bureaucracy, they provide a sanction for privatization. Second, fractured political groups and social fractions have made the State apparatus weak because the State functionaries keep on balancing the conflicting interests of multiple class fractions. The State has become a kind of middleman among the contending class fractions. Third, since multiple class fractions are in power in the Indian State, their demands and interests have become dominant guiding principles of State policies. Food processing industry is the priority of capitalist farmer and automobile industry is the favourite of surplus earning social groups. For this they look towards international capital.

In spite of conflict among the fractions of rural and urban classes, all agree to encourage foreign capital, foreign investment and foreign technology. The change of Government in India in June 1996 did not create any problems for global investors. On the contrary, every political formation was in a hurry to assure that foreign investments will continue and even more foreign funds will be welcomed. The political economy of the Indian State in the 1990s was determined by the interests of the exploiting classes who did not want to grapple with the basic crisis of accumulation in India, and who wanted to cushion this crisis by inviting transnationals. In a country of 890 million people, the annual Income Tax collected by the Indian State is only Rs. 15,000 crore to Rs. 18,000 crore. This domestic resource mobilization is absolutely inadequate to deal with the complex problems of a continental economy. Hence, an invitation to foreign capital to fill in the gaps of low domestic saving rates. This real crisis is the result of *consensus* among all important fractions of the exploiting classes in India.

REFERENCES

1. Jagdish Bhagwati, *India in Transition, Freeing the Economy,* Oxford University Press, New Delhi, 1995, p. 5.
2. Pranab Bardhan, *The Political Economy of Development in India,* Oxford University Press, Oxford, U.K., 1984.
3. Sukhamoy Chakravarty, *Development Planning: The Indian Experience,* Oxford University Press, Oxford, U.K., 1987, pp. 82-89.
4. Pranab Bardhan: "A Political-Economy Perspective on Development," in Bimal Jalan (ed.). *The Indian Economy: Problems and Prospects,* Viking Penguin Book India (P) Ltd., New Delhi, 1992, p. 325.
5. Peter B. Kenen, *The International Economy,* Cambridge University Press, Cambridge, U.K., 1996, Third Edition, p. 14.
6. Barbara Stallings, "The New International Context of Development" in Barbara Stallings (ed.). *Global Change, Regional Response: The New International Context of Development,* Cambridge University Press, Cambridge, U.K., 1995, p. 350.
7. Amit Bhaduri & Deepak Nayyar, *The Intelligent Persons's Guide to Liberalization,* Penguin Books India (P) Ltd., New Delhi, 1996, p. 75.
8. D.H. Pai Panandikar, "How Vulnerable are We to FIIs? *The Hindustan Times,* New Delhi, May 13, 1996, p. 15.
9. Also see Deepak Nayyar, *Economic Liberalization in India: Analytics, Experiences and Lessons,* Orient Longman Ltd., New Delhi, 1996, pp. 58-61.
10. See C.P. Bhambhri, *World Bank and India,* Vikas, New Delhi, 1980. Also see C.P. Bhambhri, *Foreign Policy of India,* Sterling, New Delhi, 1987.

11. S. Guhan, *The World Bank's Lending in South Asia.* The Brookings Institution: Washington D.C.: 1995, p. 69.
12. See John P. Lewis, *Essays in Indian Political Economy: Governance and Reform,* Oxford University Press, New Delhi, 1995.
13. Dietrich Rueschemeyer, Evelyne Huber Stephens and John D. Stephens, *Capitalist Development & Democracy,* Polity Press, Cambridge, U.K., 1992, p. 73.
14. *Economic Survey: 1995-96,* Government of India, New Delhi.
15. R.M. Lala, *Beyond the Last Blue Mountain: A Life of JRD Tata (1904-1993),* Penguin Books, New Delhi, 1993, ed. p. 2.
16. John P. Lewis, *Governance and Reform: Essays in Indian Political Economy,* Oxford University Press, New Delhi, 1995.

10

New Economic Policy: Indian State and Bureaucracy

The New Economy Policy of the Narasimha Rao Government was situated on a perspective which was fundamentally different from the model of economic development of Jawaharlal Nehru and Mrs. Indira Gandhi. Any basic shift in the path and strategies of economic development of a country deserves serious analysis because any break with the past cannot be attributed to the subjective feelings of the public policy makers. It is also essential to keep in mind that the Narasimha Rao Government did not receive any electoral or popular mandate for the package of new economic policies. The Lok Sabha elections of 1991 were not contested by the Congress Party on its economic programme. The political and economic developments of India of the 1990s may be contextualised by linking the domestic scene with global political and economic developments of the post-Cold War phase of the 1990s. It deserves to be mentioned that every major global development exercises a direct impact on the functionaries of the Indian State and many a time the distinction between the global and the domestic gets blurred. The Rao Government's policies of global integration of the Indian economy have consciously permitted the global decision-makers to exercise a direct impact on the policy making state apparatuses of India. The very first step of the Rao Government in July 1991 was to invite advanced industrial countries to resolve the so-called Balance of Payments crisis of India. The *quid-pro-quo* between the Rao Government and the advanced industrial countries was that India will open its market to the foreign investors for the resolution of the so-called economic crisis of the 1990s. The Nehru Model of economic development of India was based on relative self-reliance, import substitution, industrialization and bargaining with powerful industrial countries on terms and conditions for foreign assistance in India's economic development. The Nehru Model was based on the principle of the relative autonomy of the Indian State while dealing with other nation-states. The proclaimed goal of Narasimha Rao's Model is global integration of India with advanced industrial countries. This new globalization of the Indian economy was a decisive break with the Nehru-Indira Gandhi phase of political leadership of the Indian State. What are the explanations for such a new turn in the political economy of India?

A few salient features of post-1990s changes in the global correlation of social forces may be mentioned to understand the context in which the new economic policies of India had to operate.

First, the collapse of East European socialist systems had qualitatively changed the global power equations because the non-aligned countries of Asia, Africa and Latin America received great political, military and economic support from the erstwhile socialist countries and on this basis, they could bargain with the advanced Western industrial countries. India maintained its relative autonomy in world affairs and effectively bargained in every global institution because of its special friendship with the erstwhile Soviet Russia and other East European socialist countries. The Movement of Non-Aligned countries suffered a serious setback because of collapse of the East European socialist countries.

Second, the Transnational Corporations (TNCs) had emerged as very powerful global players and they were looking for markets, cheap labour and cheap raw material in every developing country of the world. The United Nations Conference on Trade and Development (UNCTAD) in its World Investment Report 1994: *Transnational Corporations, Employment and the Workplace* (WIR 94) has mentioned a few important features of the operations of the TNCs in global economy: (i) The global sales of the TNCs exceeded US$ 4.8 trillion, and this contributed to the "growing internationalization of the production of goods and services", (ii) The TNCs have 37,000 parent firms and more than two lakh foreign affiliates, (iii) The TNCs employ some 73 million persons at home and abroad, (iv) The world's largest 100 TNCs held US$ 3.4 trillion in global assets in 1992. Forty per cent of these assets were located outside their home countries. The UNCTAD Report observes: "Transnationalization influences employment, human resources development and industrial relations.... Today, the policy response to unemployment must take place against the background of a vastly more integrated world economy in which TNCs are playing an increasingly more important role."[1] The direct consequence of this globalization of capital is that the advanced industrial countries are demanding every facility from the developing countries for Foreign Direct Investment.[2]

Third, the post-World War II institutions like the International Bank for Reconstruction and Development (IBRD or World Bank) and the International Monetary Fund have also changed their role during the 1990s. A World Bank-IMF Censensus has emerged on the paradigm of the so-called structural adjustment which has to be followed by the states which approach Bank-IMF for assistance for development and fiscal stabilization. The new conditionalities which the Bank and IMF have evolved have a definite ideological approach based on the philosophy of *free market economy* and retreat of the State from its central role in the productive system of the country.

This discussion of new global developments of the 1990s will be incomplete without highlighting some significant developments within the advanced industrial countries of the West. The advanced industrial countries are re-arranging and re-structuring relationships among themselves because the United States of America has ceased to be the leader of global industrial economy and Germany and Japan have emerged as important centres of industrial economy. The first attempt to work together was made in 1980s by the so-called G7 countries of USA, Japan, Germany, UK, France, Italy and Canada. The 1990s have witnessed the marginalization of the cooperation among the G7 countries and in its place there have emerged powerful *'trading blocs'*. The European Union of fifteen countries, the North American Free Trade Area (NAFTA) of USA, Canada and Mexico, the Association of South East Asian countries and the Asia-Pacific Economic Cooperation Forum (APEC) are new groupings in search of "Free trade" among themselves. If, on the one hand, globalization of production and services is a growing reality, on the other, emergence of *'trading blocs'* is the other side of this new global reality of the 1990s. Foreign Direct Investment in the complex productive systems of Third World countries is a new reality of the 1990s. Michel Hansenne, Director General of the ILO, while releasing a *Report on World Employment* (1995) observed that: "In the eighties about 80 per cent of the FDI flowed to developed countries. It has changed. In 1992, the share of the developing countries in FDI flow rose to 30 per cent as against an average of 24 per cent during the 1970s. It increased further to 40 per cent in 1993." The ILO Report (1995) further stated that "If present trends continue, annual flows of FDI into the Third World would, in the medium term, exceed those into the developed world. This would represent a major structural shift in the pattern, not just of investment, but also of the production and trade that arise from it."[3]

Thus the UNCTAD Report of 1994 and the ILO Report of 1995 have clearly brought out the salient features of the changing role of global capital in the 1990s, and their impact on the economic policies and productive systems of the developing countries including India. It may be mentioned here that the Transnational Corporations or other foreign investors from the advanced industrial countries will decide their own priority areas for making investments in India. The 'Finance Capital' of the United States is interested in the Indian market in service sectors like the Insurance Business and Banking Operations. The opening of the Indian market to the global capital has brought a sea change in India's political and economic relations with the United States of America, the European countries and Japan. In addition to many business delegations and junior administrative functionaries, four top functionaries of the United States visited India during the new phase of globalization of the Indian economy. The US Commerce Secretary, Ron Brown, the Defence Secretary, William Perry, the Energy Secretary, Mrs. Hazel O. Leary, and the Treasury Secretary, Robert L. Rubin have visited India to promote the economic and political interests of their country and they found that the Indian policy makers were very hospitable to the US economic involvement in the Indian market. The total repayment of principal of India was US$ 2826.236 million up to March

31,1994. The total debt of India to US up to March 31, 1994 was $ 2,201.067 million. In 1994-1995, the repayment of principal by India to the US is US$ 121.781 million and the payment of interest is US$ 60.927 million.[4]

India is on the march on borrowing money from abroad and for establishing large number of collaborative arrangements with foreign financial and trading companies. The merchant bankers like the Chairman of Morgan Stanley, J.P. Morgan, Merrill Lynch, Jardine Fleming of Deutsche Bank, Bank Paribas, Namura Securities and Barclays visited India to seek expansion of their activities.[5]

Further, the foreign firms are earning good profits in India and this encourages other foreign companies to seek entry and India is very willing to allow such companies to start business. A Reserve Bank of India survey of the annual accounts of 313 selected foreign-controlled companies showed their higher profit margins and comfortable liquidity position during the period 1987-88 to 1989-90. The foreign-controlled companies registered a higher profit margin on sales of 11.9 per cent against 9.9 per cent of the Indian controlled companies.[6] A Document on *"Indo-US Trade and Economic Cooperation"* mentions that "Traditionally, India has never been a favourite destination for the US foreign investors. It shared only 0.07 per cent of US FDI stock in 1990 which increased to 0.98 per cent in 1992. However... US investment increased from $ 22.38 million in 1986 to $ 1135.41 million in 1993. In 1993, $ 1,135.41 million of US investment was approved which was 39 per cent of the total."

The Document further observes that "The average rate of return on total US FDI abroad in the manufacturing sector is 8 per cent for 1991. However, the same in India is 16.4 per cent. This is more than double the average rate of return of US FDI in the manufacturing sector in the world."[7]

The above Documents reveal *profitability* of foreign investments in the Indian market, and it is not surprising that the United States of America sent large "presidential missions comprising key officials and representatives of top business and industrial houses" to India in January 1995 under the leadership of US Commerce Secretary Mr. Ron Brown. The United States has identified ten Big Emerging Markets like India, China, South Korea, Indonesia, South Africa, Poland, Turkey, Mexico, Argentina and Brazil. The US Under Secretary of Commerce for International Trade, in an interview in the *Wall Street Journal,* observed that "The race between US and European companies for footholds in promising markets from Brazil to India to China has become quite hot. At stake,... are billion-dollar contracts for mass transit systems, telecommunications, power generation, airports and other infrastructure projects that have become scarce in Europe". He further observed that this would intensify competition between US and Europeans. He also warned that "Race for emerging markets may open fresh rifts".[8] The governments and capitalists of advanced industrial countries are ruthlessly promoting their interests in India. Like the US Presidential Mission, the Indo-British Partnership Initiative was launched in January 1993 by the British Prime Minister, John Major. The Government of India has completely diluted the Foreign Exchange

Regulation Act; foreign equity participation up to 51 per cent is automatically approved, and excess of 51 per cent foreign participation requires formal approval of the Foreign Investment Promotion Board of the Government of India.

The Indian State has not only dismantalled its regulatory arrangements for restricting the flow of 'foreign capital' into India, it is encouraging Indian Big Business to launch joint ventures with the multinational corporations. A few illustrations will prove the point that the MNCs are expanding their social base in India: (a) ATOT, the leading US-based telecom MNC and Aditya Birla Group have signed Memorandum of Understanding (1995) "to jointly explore business opportunities in telecom sector" including basic and mobile cellular services.[9] (b) Reliance-Enron Consortium for coal-fed methon exploration and development in Madhya Pradesh and Orissa. (c) The German Automobile Giant, Daimler-Benz Ag. has invested DM 300 million in Rahul Bajaj's Bajaj Auto. (d) Tata Group has negotiated collaboration with Daimler-Benz. Raghupati Singhania of the JK Tyres is negotiating for a "tie-up" with Schellenberg, Germany "to market and distribute Audi cars in India."[10]

It was assumed that the package of New Economic Policies of the Narasimha Rao Government would receive a sharp opposition from the *Indian bourgeoisie* because their own class interest would be hurt. India's structural adjustment programme, fiscal stabilization, deregulation of industry, globalization and opening of economy to market mechanism, the equity sale of public sector undertakings and open invitation to Foreign Direct Investment would lead to a situation of "unequal" competition between the foreign capital and the Indian capitalist classes. A little protest came from Bombay Club which demanded 'level playing' by the Indian companies, but even this opposition could not stand the aggressive pursuit of new economic policies by the Rao Government and the Indian Bourgeoisie fell in line with the new economic regime of globalization. Mr. A.K. Rungta, the President of the Federation of Indian Chamber of Commerce and Industry wrote a letter to the Prime Minister urging him to continue with the New Economic Policy. Rungta wrote that: "Ephemeral emotive appeals cannot wish away India's irreversible commitment to reforms." He further wrote that "huge investment is required in sectors like power, transport, ports and telecommunication" to bridge the resource gap.[11] The Government of India is encouraging Industrial Houses to take loans in foreign markets and attract foreign collaborators.

The above discussion clearly shows that a qualitative change has taken place in the nature and role of global capital and India has also opted for reversal of its Nehru-Indira Gandhi Model of relatively self-reliant State Capitalism. It is essential to understand and analyse the *implications* of the Rao Government's policies for the sovereignty of India. Further, explanations have to be attempted to grapple with the nature of shifts brought by the policies of the Rao Government.

Implications for National Sovereignty

The globalization of Indian economy undertaken by the Narasimha Rao Government has encouraged the advanced industrial countries to demand concessions in the field of legitimate security concerns of India. The United States imposed its Missile Technology Control Regime (MTCR), pressurised Russia not to transfer cryogenic engines to India for Space Research Organization because such a 'transfer' was violative of the US laws. This action of the United States established that the laws passed by the sovereign Parliament of India were subordinate to the laws of the Government of the United States. The United States also put India on notice under its Super 301 for violating patent laws and copyright laws of the United States. The United States had demanded that India should amend its patent laws and bring its laws in harmony with the laws of the United States.

On January 1, 1995, the World Trade Organization was established by replacing the General Agreement on Tariffs and Trade. This World Trade Organization will act as a 'watchdog' of Trade in Intellectual Property Rights (TRIPS) and Trade in Investment Matters (TRIMS). In an inter-dependent world, every sovereign state has to come to terms with the demands of interaction with other sovereign states but in the existing 'hegemonic' world, some states are more sovereign than the others. The laws of some sovereign states are superior to the laws of other sovereign states and India has experienced this new reality under the Narasimha Rao Government's policies of globalization. The advanced industrial countries have asked India to improve its *governance* and allow market mechanisms to determine its macro-economic arrangements. The advanced industrial countries have served notice to the Indian State to maintain a good record on *'Human Rights'*. The Indian State is expected to implement the ideology and agenda *of good governance* and *free market economy* in return for private foreign investments. The World Bank, the IMF, the Asian Development Bank are also important instruments of the advanced industrial countries which have started *'auditing'* the policy framework and performance of the Government of India. The issue of 'subsidy' to the Indian farmers has ceased to be a domestic problem of the Indian State. The World Bank, the IMF, and the advanced industrial countries have strongly objected to the 'subsidization' of the Indian agriculture because it creates fiscal deficits in India and leads to bad management of the Indian economy. Thus, the good management of the Indian economy has become the concern of aid-giving countries and global aid-giving institutions. Even while accepting an instrumental view of State in class divided societies, Marxists are unanimous on the concept of 'relative autonomy of the State'.[12] The concept of relative autonomy of the State has domestic and international dimensions but globalization of the Indian economy under hegemonic world situation knocks down the concept of sovereignty of the Indian State.

European Marxists like Althuser, Gramsci and Poulantazs while referring to 'structural' aspects of late capitalism have drawn attention to the role of the *state apparatus* with special reference to the role of State bureaucracies. Populantaz claims that 'the political, economic and ideological structures have a relative autonomy' of social classes and there is a competition and conflict among the fractions of the classes, 'within the power bloc' and the State in such a situation plays a 'cohesive role'. Conflicts are between competitive versus monopoly fractions, finance versus industrial fractions and international versus local bourgeoisies and State has to play a cohesive and integrating role in such a situation."[13]

If State bureaucracy is important for late capitalist European countries, it is crucial and critical for the administration of peripheral capitalist countries like India. It is relevant to examine the impact of the policy of globalization on the role of Indian bureaucracy and their linkages with the advanced industrial countries and global institutions like the World Bank and the IMF.

The higher echelons of Indian bureaucracy were always integrated with the Indian capitalist classes. Indian bureaucracy believes in the fundamental social institution of 'private property' and it has actively participated in managing State capitalist sector and has facilitated the promotion of private corporate sector in India. A few illustrations may be given to expose the close linkages between Indian bureaucracy and Indian capitalism. V.P. Menon, who worked with Sardar Patel for the integration of the Indian states, was himself a Founder Chairman of the Leela Group. The Group consists of Leela Scottish Lace Ltd., Leela Fashions Ltd., Leela Kenapinshi, Bombay, and the Leela Beach, Goa. Usha (India) Ltd. 1993 (formerly Usha Rectifiler Corp. Ltd., 1962) is a multi-product company and has three directors on the Board who were closely linked with the Government of India. Baldev Pasricha was former Chairman of the Industrial Finance Corporation of India, Lt. General J.K. Khanna (Retd.) was former Director of Minerals and Metals Trading Corporation of India, and M.C. Sarin was former Secretary, the Government of India. Mr. Gyan Prakash, Retired IAS and former Comptroller and Auditor-General of India is the Chairman of Parsarampuria Synthetics, Srinivas Fertilisers, and Director with Modi Cement Ltd., P.S.B. Finance and Leasing Ltd., Thapar DuPont Fibres Ltd. and P.S.B. Housing Finance Co. Ltd.[14] Flexible Packaging Flex Industries Ltd (Delhi) deals with printed, laminated, metallised plastic film and paper and mettallising of plastic film. It has on its Board, Directors P.L. Punia and R.C. Thakkru, retired IAS.[15]

CIFCO Finance Ltd., incorporated on February 16,1994, deals with hire purchase, leasing, investments, under-writing, venture finance etc. One of the Directors of this Company is Field Marshal S.H.F.J. Manekshaw who was former Chief of the Army Staff. The higher echelons of civil and military bureaucracy have always been actively associated with private corporate sector in India.[16]

If Indian capitalist classes have recognized the utility of State bureaucracy in the building of private corporate sector, the advanced industrial countries also recognize that the linkages with the higher echelons of Indian bureaucracy are essential for the promotion of the interests of the transnational corporations in India. Global capitalism has to penetrate the policy making levels of the Indian State by establishing appropriate linkages with State bureaucracy. These international linkages of Indian bureaucracy and crucial policy makers were revealed dramatically by the Parliamentary Committee which was established to investigate the corrupt activities indulged by some stock brokers. The Ram Niwas Mirdha Committee (1994) indicted some important foreign banks in India for indulging in corrupt activities in league with stock brokers, but these *foreign banks* were fully protected because they had provided jobs to the family members of important and influential public policy makers in India. Further, important Ministries of the Government of India like Finance, Industry, Commerce and Trade and also the Planning Commission are the target of multinational corporations and they make every effort to establish linkages with higher echelons of bureaucracy in these crucial Ministries of the Central and the State Governments. *Internationalization* of important public policy makers of India has emerged as a logical consequence of the Rao Government's policy of globalization of the Indian economy. Since every advanced industrial country promotes the interests of its own capitalists, these countries are competing in India for coopting and winning the support of Indian decision-makers. Every important project creates international competition, and international lobbies are quite active in the Ministries of the Government of India and the state governments in the country. To sum up, two interrelated implications of globalization are the erosion of the sovereignty of the Indian State and international cooptation and linkages of state apparatuses of the country. Globalization cannot succeed in India without the willing cooperation of the State bureaucracy. And this has happened in India. Ideological orientations and career perceptions of the Indian bureaucracy have made them willing partners of global capitalism.

Another important *implication of* globalization of Indian economy is for the state governments of India. India has serious regional imbalances and developed and underdeveloped states have to follow different strategies of economic development and inter-state cooperation. The opening of the Indian economy to foreign capital and the retreat of the Central Government from its leadership role has compelled the state governments to compete for the flow of foreign capital and collaborations with multinational corporations. The last four years of globalization of the Indian economy have further deepened the difference between the developed states like Maharashtra, Karnataka etc. and the underdeveloped states like Bihar, Uttar Pradesh etc. Similarly North-Eastern states like Assam, Meghalaya, Manipur, Tripura, Arunachal Pradesh, Mizoram and Nagaland have been further pushed towards underdevelopment because the foreign investors are attracted towards developed states and not towards really backward states. Every Chief Minister of the different Indian states' governments is offering maximum incentives to foreign investors for investment in his or her particular state. Chief Ministers are competing among themselves in their bid to attract foreign investors and a *deep divide* has occurred between the backward and industrially advanced states of India. Thus, globalization of the Indian economy has directly affected sovereignty of the Indian State and cooptation of the higher echelons of bureaucracy with global capitalism. It has also aggravated regional imbalances and generated ruthless inter-state competition to attract foreign capital.

New Economic Policy and Crisis of the Indian State

The foreign debt of India amounting to US$ 90.27 billion is not the cause but a consequence of the structural crisis of the path of capitalist development of India. The Balance of Payments crisis of India will persist and debt service on external debt would go up from US$ 10.5 billion in 1994-95 to US$ 13 billion in 1995-96, and export-led growth or global integration of India will not resolve the balance of payments crisis.

The Indian State is a product of powerful anti-colonial Third World nationalism. After independence the State became very active in building capitalism as a logical extension of the social essence of Indian nationalism. The anti-colonial Third World nationalism of India has to be taken in its totality with all its strong and weak points. It is essential to keep in mind here that the concept of bourgeois revolution according to Karl Marx is which "reconciles all levels of historical reality and every aspect of the French Revolution". The Indian State began its journey by evolving a broad class coalition of the national bourgeoisie, the working classes and the peasantry to build "import-substitution" based capitalism with a view to promote relative self-reliant economy for the country. Another pillar of this path of capitalist development was that the Indian State maintained "relative autonomy" in global affairs. This tenuous class coalition broke down and structural crisis of Indian path of capitalism emerged in a big way from the middle of 1960s.[17]

Mrs. Indira Gandhi, as the political leader of the Indian State faced the consequences of structural crisis of India by ruthlessly suppressing the Railway strike of 1974 and by imposing the Emergency in 1975-77. The electorate of India rejected the authoritarian regime of Mrs. Indira Gandhi in the elections of 1977. The authoritarian solution to deal with deepening of economic crisis failed to achieve the desired goals of the political regime of Mrs. Indira Gandhi. Three important studies examined the causes of deceleration of industrial growth and reasons for economic crisis of 1970s. Isher Judge Ahluwalia in her study *Industrial Growth in India: Stagnation since the Mid-Sixties* identified three reasons for stagnation of Indian economy. First, slow growth of agricultural incomes had their effect on limiting the demand for industrial goods. Second, there was a slowdown in public investment after mid-sixties which had a particular impact on infrastructural investment.

Third, poor management of the infrastructure sector which led to severe infrastructural constraints. The real villain of the piece according to Ahluwalia was the industrial policy framework which saddled India with high cost economy and her recipe for resolution of crisis was deregulation and globalization of the Indian economy.[18] Another important book was written by

L.K. Jha, who was Chief Economic Adviser to Lal Bahadur Shastri and Mrs. Indira Gandhi.[19]

On her return to power in 1980s, Mrs. Indira Gandhi arranged mega IMF loan of US$ 5 billion and declared 1982 as "the year of productivity". Prabhat Patnaik's *"An Explanatory Hypothesis on the Indian Industrial Stagnation" (1981)* in the Bagchi and Banerjee's edited volume took a very different view from that of Ahluwalia, Jha and many economic advisers of Mrs. Indira Gandhi.[20]

The deepening of economic crisis completely shattered the post-independence class coalition of national bourgeoisie, working classes and peasantry. The Indian Communist parties launched a strong opposition against Mrs. Indira Gandhi's decision to go in for mega IMF loan in 1980. While parties of the working classes were critical of the Indian State for inviting foreign capital, land-owning middle caste peasantry also opted out of coalition of classes. The powerful surplus producing peasantry launched movements for changing the terms of trade in their favour and during 1970s and 1980s peasant movements for promoting the interests of land-owning peasantry have been the order of the day. The *ad hoc* remedies evolved by Mrs. Indira Gandhi and Rajiv Gandhi to tackle the crisis of Indian economy failed to find appropriate answers because none of the political leaders were interested in pushing land reforms to tackle the deepening of the crisis in the rural markets in India. When this crisis burst in 1990s, the Narasimha Rao Government followed the road towards global capitalism for rescuing India from its crisis.

The Indian State of 1990s was weak and internally fragmented because it did not enjoy popular legitimacy in the minds of the people. It is essential to refer to three developments which had a direct bearing on the political and economic crisis of the Indian State. The India of 1990s has witnessed the emergence of powerful *Hindutva,* the great assertions by the upwardly mobile middle caste peasantry, and a powerful urban and rural middle class which is exercising disproportionate claim over national resources. Thus *Mandal* assertion, *Mandir* (Temple) assertion and *Middle Class* assertion have emerged as the realities of the 1990s India.

Marxist and non-Marxist analysis of the political and economic crisis of the Indian State as reflected in the New Economic Policy of globalization has different concerns and perspectives.

Mao-tse-Tung elaborated Marxist-Leninist theory of "Contradictions"; he observed: "There are many contradictions in the course of development of any major thing. For instance, in the course of China's bourgeois democratic revolution, where the conditions are exceedingly complex, there exist the contradiction between all the oppressed classes in the Chinese society and imperialism, the contradiction between the great masses of the people and feudalism, the contradiction between the proletariat and the bourgeoisie, the contradiction between the peasantry and the urban petty bourgeoisie on the one hand and the bourgeoisie on the other, the contradiction between the various reactionary social groups, and so on. These contradictions cannot be treated in the same way since each has its own peculiarity; moreover the two aspects of each contradiction cannot be treated in the same way since each has its own characteristics".[21]

While it is essential to keep in mind principal and non-principal contradiction, the final stage of maturity of these contradictions has to go through a zigzag process of struggles. India's heterogeneities can be viewed from structural, analytical and descriptive perspectives for the identification of vertical and horizontal conflicts in society. The essence of Marxist approach is to identify the potential of proletarian revolution in India and identify social obstructions in the way of the emergence of the Indian proletariat. Marx observed:

> "As philosophy finds its *material* weapons in the proletariat, so the proletariat finds its *spiritual* weapons in philosophy .... The *head* of... (human) emancipation is philosophy, its *heart* is the *proletariat*. Philosophy cannot be made a reality without the abolition of the proletariat, the proletariat cannot be abolished without philosophy being made a reality".[22]

A conscious attempt is going on in India to accelerate the process of growing fragmentation of the *proletariat* by social and political forces of various kinds. Religion in public life, casteization of society and aggressive promotion of religious-ethnicities in 1990s has helped the processes of social fragmentation. According to classification of contradictions made by Mao, contradictions between the various reactionary social groups' in India are getting reflected in the form of heightened religiosity or aggressive casteism or exclusive ethnicism.

The on-going process of fragmentation of Indian politics is giving rise to the emergence of new identities in the name of multi-religious, multi-caste, multi-ethnic and multi-cultural reality of India. The fractions of the bourgeoisies and the land-owning classes or to use Mao tse-Tung's description of 'social reactionary classes' are creating their own specialised social constituencies in the name of plural identities of India and these social constituencies are sectional and primordial. The theoreticians of the fractions of the bourgeoisie and the land-owning classes are also justifying religious, cultural, ethnic and caste plural identities in India. It must be maintained that pluralism is a positive social arrangement because it safeguards homogenization and hegemonization of plural diversities by the majority community. Pluralism becomes negative if it is extended beyond a point because it facilitates fragmentation of society into numerous sectional and segmentary groups. Its result is that a society becomes "volatile plural society composed of discrete groups with no shared values" and this is the reason that Eriksen has warned against 'one sided focus on ethnicity'. Eriksen observes that "In this regard, the theory of the pluralist society seems to be flawed in that it assumes in a rather axiomatic way that ethnic alignments are the most basic ones in polyethnic societies".[23] Karl Marx reminded us that "The ideas of the ruling class are in every epoch the ruling ideas, *i.e.,* the class which is the ruling *material* force of society is at the same time its intellectual force".

It is not without reason that pluralism is an ideology of ruling class in the United States of America. "Dewey spent his life trying to lend a hand in these little fights, and in the course of doing so he worked out the vocabulary and rhetoric of American *'pluralism'.* This rhetoric made the first generation of American social scientists think of themselves as apostles of a new form of social life."[25] Pluralism, ethnicism, casteism and communalism do not operate at the level of ideas, they are practised by fractions of the socially reactionary classes in India as in the United States of America to "fragment" the proletariat. While referring to the United States reality Paul Sweezy observed that the working classes were "divided" between black and white and later into many ethnic and immigration groups and that instead of two antagonistic classes, the US ruling classes had full opportunity to play "divide and rule". Sweezy observed: "I think it is probably accurate to say that there has never been in history a ruling class as well placed as that of the US to pursue this course, *i.e.,* "Divide and rule".[26]

Another warning is that the crisis of capitalism and especially *inflation* fragments the proletariat. According to Goldthorpe, "inflation may well be an alternative to revolution. Creeping inflation permits the class struggle to proceed in a politically blind direction and encourages sectarianism rather than solidarity as powerful sections of the working class attempt to preserve differentials".[27]

While the believers of pluralism spread the message of identities on the basis of false consciousness, but the message of Karl Marx is that 'we - are - not - necessarily - what - we - define - ourselves - as - being'.[28]

The upshot of the above discussion is that the crisis of Indian capitalism has created conflicts within the Indian State and fractions of the bourgeoisies, and the land-owning peasantry are fighting their *sectional* battles by adopting strategies of political mobilization on the basis of fragments like religion or caste or ethnicity. This crisis-ridden weak State instead of restricting the agrarian relations and deepening of the crisis in the Indian market has taken the option of globalization of the economy. The Narasimha Rao Government has won over the support of the rising rural and urban middle class by making an illusory promise of liberating them from the shackles of Indian bureaucracy. The New Economic Policy has been projected within the country on the plank of 'debureaucratization' of India. Bureaucratic power never dies. It expands in every regime and assumes 'relative autonomy' of its own especially in the name of management of crisis of the Indian State. Bureaucracy in India has not vacated its power space in the so-called new regime of deregulation of the Indian economy. On the contrary, it has increased its powers because of its global connections and by championing the cause of transnationalization of Indian market economy.

Summing up

India is experiencing multi-dimensional crises in a global situation which is under the complete leadership of the advanced industrial countries of the West. Since the Indian State has not decided to operate in a relative autonomous manner in global affairs, it has allowed itself to be pushed around by global capitalism. The only social constituency which supports this globalization of India is upwardly mobile middle classes, sections of the bourgeoisies and land-owning classes and the powerful sections of the bureaucracy who see new career opportunities under globalism. The Indian masses who are the real victims of the serious crisis of economy, *i.e.,* the real proletariat classes are victims of ideologies of sectionalism like communalism, casteism, ethnicism and parochialization. If, on the one hand, under the impact of false consciousness Indians are becoming highly 'sectarian', the fractions of the ruling classes, on the other hand, are globalising the economy of India.

REFERENCES

1. Growing Global Influence of Transnationals, *The Business Standard,* New Delhi, September 1, 1994, p. 3.
2. See Strong Support for India's Policies: UNCTAD Report, *The Economic Times,* Delhi, August 31, 1994, p. 1.
3. Job Growth Prospects Gloomy World Over, *The Economic Times,* New Delhi, February 23, 1995, p. 3.
4. Answer to the Lok Sabha Question, *The Business Standard,* New Delhi, August 6, 1994.
5. See Top Merchant Bankers to meet FM, *The Times of India,* New Delhi, September 25, 1994.
6. Foreign firms posted more Profits in 1987-90, RBI, *The Economic Times,* New Delhi, November 8, 1994, p. 3.
7. Document/US Foreign Investment, *The Economic Times,* New Delhi, January 9, 1995, p. 6.
8. Jeffrey Caeten's Interview: *The Economic Times,* December 21, 1994, p. 6.
9. *The Economic Times,* New Delhi, January 6, 1995, p. 24.
10. *The Economic Times,* New Delhi, January 12, 1995, p. 1.
11. FICCI asks PM to go ahead with Reforms, *The Economic Times,* New Delhi, December 19, 1994, p. 1.
12. Etinne Balibar, *Masses, Classes, Ideas: Studies on Politics and Philosophy Before and After Marx* (Translated by James Swenson), Routledge, New York, 1993.
13. See: Bryan S. Turner, *For Weber: Essays on the Sociology of Fate,* Routledge and Kegan Paul, 1981, Boston, p. 58.
14. *The Economic Times,* New Delhi, December 22, 1994, p. 2.
15. *The Hindustan Times,* New Delhi, December 31, 1994, p. 17.
16. See C.P. Bhambhri, *Bureaucracy and Politics in India,* Vikas, Delhi, 1971, Also see: *Administrators in a Changing Society,* National, Delhi, 1972; *Politics in India: 1947-1987,* Vikas, Delhi, 1988.

17. See: James Petras and Todd Cavaluzzi, Latin American Liberalization and US Global Strategy, *Economic and Political Weekly*, Bombay, vol. XXX, no. 1, January 7, 1995, pp. 26-30.
18. See Isher Judge Ahluwalia, *Industrial Growth in India: Stagnation since the Mid-Sixties*, Oxford University Press, Delhi, 1985, pp. 166-72.
19. See L.K. Jha, *Economic Strategy for the Eighties*, Allied, New Delhi, 1980.
20. See A.K. Bagchi and N. Banerjee, eds. *Change and Choice in Indian Industry*, Bagchi & Co., Calcutta, 1981.
21. Mao tse-Tung, *Selected Works of Mato-tse-Tung*, Vol. I, Foreign Languages Press, Peking, 1967, edn 2, pp. 322-23.
22. Alien Oakley, *The Making of Marx's Critical Theory: A Bibliographical Analysis*, Routledge and Kegan Paul, London, 1983, p. 1.
23. Thomas Hylland Eriksen, *Ethnicity and Nationalism: Anthropological Perspectives*, Pluto Press, London, 1993, p. 156.
24. Eriksen, *ibid.*, p. 157.
25. Richard Rorty, Method, Social Science and Social Hope, in Michael T. Gibbons, ed. *Interpreting Politics*, Basil Blackwell, Oxford, 1987, p. 257.
26. Paul Sweezy, GATT is Instrument of Global Capitalism, *Mainstream*, New Delhi, January 14, 1995, Vol. XXXIII, no. 8, pp. 11-13.
27. Fred Hirsch and John H. Coldthrope, eds. *The Political Economy of Inflation* (London, 1978), quoted by Bryan S. Turner, op. cit., p. 362.
28. Also see, Tom Brass, Postscript: Populism, Peasants and Intellectuals or what's left of the Future, *The Journal of Peasant Studies*, Vol. 21, Number 3/4, April/July 1994, pp. 246-86.

11

Globalization, Liberalization and Welfare State

The Constitution of India established a Welfare State and a very detailed agenda for promotion of social sector and human capital was mentioned in the chapter on the Directive Principles of State Policy. The underlying philosophical orientation of the Indian Constitution-Makers was that an activist state through positive action could promote the quality of life of the underprivileged, deprived and vulnerable strata of society. The new vocabulary of globalization, liberalization and social sector has new meanings because the philosophical postulates of the promoters of liberalization are fundamentally different from the world-view of the Indian Constitution-makers. The central argument of our discussion is that the development of social and human sector is closely linked with the role of the State in development of economic and productive sector of Indian society and the newly emerging area of social sector as a concern of the State is based on a delinking between the social, productive and economic sectors. It is essential to examine the process which has brought a new thinking in the 1990s that the States of late peripheral capitalism of the Third World should *'retreat'* because "bureaucracy cannot do business" but concentrate on social sector like development of human material. This new thinking of the 1990s regarding the role of the State raises some fundamental questions with specific reference to the problems of 'development' of developing societies like India.

The European experience of development of Welfare State may be referred to here because it helps us to situate social problems in a proper historical context. Theories on Modern Industrial State, beginning from Adam Smith to John M. Keynes, enlighten us on the inter-related issues of the *State* and the *market*, the individual interest and social interest.[1]

The theory and practice of modern industrial States clearly reveals that *laissez faire* doctrine has been a pure rhetoric and every State has regulated the market and individual interest and collective social interest has always been the concern of the theorists of political economy and actual praxis of the Western State systems. Amit Bhaduri observes:

"The very existence of an organised market pre-supposes some basic

> economic role of the State which economic conservatism prefers to overlook. Adam Smith was the first economist to provide systematic arguments against intervention by the State in the functioning of the market — which still serve as the basis of conservative economic ideology. At the same time, unlike modern conservative economists. Smith did not ignore the essential role that the State has to play for ensuring the very existence of organized markets".[2]

At the same time, role of the State has changed from the 18th to the 19th and the 20th centuries.

A panoramic view of growth in the role of the State will validate the statement that stages of development of society determined responses of the State with an overall goal that the State is the preserver of the social and economic order of society:

1. The nineteenth century history informs us about existence of the old Elizabethan Poor Law.
2. The rights of mill-owners to employ children was restricted in 1819.
3. The Ten Hours Act was passed in 1847.

The above-mentioned few illustrations have been mentioned only to prove the general point that regulatory activities of society and economy by the State were fully recognised by the capitalist class of the 19th century, and the so-called mythology of *laissez faire* and freedom to market were always practised in written pamphlets but never in reality.

Allan Lockframe observes:

> "Although the new industrialists and their liberal ideologists opposed the continued existence of irrelevant and unnecessary State activities, they did not want a weak and powerless State. Certainly they turned a jaundiced eye on the State machine with a view to making its operation rational and more efficient, but they still had important work for State institutions to perform. In the nineteenth century the State became a better organized, centralised and coherent force"[3].

Two inter-related facts that emerge from the experience of nineteenth century State-formation in capitalist countries is that while the capitalist classes wanted State support for appropriating surplus value, the working classes were involved in a struggle to demand from the State regulation against the inhuman conditions of work. Thus, in a class-divided society, classes look differently on the role of the State. This story continues and the twentieth century Welfare State in the capitalist countries has been projected as a moral and "Human face of capitalism".

E.J. Hobsbawm, the greatest living Marxist historian, in his latest work, has described the post-World War II phase as the short but Golden Age of Capitalism, and its implication is that the Capitalist State practises welfarism when its rate of growth is high. After World War II, the USA had decisively emerged as the leader of World Capitalism and the liberal White's heart was bleeding for the Blacks.[4] Martin Luther King got a positive response from the liberal Whites because of economic boom, and in 1995, half a million Blacks marched in Washington, D.C., to express their anger and resentment against racial discrimination and economic deprivations. Post-World War II Germany welcomed foreign labour with open hands for its economic reconstruction, but the economic giant, *i.e.*, Germany of today is inhospitable to the children of foreign workers who were born in Germany. J.M. Keynes, the most important economist of the capitalist world whose ideas shaped governmental policies of the capitalist States, assumed that his policy prescriptions would achieve the goal of full employment. The current on-going recessionary period (in reality Economic Depression) has generated unemployment in every Western capitalist country and this phenomenon is threatening the survival of capitalist Welfare State. While socially racialism is rising high because of growing unemployment and perceived threats from the presence of the so called "outsiders", the ideology of New Right does not believe in welfarism. If taxes are lowered, the public health programmes will have to be discontinued. Margaret Thatcher hated the concept of Welfare State which was described by her as "the Nanny State". Serious crisis ridden capitalism is the fertile ground for the New Right who are internally against the poor and the unemployed, and externally they are war-mongers because defence production brings them huge profits. We have the testimony of John Kenneth Galbraith that:

> "The year 1929 and the events of that unhappy October were in marked contrast ... after the stock market crash came the Great Depression. This was to last a full ten years and extend to all the industrial world. It was eased by public policy, but it was ended only by the different drama of World War II. War, not economic wisdom, brought the depression to an end".[5]

The New Deal of the former United States President Franklin D. Roosevelt and the post-World War II Marshall Plan for Reconstruction of War devastated Europe clearly shows that an active management of economy by the State is essential to meet crisis situations arising out of either Economic Depression of the 1930s or World Wars or to overcome the inherited problems of underdevelopment of the newly decolonised societies. While Marshall Plan was launched to reconstruct European economies, Keynesian prescriptions of government investment, deficit financing, full employment and demand generation brought States in active picture like the 'New Deal'. Professor Harris observes that "*more* money, lower rates of interest, lean expenditure, measures to raise the propensity to consume, some freedom from dictation from abroad all of these were the ingredients out of which the New Deal Cocktail was made".[6]

The Keynesian system as propounded by his classic General Theory not only revolutionalized the capitalist development in post-World War II Europe, it also influenced global thinking and Jawaharlal Nehru-Mahalanobis Model and Indira Gandhi Model of development was claimed as India's Third Path of Development, *i.e.*, Democratic Planning and Welfare State.

It seems to be a coincidence that when Friedmann, Reaganewnomics and Thatcherism rejected Keynesianism and the State's great concern for "collective social interest", at the same time India was also struggling to restructure its Model of Development in the 1990s. While the Keynesian crisis is the crisis of Welfare Capitalist States, India is struggling to cope with the global changes and to redefine role of the State and State institutions.

Two inter-related issues have emerged for the changing role of the Indian State in the 1990s and any reappraisal of the Model of Indian Development will have to grapple with these issues.

First, a basic contradiction has emerged between the Nation State and the transnational corporations and globalization of their activities. Dick Bryan clearly brings out this contradiction by stating that the real centre for economic power decision-making now lies with the transnational corporations and not with the nation states.[7] At the same time, the citizens of a State demand from their own State economic relief which cannot be provided by the 'retreating States'. The situation becomes very clear if we consider the issue of poverty, the Indian State, and Globalization-Liberalization Model of Development.

Table 10.1: Poverty

(in millions)

Category	*1989-90*	*1990-91*	*1991-92*	*1992-93*
Rural	232	228	267	310
Urban	67	69	71	77
Total	299	297	338	387

If this is the nature of mass poverty, the State in India cannot rest at peace either with the demands of transnational corporations or the domestic liberalizers. The Indian Minimum Wages Act was passed in 1948, but in many states the actual payment of revised minimum wages is still not made to the poor in India. Many schemes have been launched to create assets and generate jobs for the poor. There are the Integrated Rural Development Programme, the Employment Guarantee Schemes, the Public Distribution System but in spite of all this much remains to be done in making a real dent in poverty eradication in India. *How can a State which withdraws from the productive sector of the economy promote social welfare sector?*

It is again essential to come back to the inside story of the Western capitalist States for support to the argument that the Welfare State of India cannot grow further if the State withdraws from the productive sector of economy or it fails to protect its relative autonomy from Transnational Corporations. Goran Therborn suggests that in the 1960s and 1970s "advance capitalism underwent a silent yet major transformation, the full economic, social and political range and impact of which remains to be explored" and he calls this as *"Welfare State Capitalism"* under which "a growing part of people's incomes is determined by political rules and rights, and the routine activities of the State are increasingly devoted to regulation and provision of social security, health and social care and education"[8]

If the 1960s, 1970s and 1980s capitalism was 'welfare', the 1990s Capitalist States are rejecting welfarism to their citizens; the capitalist countries are in crisis because of breakdown of the 'Social Contract' between the capitalists and the working classes. India is also being given the same prescriptions of deregulation, globalization and consequences of these prescriptions will deepen the Indian crisis.

Reagan/Thatcher neoliberalism produced oligopoly and class polarization. Will neoliberalism promote real democracy or elitism? In India, the task is to strengthen the Welfare State as demanded by the Constitution-makers, and this task cannot be performed either by too much dependence on the transnationals for capital, technology, and market or by freeing the domestic markets and entrepreneurs from State control. Robert Wade observes that "... the confidence with which the neoclassical school prescribes liberalization and privatization cannot be grounded in theory" for the theory which shows how liberalization and privatization generate growth is scarcely developed. We have also seen that it cannot be grounded in the experience of the new East Asian industrial countries for, with the partial exception of Hong Kong, they have pursued a mix of policies — many of which are inconsistent with neoclassical prescriptions.[9]

Raja J. Chelliah claims that 'inward looking strategy' and regulatory mechanism of the period of planning are important factors for the retarded growth of post-Independence Indian economy. His reform agenda is that the State should liberate the industrial economy and concentrate on 'irrigation, education, health, flood control, environment, railways, roads and bridges, space, defence, and power.[10]

Our argument is that neither the productive sector can be delinked from the social welfare sector, nor the weakening of the State institutions will help in creating a situation for sustainable growth with equity and justice. It is always the inefficient State which promotes the forces of market-friendly *laissez faire* economics. Without State intervention, social equalization cannot take place and if the State does not control national economic and productive resources, it cannot implement welfare programmes, like food security and job guarantees. India has to follow the model of economic development and welfarism of Keynesianism and if it follows the neoliberalism of Friedmann and increases its dependence on the transnationals, the vulnerable strata of society will be deprived of the benefits of national development. The evidence from advanced capitalist countries clearly points out that neoliberalism is creating elitism and the Welfare State is under serious attack. India should learn from the experiences of other societies, because we launched our developmental journey quite late and under adverse historical and contemporary global situations. The Indian State has to be actively involved in the total process of production and equitable distribution and this is the only method to promote real social welfare sector. Liberalised economic reforms are based on serious social inequalities and India has to rectify inherited social and economic inequities. *How can the democratic State of India abandon agenda of economic development for achieving the goals of real social justice?*

REFERENCES

1. *See* Amit Bhaduri, *Macro Economics: The Dynamics of Commodity Production*, MacMillan, New Delhi, 1990 (Rev. Indian Edition), pp. 261-87. Also *see* Eric Roll, *A History of Economic Thought*, London, Faber and Faber, 1953.
2. *Ibid.*
3. Allan Lockframe, Industrialization and Nineteenth Century States, in James Anderson (ed.). *The Rise of the Modern State*, Harvester Press, Sussex, 1986, p. 71.
4. E.J. Hobsbawm, *Age of Extremes: The Short Twentieth Century, 1914-1991*, Viking London, (Penguine India), 1995.
5. J.K. Galbraith, *The World Economy Since the Wars: A Personal View*, Mandarin Paperbacks, London, 1995, p. 78.
6. S.E. Harris, *The New Economics*, p. 18 (quoted by Eric Roll, *A History of Economic Thought*, 1953, p. 503).
7. Dick Bryan, *The Chase Across the Globe: International. Accumulation and the Contradictions for Nation State*, Westview Press, Boulder (Sanfrancisco), 1995.
8. Goran Therborn, *The Prospects of Labour and the Transformation of Advanced Capitalism*, quoted by Ralp Miliband, *Socialism for a Sceptical Age*, Polity Press, Cambridge (UK), 1994, p. 8.
9. Robert Wade, *Lessons from East Asian Miracle*, The World Bank, Washington DC, 1993, p. 312.
10. Raja J. Chelliah, *Towards Sustainable Growth: Essays in Fiscal and Financial Sector Reforms in India*, Oxford University Press, Delhi, 1996, p. 205.

12

Globalization, Market and the State

Eric Hobsbawm, the most important historian of European capitalism, has warned that 'the specter of globalization haunts us' in the last decade of Twentieth Century.[1] What is specific about globalization of the decade of 1990s and the beginning of Twenty First Century? Globalization and internationalization of world economy is the logical product of the growth of capitalism from the beginning of the Fifteenth Century to the end of Twentieth Century. Not only this. Industrial capitalism, differentiated from its predecessor feudal mode of production, needs global markets for raw material and finished products because industrialism means large scale production of commodities for consumption. The history of five hundred years of growth and development of industrial capitalism is based on the emergence of nation-state or national capitalism, colonialism, imperialism and in spite of the Treaty of Westphalia, European countries fought wars among themselves for the establishment of colonies in Asia, Africa and Latin America. The only long period of peace in Europe has been from the end of the Second World War and up to December 1991 when the erstwhile socialist state system of Russia and other East European countries collapsed. President George Bush Sr. declared in 1991 the birth of a new global era and characterised it as New International World Order. The collapse of erstwhile socialist state systems from 1991 was interpreted by the Western, especially the American, State leaders and intellectuals as a victory for Western value system as opposed to one party socialist state system. Francis Fukuyamas' Essay *"The End of History"*, published in *National Interest* of July 1989, stated that the values of 'liberal-democratic civilization' have been globally vindicated and it has 'marked the end of the ideological evolution of mankind'. In 1991-1993 Samuel P. Huntington brought two books in which he, like Fukuyama, celebrated the victory of democracy over all other political systems and perceived the future faultines based on religious hostilities and concluded that it will be an era of 'the West and the Rest'.[2] Huntington has interpreted the last decade of the Twentieth Century around the victory of Western democratic values; and the other motivating force according to him is 'religion' which is 'perhaps the central force that motivates and mobilises people'. American experience of September 11, 2001 confirmed the Western capitalist democracies and their scholars that 'Christian West' and 'Islam' are involved in struggle against one another as the new Twenty First Century opens its account. It has led Sheldon Wolin, the Biographer of Tocqueville, to conclude that "Far from being valued as symbolising an aspiration towards the democratization of power and a participatory society of political equals—democracy would come to be regarded by late-modern power elites as an indispensable yet valuable myth for promoting American political and economic interests among pre-modern and post-totalitarian societies. At home democracy is touted not as self-government by an involved citizenry, but as economic opportunity serves as the means of implicating the populace in anti-democracy in a politico-economic system characterised by the dominating power of hierarchical organization, widening class differentials, and a society where the hereditary element is confined to successive generations of the defenceless poor."[3]

The specific and real meaning of the current phase of capitalist globalization lies in the proclamation of the ideology of Western democratic values of individualism, liberalism, freedom for market, and free competition at global level. In concrete terms, instead of state activism in managing economies of the late developing countries, the shift is from state to market and to non-state civil society interventions especially by the non-government institutions. In the context of India, the decade of 1990s brings an end to Nehru-Mahalanobis model of economic planning and 'retreat of the state' from activities connected with major areas of Indian economy.

The central position which the state occupied in Indian national economy has to be vacated and it is replaced by free market economy both domestic and international. The new emphasis on market as a mediator in economic transactions is based on an indictment of planned economic development of India and of the four decades of post-independence struggle for nation-building. The inspiration for the New Economic Policy of liberalization, privatization, deregulation, disinvestment of public sector undertakings, and the opening of national economy to international players has come from the west-controlled global institutions. The World Bank, IMF, World Trade Organization *et al* are selling the American Model of Capitalism of free market economy for the whole world, and it can be substantiated by just referring to the titles of annual publications of the World Bank beginning with its *World Development Report* (1991); *The Challenge of Development* (1995); *Bureaucrats in Business—The Economic and Politics of Pubic Ownership* (A World Bank Policy Research Report) (1996); World Development Report: *From Plan to Market* (1996). World Development Report. *The State in a Changing World (1997) et al.*[4]

The continuing focus of World Bank and other global agencies is to highlight the serious deficiencies of state-led planning model of economic development and promote global integration of economies by replacing and displacing the 'state' by the market. What is the new role for the state in the management of national economy under the new dispenzation of neo-liberal classical economic ideology as propagated by the globalizers, liberalizers and deregulators? The state should regulate competition, regulate market, negotiate on behalf of the private corporate sector, promote the interests of domestic corporate interests, arbitrate in inter- and intra-corporate disputes, manage inflation and interest rates and control fiscal deficit.[5]

A few statements from authentic sources may be mentioned here to firmly state the argument that the globalizers are projecting states and their bureaucracies as the real villain of the piece for road blocking economic growth which should be left to market forces and private corporate sector of the economy. The World Bank President James D. Wolfensohn while introducing the *World Development Report* (1996) states about the Report: "It drives home the utter necessity of both liberalizing economies through opening trade and market opportunities and stabilizing them through reducing inflation and practising fiscal discipline—and then of sticking to these policies consistently overtime...the necessity of reforming enterprises and expanding the private sector, while restructuring social safety nets to deal with the social impact of the move to the market.'[6]

The upshot of this Report is a total indictment of public sector and complete faith in free market and private sector. The World Bank President Wolfensohn further elaborates his views in the Twentieth World Development Report (1997):

> "For many, the lesson of recent years has been that the state could not deliver on its promises: transition economies have had to make a wrenching shift toward the market economy, and much of the development world has had to face up to the failure of state-dominated development strategies. Even the mixed economies of the industrialized world, in response to the failures of government intervention, have opted for a decisive shift in the mix in favour of market mechanism that development requires an effective state, one that plays a catalytic, facilitating role, encouraging and complementing the activities of private business and individuals. Certainly, state-dominated development has failed."[7]

It is no one's case that under the new ideology of free market economy the state will wither away. The argument is that national economies of developing countries will be fully integrated with world capitalist system in the absence of effective control of the national sovereign states over its own economic wealth. Further, this is new globalization of the last decade of Twentieth Century which is premised on the denial of relative autonomy to the states of developing countries to manage their own public affairs as decided by their own democratically elected Parliaments and Political Executives. Hence, the issue is not about 'minimalist' versus 'maximalist' state but it is about the role of the state in decision making about national economic goals and strategies of economic development.

It is essential to have a brief look at a shift of nuances from 1991 World Development Report on "*The Challenge to Development*" to the Millenium goals of development based on Millenium Declaration adopted by 189 countries at the UN Millenium Summit in September 2000. Human Resource Development for economic growth has emerged as the new concern and a *mantra* of globalizers because 'labour as a factor of production' is a recognised pillar of industrial economy. From David Ricardo, Karl Marx to the Twentieth Century Welfare capitalist and socialist states, the conditions of industrial working classes have occupied a centrestage in the thinking and praxis of every industrial society of Western Countries. The history of industrial capitalism clearly tells us that the concern for the social welfare of the labouring classes is in the enlightened self-interest of capitalist classes and their state systems. It also deserves to be stated that western industrial societies have different models of capitalist welfare states beginning with the minimalist welfare state of America with its 1935 US Social Security Law for retired and unemployed individuals to the maximalist western European capitalist states like Norway, Denmark, Sweden etc. The Human Development Report of 2003 by the UNDP is only an attempt by the globalizers and believers of free market economy that human beings as 'capital' can not be ignored and this brings back a truncated National State as the Report maintains: "The Goals must become a national reality, embraced by their main stake-holders people and governments."[8] In spite of this new concern for human welfare, the globalizers are not abandoning their commitment to free market economy; this tight rope dancing becomes clear when the Human Development Report 2003 states that: "In the 1980s and much of the 1990s many development efforts by international financial institutions and major donor countries were guided by the belief that market forces would lift all poor countries on to a path of self-sustaining economic growth. Globalization was seen as the great new motor of world-wide economic progress. Poor countries were assumed to be able to achieve economic growth as long as they pursued good economic governance based on the precepts of macro-economic stability, liberalization of markets and privatization of economic activity....

"Though this optimistic vision has proven hugely inadequate for hundreds of millions of poor people, it still has considerable merit for much of the world. Despite protest against globalization in recent years, world market forces have contributed to economic growth...".[9]

The Other Side of Market-led Globalization and Liberalization Economic Model

The critics have faulted the centrality and primacy accorded to 'free market' and the demand for replacement and displacement of 'state-led' economic growth on many grounds. The first ground of indictment of the economic theology of the decade of 1990s is built on the argument that 'economics and politics' of the new globalism is directly beneficial to American capitalism, and the New Economic Policy and ideology of the liberalization of financial markets and trade and the deregulation of capital markets in the name of 'macro-economic stability' is disastrous for the developing countries. Joseph Stiglitz, a former Chief Economist at the World Bank, makes it clear that the ongoing globalization process is beneficial for the capitalist countries and it has disastrous social and political consequences for the developing countries Stiglitz observes: "When US Secretary of Commerce Ron Brown travelled abroad, he was accompanied by US business people trying to make contacts and gain entry into these emerging markets. Presumably, the chances of getting a seat on the plane were enhanced if one made significant campagin contributions."[10] Government of every western country is actively promoting the interests of its own capitalist classes by influencing the economic decisions of recipients of Foreign Direct Investments. Further, pressures are exercised by capital surplus countries on the capital deficit countries for securing 'unfair contracts'. Stiglitz observes: "The Foreign direct investment comes only at the price of undermining democratic processes. This is particularly true for investments in mining, oil, and other natural resources, where foreigners have a real incentive to obtain the concessions at low prices."[11] Stiglitz dramatises it by observing that the United States' national interests are equal to the Wall Street interests. A President of General Motors, Charles E. Wilson, was Secretary of Defence and it does not need any logic to maintain that "What's good for General Motors is good for the country."[12]

Consequences of the Phenomenon of the Retreat of the State

An important negative impact of the 'opening of national economy' to foreign capital has been the growth of speculative capitalism at the cost of productive capitalism because the Foreign Exchange Regulation Act of India has been debunked by the liberalizers without creating any capability of the Indian State to control speculators and 'fly by night capital' investors like George Soros and others. Stiglitz, while attracting attention to the menace of international speculator capital investors, warns that: "..., neither theory nor evidence supports the view that opening markets to short term, speculative capital flows increases economic growth. But there is considerable evidence and theory that it increases economic instability, and that economic instability contributes to insecurity and poverty. So, such forms of capital market liberalization might in some ways increase 'globalization'. But they do not enhance growth...".[13]

The second consequence of the policies of liberalization and free market economies has been the emergence of regional disparities, income inequalities, disparities among social groups, widening of rural-urban gap and forced migration of the poor from their homes to unwelcome and inhospitable large cities and metropolitan cities. We have authentic evidence from the Human Development Report (2003) about economic and social distortions which have emerged in developing countries following the New Model of Free Market Economy. The Human Development Report (2003) informs:

> "But stark differences are emerging between regions, with some pulling ahead and reaching new levels of development—while others are left behind. The same pattern is occurring within regions: some countries are succeeding amid disappointing regional trends, while others are falling behind in regions making good overall progress".[14]

The Indian policy makers are grappling with the problems of regional imbalances accentuated by the policies of the 1990s. During the period of Economic Planning, removal of regional imbalances was accepted as one of the most important goals by the Indian state and economic planners. This claim has been abandoned by the Central governments of the 1990s. Not only this. The Indian Constitution created a very important institution of Finance Commission for the task of distributing financial resources among the states of India on the basis of very objective criterion. Its recommendations were sacrosanct and never challenged except, for the first time, in the decade of 1990s when Chandra Babu Naidu, the Chief Minister of Andhra Pradesh, raised the issue of 'developed' versus 'backward' states and asked that the Finance Commission should not punish the 'economically developed states' by conceding to the needs of 'backward states'. Is India moving towards 'islands of development' versus mainland of poverty? Can such an India be stable?

The most telling example of growing regional and sub-regional imbalances is reflected in the demand for the creation of new states like Chhatisgarh, Jharkhand, Uttaranchal, Telegana, Vidarbha because these sub-regions feel that they have been neglected by their own developed neighbouring districts. The Human Development Report (2003), on the basis of gender literacy, infant mortality and health concludes that India has 'progressive states' and extremely 'backward states'. While a few states have positively responded to the various aspects of Human Development, some others are laggards. What more evidence is required to substantiate the argument that many Indias are co-existing in the absence of an effective central planned growth model.

Another serious development which has disastrous social consequences is the growing gap between the developed and developing countries. The growing inequality among nations like the OECD countries and the others and also within the nations is likely to sharpen inter-nation and intra-nation conflicts. Milnovic, on the basis of his measurements of 'income inequality' informs that: "The richest 5 per cent of the world's people receive 114 times the income of the poorest 5 per cent. The richest 1 per cent receive as much as the poorest 57 per cent. And the 25 million richest Americans have as much income as almost 2 billion of the world's poorest people."[15]

A significant implication of the growing income inequalities among the nations is that the rich countries need global resources to maintain their standards of economic prosperity. How do developing countries protect their natural national resources from the greed and constant demands from the prosperous western countries? The decade of 1990s has not only witnessed the collapse of the erstwhile European socialist state system, it has also seen the emergence of a 'unipolar world' under the supreme leadership of America, which has emerged as the sole military super power and a global policeman. America and its European Union allies need to control global resources for the economic prosperity of the OECD countries. How can the vulnerable developing countries protect economic resources found in their recognised national geographical territories? Only a national state which is capable of protecting its national economy can bargain effectively with powerful western global players. Only a democratic state can act as an effective buffer between the capricious demands of the advanced capitalist countries and national interests. The ongoing process of globalization is precisely aimed against the state systems and their capacities to manage national economies on the basis of relative autonomous relationships among the nation-states. The democratic nation-state is not only involved in a conflict situation with other powerful western states, the growing national income inequalities and social disparities create serious conflict situations within these societies. How can any state manage its own domestic affairs without a positive response to the felt needs of the absolute alienated majority in an unequal society? The globalizers and liberalizers have to accept that it is only a democratic state and not a free market which can perform the role of resource allocation among regions, social classes and groups. And in the absence of an effective state intervention in favour of the deprived majority, social disorder will become an order of the day. Stiglitz observes that:

> "Civil strife in Africa has been a major factor setting back its development agenda. Studies at the World Bank show that such strife is systematically related to adverse economic factors, including unemployment that can be produced by excessive austerity. Moderate inflation may not be ideal for creating an environment for investment but violence and civil strife are even worse."[16]

Such a warning deserves serious attention from the western public policy makers. It can be reasonably stated that active state interventions are essential to control and contain serious distortions in economic development created by the market forces not amenable to state control. Bhanoji Rao offers an explanation on the basis of data of 50 economies that "(1) ...there is no convincing evidence that economic growth per se could lower income and wealth inequalities. (2) ..., with acceptance and emulation of socialism and/or welfarism on the decline, institutions that work for the decline of inequalities such as land reform and fully government funded public and social services get marginalised....[17] Eric Hobsbawan has also warned about the disastrous consequences of American-led free market model of capitalism. He states that: "It (US) has deliberately sabotaged the EU, and also aims at ruining another of the great world achievements since 1945: prosperous social welfare states.'[18]

It is not market but only a democratic state with appropriate economic policies and strategies that can deal with social inequality and if it is not done, the state will be involved in fire fighting operations to control violence and social anarchy.

Further, in developing countries, employment generation programmes have to be undertaken by the state because human resource planning is not the task of market. The market is not responsible for undertaking economic activities for providing employment opportunities to millions of people in labour-surplus populated developing countries. *Public Enterprises Survey, (1995-96)* mentions the following objectives of economic planning by the state:

"(a) To help in the rapid economic growth and industriali-zation of the country and create the necessary infrastructure for economic development;
(b) To earn return on investment and thus generate resources for development;
(c) To promote redistribution of income and wealth;
(d) To create employment opportunities;
(e) To promote balanced regional development;
(f) To assist the development of small-scale and ancillary industries; and
(g) To promote import substitution, save and earn foreign exchange for the economy."

This comprehensive agenda of social and economic planning of India was arrived at by the democratic state on the basis of existing social realities of a diverse continental country. Employment crisis has emerged in the 1990s because generation of new employment opportunities has ceased to be public policy agenda. One of the consequences of growing unemployment is forced migration of the helpless and hapless labouring groups. According to Tushar Mahanti *"Waning job market makes 14 lakh Indians scurry abroad in last five years."*[19] Migration within the country and outside the national territorial borders is a consequence of complex factors which can be positive as well as negative. Migration of labour is a welcome step if it is a product of expanding and booming economy. If economy is growing, migration is a 'pull' factor as it happened in the earlier stages of British industrialization when the process of migration was "from farm to factory". Migrants are attracted towards new opportunities for gainful employment. Migraton can be a consequence of negative factors when the labouring classes are pushed out of their 'home' because job opportunities nearer home are not available because of absence of economic growth. In Indian migration, both 'pull' and 'push' factors are at work because workers are migrating in search for new job opportunities in new places, both domestic and foreign, and there is large scale 'distress' migration especially from backward regions and districts to relatively developed cities or towns. Every large metropolis has huge migrant working population in the slum areas and shanty towns.

Tusher K. Mahanti informs us that, "...India's job market has shrunk dramatically in the post-reforms years. Most of the big companies, both in the public and private sector, have introduced various separation schemes of late and reduced work force significantly".[20] He further informs that "The number of employed in the organised sector has fallen unchecked from 282.45 lakh in 1997 to 227.89 lakh in 2001. The fall was sharper in the public sector, where the number of employed has fallen by 4.20 lakh or 2.2% during the period. The number of employed in the organised private sector during the same period has fallen by 0.4% from 86.86 lakh in 1997 to 86.52 lakh in 2001."[21]

India is witnessing an inverse relationship between employment growth in the post-reform phase and the output growth. The National Sample Survey Organization (NSS) confirms that the 'growth rate of employment has declined from 2.7 per cent per annum during 1983-94 to 1.07 per cent during 1993-2000 when the growth of output, that is gross domestic product, accelerated from 5.2 per cent to 6.7 per cent.' In such a gloomy employment situation, unskilled and semi-skilled working class migrants are moving from an inhospitable situation at home to a little less socially acceptable situation in new neighbourhood. Such a phenomenon has been described by Jermy Seabrook as 'creating economic migrants.' He observes that: "The International Monetary Fund has been criticized for imposing its uniform structural adjustment programmes upon every country that has fallen within its superintendence. In every case, they have included mechanism for making the poor even poorer: Cuts in government spending which have focussed on nutrition programmes, education, healthcare and welfare services, have compelled more and more poor people to seek a livelihood far from home".[22]

Social consequences of rising unemployment situation are giving rise to negativism and violence both within the country and foreign countries of the migrants. The 'village vagabonds' and the 'lumpen proletariat' of the early British industrial social history are the new phenomenon of the 1990s as a consequence of New Economic Ideology of neo-classical liberal variety. Advanced western countries are facing backlash against foreign migrants (immigrants) either in the form of race-riots or a demand to restrict migration. In the United States of America, unemployed workers are asking their political representatives to legislate against 'outsourcing' of production by American owned companies because establishing 'assembly lines' in foreign countries creates jobs for the workers of the host countries while it leads to joblessness in America. The Information Technology Association of America, a high power American industry body, has 'made a strong pitch for outsourcing the jobs so that the United States can remain competitive'. ITAA President, Harris Miller, says that: "This is the new global reality for US information technology companies and workers, and we must meet it with a new spirit of competitiveness". Since American IT companies are global, 'product or service localization' is needed.[23] While high technology jobs through outsourcing are a drop in the ocean of growing unemployment, the Indian immigrants in America face hate campaigns. Public sector enterprises in India were assigned a goal to generate employment, but in the phase of the dismantling of state enterprises, employment as a public policy is confined to the corridors of policy makers and it has become a part of political rhetoric as shown by the NSS data of the Government of India.

Another socially adverse impact of New Economic regime is the emergence of great social disparities and the impact of these sharp social divisions of status are visible in the changing character of the consumer products.[24] The best example of the emergence of a socially narrow based Indian elite in the post-reform phase is provided by the availability of private cars by the global car makers, the General Motors, Ford, Toyota, Honda, Suzuki, Hyundai-Mitsubishi, Fiat *et al.* Not to be left behind, the new status symbol of the elite, BMW, is also planning to open shop in India. The management of Bayerische Morton Werke (BMW) announced the establishment of a Joint Venture car plant in India in 2003 which "can either be assembly or a manufacturing unit." The story does not end here. The government has opened financial sector of economy like banking, insurance and pension to foreign private investors because it is global capital which is a real player in the current stage of centralization-cum-globalization of economy and it is foreign banks and multinational corporations which want to open their shops in every developing country. This opening of Indian economy to foreign capital investors has been justified on the plea that India is capital-deficit and capital-surplus western countries deserve to be welcomed for accelerating the rate of economic growth. While the national financial sector is liberalized, deregulated and opened to foreign competition for the need for attracting Foreign Direct Investment for economic development; the opening of insurance sector and the market of milk products like yoghurt, cheese and butter to multinationals such as USA's Dean, Dairy Farmers of America, Scheiber and Land O Takes, and Europe based Arla, Parnalaat, Lactalis, and Compania can only serve the interests of a social minority of Indian elite. Nidhi Nath Srinivas observes: "With a market size of $ 2.5 billion for curd and curd-based products, and $ 375 million for *paneer* alone, MNCs are quickly realising the peril of ignoring these money-spinners."[25]

Even the opening of insurance sector to international insurance companies is to cater to the preferences of the status oriented elite because Life Insurance Corporation of India played a Yeoman role by creating the culture of insurance among the lower middle classes. The market is captured by foreign insurance companies because elite consider it as a status symbol. ICICI Prudential Life, a joint venture between ICICI and Prudential is first private insurance company to have crossed the Rs. 10,000 crore mark while premium income had already touched Rs. 680 crore on July 31, 2003. Ms. Shikha Sharma, Managing Director and CEO, ICICI Prudential said, "Among the private life insurance players we have captured a 38 per cent market share, while in the industry as a whole we have 3 per cent share. In fact, our market share for pensions is 23 per cent. The brand acceptance has been extremely positive".[26]

Another adverse consequence of the current phase of globalization of the 1990s is that in an asymmetrical international political system, the state sovereignty of the developing countries is under threat from the real sovereign western countries which are the headquarters of surplus capital for investments and superior technology. It deserves to be stated here that Nehru-Mahalanobis model of economic development based on import substitution industrialization was not "autarchic" or isolationist but it was an assertion of national interests being nationally defined by the Indian state and linkages with the world system were based on relative autonomy of the Indian state in conducting its international relations. The best illustration to prove this point is that it was an Indian decision to establish steel plants in public sector and after arriving at this basic decision, the Nehru government started negotiations with foreign countries. The Americans were the first to be approached with a proposal for a steel plant for India but the American offer was declined because America was offering a steel plant to be managed by private entrepreneurs. The Russians, the Germans and the British agreed to India's request for steel plants in public sector and Bhillai, Rourekla and Durgapur steel plants were launched by foreign countries in India.[27] This situation of sovereign decisions by India does not exist any more in the trade regime of World Trade Organization. A telling example of quasi-world government role of the WTO is the response of the Indian government on Indian Patent Law and meeting the demands of TRIPs[28] before 2005. The Patent Act of 1970 was first amended in 1999, the second amendment was made in 2002 and the third amendment to patent law is before parliament. The purpose of this third amendment is 'the introduction of the TRIPs-mandated product patents regime in the country for food, drugs and pharmaceuticals and chemicals.'[29] On the eve of discussion in Parliament, the Organization of Pharmaceutical Production of India (OPPI) which comprises MNCs such as Pfizar, Glaxo-Smithkline, Novartis, Antra Zenera et al made a representation to the Government of India that 'not a single exclusive marketing right (EMR) has been granted by India's patent controller after its introduction in 1999, which shows that the country's EMR norms are flawed and not TRIPs compliant'.[30]

It is not only that the MNCs are openly pressuring the Government of India for concessions, their powerful western nation-states also put pressure over the states of the developing countries to extend concessions to foreign-owned MNCs. Foreign and domestic capital many a time combine together to pressurise host country's government for favourable trade concessions. This new development of the globalized 1990s world has made some scholars, state leaders and foreign and domestic Big Business and global institutions like the World Bank, IMF and WTO to make unsubstantiated and fundamentalist statement that capitalist global market has 'an intrinsic tendency to transcend any national institutions.'[31]

The crux of the issue is not the logic of capitalist global market but the capabilities of a state to manage its own national affairs in a relatively autonomous inter-national global system where spaces for autonomy are available if the states have the intention to decide on their own and have the 'capability' to negotiate with Western capitalist countries. This is the reason that the decade of 1990s has created a situation in which middle classes of developing countries have been persuaded by the free market ideology that state-in-economy is a villain of the piece and pubic services should be either privatized or handed over to the institutions of civil society like the NGOs. The idiom of governance has changed in the 1990s and preference is for 'public-private partnership' and Non-Government Organizations providing public services and the consequence of this thinking is felt on the morale of public services whose capacity to govern is getting gradually eroded. The Indian state has greater competence than NGOs to regulate social aspects of economy, but it is made to surrender this role to the NGOs and in the process state's capabilities are getting eroded and making it more vulnerable to powerful foreign and domestic pressure groups.

The dramatic exposure of the states' unwillingness to manage and regulate the Big Business, external and internal, came from the Centre for Science and Environment (an NGO) on August 5, 2003, when 'it rocked the corridors of Pepsi, Coca Cola MNCs by claming that their laboratory tests show traces of pesticide in the drinks sold in Delhi.' This statement of Sunita Narain, the CSE Chief, rattled the two MNCs and Parliament demanded an answer from the government, and till the answer was authoritatively given the parliamentarians demanded a ban on the sale of Pepsi, Coca Cola drinks.[32] The Indian state was put on the defensive by a NGO while it has institutions like Central Food Technological Research Institute, Mysore and Central Food Laboratory, Kolkata for performing tests on food stuffs and drinks. When the Health Minister Sushma Swaraj told parliament on August 21, 2003, that the tests conducted by government agencies 'clearly show that all the 12 samples do not have pesticide residues of the high order as was alleged by the Centre for Science and Environment (CSE) Report', it did not carry conviction because a sea change has taken place in the mindset of the elite including political class that somehow the state is not worthy of trust. The NGOs as voluntary agencies have won over the trust of the public which has developed a feeling of alienation from pubic services and public institutions. It deserves to be stated that the mushroom growth of the non-government organizations as voluntary bodies providing public services has been legitimized on the basis of an ideological myth that public services can not deliver the goods. On the contrary, in a democratic country, accountability is imposed on pubic services and institutions and NGOs are not accountable to any public.[33] The government of India can be compelled to respond to public criticism for its acts of omission or commisison but non-government voluntary agencies, funded by Indian or foreign donors, are not at all answerable to Indian public. Accountability of public services and institutions is built around constitutional arrangement of Indian democracy. The NGOs operate and function outside the preview of parliamentary or judicial accountability.

The State and Social Justice

In a democratic country, citizens look towards the state and not free market forces or multinationals or global institutions for social justice and it is the sole responsibility of a democratic state to establish just social order. The ideology of liberalization and globalization by ejecting the state from its central role in the management of national economy leaves little space for the state to manage social inequities created by the New Economic Regime. Not only this.

John M. Keynes had suggested public investments as the motor force of economic development for the generation of gainful employment in a country. It is not only Nehru-Mahalanobis model that has been discarded by the globalizers, Keynesian economics of public expenditure as the fountain source of economic and social growth has been also burried by the IMF, World Bank and neo-classical liberal economists who are concerned with 'fiscal deficit', 'fiscal balance' and structural adjustment. Since India is following the model of growth on the lines suggested by western global institutions and western capital investors, it has followed their suggestion of structural adjustment and on July 29, 2003 the Rajya Sabha approved the Fiscal Responsibility and Budget Management Bill 2003. Finance Minister, Jaswant Singh, promised to implement schemes to control public expenditure and he also promised to regularly report to Parliament on the status of fiscal deficit. It is on the pattern of the Stability and Growth Pact of the European Monetary Union to cut spending.

The rise in government spending is a useful way to achieve national economic growth with justice in a developing country in spite of budget deficits. There is nothing automatic about fiscal 'stability' and democratically elected governments should have the autonomy to manage their own budgets and define their own social goals depending on the existing and prevailing social situation in a specific country. Even Americans do not do what they are prescribing to the Indians. J. Braford Delong observes that: "On the American side of the Atlantic, the usefulness of these automatic fiscal stabilisers is unchallenged. On the contrary, whenever recession threatens, political debate revolves around whether they need to be reinforced by *additional* stimulus via discretionary fiscal policy. No one considers how to put further downward pressure on the economy back on spending programmes. Neither Democrats nor Republicans have an interest in choking off economic activity. This is not a partisan issue".[34] When a medicine is not acceptable to the most advanced capitalist country, a poor country can hardly accept the prescriptions of automatic 'fiscal stability' because it will cut expenditures from the welfare programmes of 500 million poor and labouring men and women in rural and urban areas. The poor of India look towards the state for programmes for the eradication of poverty, malnutrition, infant mortality and other social services. The ultra rich and newly emerging upwardly mobile middle and enterprenuical classes of India have abandoned the state in favour of the ideology of free market, private enterprise and global market linkages. But the state can not be a private stock exchange company of the 250 million middle and upper middle classes who along with the Indian Big Business and global players are wanting to displace the centrality of state in economic management.[35] The majority of Indians which include rural and urban poor, marginal and small farmers, unskilled and daily wage earners, lower middle classes—all look towards a democratic social welfarist state for economic development and social justice.

The upshot of above argument is that the prevailing ideology in favour of free market and non-government organizations providing public services to the community is premised on non-empirical reality of state's failures to provide public services to the multiple groups in society. The plea is not for statism. A democratic social welfarist state which is a jealous guardian of its own sovereignty and which can be effectively held accountable for the management of social problems is a preferred option over a sate which is being marginalized both by foreign players and powerful domestic private interests. A poor country needs a Big Government which is democratically constituted and which is responsive to its own citizens and their welfare. The choice is clear—either a developmentalist state with an agenda of social justice or social disruption and chaotic violence under New Economic Regime of privatization, liberalization and globalization.

REFERENCES

1. Eric Hobsbawm, *The Age of Extremes: A History of the World*, 1914-1991, Pantheon Books, New York, 1994.
2. See Samuel P. Huntington 1991, *The Third Wave: Democratization in the Late Twentieth Century*, University of Oklahoma Press, Norman 1993. Also see his "*The Clash of Civilizations and the Remaking of World Order*, Simon of Seluestic, New York, 1993.
3. Sheldon Wolin, *Tocqueville Between Two Worlds, The Making of a Political and Theoretical Life*, Princeton: 2001; quoted by Tariq Ali in *The Clash of Fundamentalisms: Crusades, Jihads and Modernity*, 2003. Rupa and Co., New Delhi, pp. 311-312.
4. All Reports: Oxford University Press, New Delhi.
5. See Samir Amin, '*The Political Economy of the Twentieth Century*', *Monthly Review*, New York, June 2000, p. 9.
6. *From Plan to Market*, World Development Report 1996. Oxford University Press, New Delhi, 1996, p. 111.
7. *The State in a Changing World:* World Development Report 1997, Oxford University Press, New Delhi, 1997, p. 111.
8. *Human Development Report (2003)*, UNDP, Oxford University Press, New Delhi, p. 1.
9. *World Human Development Report* (2003), UNDP, Oxford University Press, New Delhi, 2003, p. 16.
10. Joseph Stiglitz, *Globalization and Its Discontents*, Penguin Books, New Delhi, 2002, p. 70.
11. *Ibid.* p. 72.
12. *Ibid.* p. 195.
13. Joseph Stiglitz, quoted in *Human Development Report*, (2003), Oxford University Press, New Delhi, 2003, p. 80.
14. Human Development Report (2003), op. cit. p. 34.
15. Branko Milnovic: "True World Income Distribution, 1988 and 1993: First Calculation Based on Household Survey Alone" *Economic Journal:* 2002, 112 (476), pp. 51-92. Also see Angus Maddison: *The World Economy: A Millennial Perspective:* Paris: Organization for Economic Co-operation and Development, 2001.
16. Stiglitz: *op. cit.* pp. 77-78.
17. Bhanoji Rao, "Explaining Cross-Country variation in Income Inequality", *Economic and Political Weekly*, Bombay, April 26, 2003, Vol. XXXVIII, No. 17, p. 1648.
18. Eric Hobsbawan, "Empire State Building", *The Guardian*, London, June 16, 2003, quoted from *The Hindustan Times*, New Delhi, June 18, 2003.

19. Tushar K. Mahanti, *Economic Times,* New Delhi, May 12, 2003, p. 10.
20. *Ibid.,* p. 10.
21. *Ibid.,* p. 10.
22. Jeremy Seabrook, *The Statesman,* New Delhi, 17, 2003, p. 9.
23. S. Rajagopalan, "US tech backs out souring trends", The *Hindustan Times,* New Delhi, August 21, 2003, p. 15.
24. See Satish Deshpande, *Contemporary India: A Sociological View,* Viking Penguin Books Ltd., New Delhi, 2002.
25. Nidhi Nath Srinivas, "MNCs to read the milky way in India", *The Economic Times,* New Delhi, July 18, 2003, p. 11.
26. "ICICI Prudential 1st Private Insurance to cross Rs. 10K-er Sum". *The Economic Times,* New Delhi, August 21, 2003, p. 8.
27. C. P. Bhambhri, *World Bank and India,* Vikas Publication Ltd., New Delhi, 1980. Also see Bhambhri, *The Indian State since Independence,* Shipra Publications, New Delhi, 2001.
28. Trade Related Intellectual Property Rights.
29. *The Economic Times,* New Delhi, August 6, 2003, p. 6.
30. *The Economic Times,* New Delhi, August 15, 2003, p. 11.
31. Immanuel Wallerstein and Etinne Balibar, *Race, Nation, Class: Ambiguous Identities,* Verso, London, 1991, p. 89.
32. *Hindustan Times,* New Delhi, August 7, 2003.
33. See Neera Chandhok, *The Conceits of Civil Society,* Oxford University Press, New Delhi, 2002.
34. J. Bradfold Delong, 'Herbert Hoover of the stability pact', *The Economic Times,* Delhi, July 29, 2003, p. 10.
35. Incidentally, these classes also gave birth to Ketan Parikhs and Harshad Mehtas, the speculators and adventurists in the Stock Exchange Market.

13

Globalization, Liberalization and Institutions for Governance in India

The Constitution of India and Jawaharlal Nehru-Indira Gandhi Model of Development provided a 'context' on the basis of which institutions for governance were established in post-independence India. The inter-related and inter-connected institutional arrangements for governance are democratic participation, decentralization of powers on the basis of federalism, State-led multiple programmes for economic regeneration and a political regime which does not show any preferences on the basis of religion in a multi-religious society. Nehru-Indira Gandhi Model of nation-building was based on relatively self-reliant economic development of the country and an active role of the State in the transformation of India. Many complex institutional innovations were made to grapple with the inherited problems of backwardness and underdevelopment. Since Nehru-Indira Model was constructed on the basis of a belief that India should have relative autonomy in global bloc politics, domestic self-reliant development was essential to safeguard the sovereignty of India which was threatened by power-bloc politics. Economic planning and policy of non-alignment were two sides of the same coin and governance of the country was directed towards State-led economic development and assertion of national independence in global affairs. The institutions for governance are created in response to the basic goals of the State philosophy and Nehru-Indira phase of leadership of the Indian State witnessed the creation of a complex network of governmental institutions, organizations, agencies for promoting the goals of planned development of the country with a view to accelerate the processes of growth.

The 1980s India witnessed a new debate on governance. Mrs. Indira Gandhi herself was becoming conscious of the dysfunctionality of many bureaucratic or quasi-bureaucratic governing institutions because the goals of rapid economic development were not achieved according to the anticipation of the public policy makers and also according to the expectations of the mass of poor people in the country. Jagdish Bhagwati, a critic of Nehru-Indira Model of economic development, observes:

> "Imagine my surprise and exhilaration, therefore, when the new minority government of Prime Minister Rao, after the June 1991 elections, finally seized the day. Abandoning the caution and hesitation that defined the earlier efforts at liberalization, the new government has frontally embraced the philosophy of liberal economic reforms. 'Reform by storm' has supplanted the "reform by stealth" of Mrs. Gandhi's time and the "reform with reluctance" under Rajiv Gandhi".[1]

Since the 1990s, India has launched a new Model of Development. A powerful critique of Nehru-Indira phase of governance has emerged both within and outside the country. The Indian State, as developed in response to Nehru-Indira model, should retreat and 'free market' forces internally and 'open economy' externally is a replacement of the earlier planned, inward-looking and globally closed economy. Hence many of the old institutions for governance have outlived their utility and new institutions have to be created to release the impulses of economic growth from the shackles of earlier governmentalization of the whole society. P. Chidambaram, who has been associated with the so-called New Economic Policy of India since 1991, has observed that:

> "Over the years, the Government has taken on far too much in areas into which it ought not to have ventured, and had accomplished far too little in areas where it ought to have entered…the reforms would be of no avail unless we rescued "governance" from the laybrinth of "government" and for that we had to first reinvent government itself…; issues like downsizing, decentaliztaion and withdrawing government from some areas may not provoke the same opposition. There will be a greater acceptance of the new role of government as a promoter and facilitator rather than the prime mover".[2]

Deregulation and globalization of India is the new policy framework for governance. Murasoli Maran, the Industry Minister in the Deve Gowda United Front Government, clearly stated that foreign capital was welcome. "If any such venture is employment-oriented and has backward linkages with agricultural sector and generates employment and brings in new technology as well as promotes exports, we would welcome it". He further stated that "we are clear in one thing while allowing foreign investment, we will give priority to employment opportunities, technological upgradation and export promotion".[3]

Freedom for market is defended not only by the promoters of the New Economic Policy of India, but a very powerful indictment of the State-led economic development has come from the neo-liberal western economists, public policy makers and international institutions like the World Bank, the IMF, the UNDP etc. The World Development Report, 1996, of the World Bank has been devoted "to the transition of countries with centrally planned economies ... to market orientation" and it is entitled *"From Plan to Market"*.[4]

While cataloguing the inefficiencies of the State-dominated economic systems, the World Bank President James D. Wolfensohn observes:

> "The Report also makes a major contribution in discussing the institutions that make a market based economy work. It describes how public agencies, legal systems, financial institutions, and education and health system can all enhance the success of market economies .... And it discusses the need for transition for countries to carry through with measures to integrate themselves further within the global economy. Integration into the institutions of the world trading system is an important way to help these countries nourish and sustain the reforms they have undertaken".[5]

The upshot of the above discussion is that new institutions for governance are required to undertake new roles in the era of global integration and liberalization. In concrete terms, the institutions for governance created in the earlier era of Nehru-Indira rule in India have to be either dismantled or renovated to perform the new roles of the new era. The basic difference between 1991-1996 and 1947-1990 is that the Indian Government should vacate its pre-eminent position from management of the productive sector of the economy, and it should concentrate on the physical infrastructure and human capital for development. India is facing serious crisis because human resource development and the development of infrastructural sectors like energy, roads, transport etc. were not properly emphasized and governmental attention was concentrated on inefficient public sector undertakings and other State-led productive sector activities. In the new era of liberalization and globalization, the State should concentrate on the "Social Sector" because "People" have been ignored under the old economic regime of bureaucratic management of the economy. The World Bank Report on *"From Plan to Market"* emphasises that:

> "In the end what matters is people. In the end a country in transition be judged by whether its citizens live better than they did before ... Labour productivity, critical for economic growth, depends on workers' knowledge, skills, motivation and health, therefore relieving extreme poverty, maintaining human capital, and adapting it to the needs of a market system support growth as well as social justice and political sustainability."[6]

The new emphasis on the development of 'human capital', skill improvement, education and health needs the creation of new institutions for governance in India. Thus 'retreat of the State', 'Slimmer Government', 'Social Sector', and open and free market economy are the new context in which governing institutions will have to play their roles. What is a Good or Bad

Government depends on the quality of performance of the assigned roles to the government institutions.

Demands of Global Integration and Institutions for Governance

The context of governance has changed not only within India, it has also changed outside India and the global changes have a direct impact on the arrangements for governance of the country. The Foreign Exchange Regulation Act of the 1970s symbolizes and dramatizes the Nehru-Indira era of 'inward looking' model of development and the system of governance. All regulatory institutions of the 1950s, 1960s, 1970s and 1980s were established to deal with our outside economic and political relations with a view to protect and promote relative autonomy of the Indian State in international relations. The collapse of erstwhile European socialist State systems, the end of the Cold War, the emergence of an ill-defined New World Order, and the crisis of Third World economies and societies brought a qualitative change in global power relations in the 1990s. Mark Rupert observes: "In the context of the post-war global order, the growth of transnational production and intra-firm exchange has 'to a significant degree' displaced international trade."[7]

This 'transnationalization of capitalist production' has transformed global power relations because capital, technology and global trade is concentrated in very powerful 'transnational corporations'. The Third World is dependent on the transnational corporations and the powerful industrial countries for capital, technology and international trade. India can dismantle its Nehru-Indira Model of planned development, and it can concentrate on the so-called 'Social Sector' and hand over the 'productive sector' to the free forces of market. In spite of this change, the Government of India will have to bargain with transnational corporations at every step for every important economic and social activity. A fundamental *contradiction* has emerged at the close of the twentieth century that the State systems have ceased to be real decision-makers on crucial national issues, and the real power of decisions has shifted to the most powerful transnational corporations. This has been the new context of governance in the last years of the Twentieth Century.

In this on-going process of the restructuring of global power relations, the Indian institutions for governance will have to develop new and powerful *capabilities* to negotiate and bargain with the real centres of world power. The real challenge to the governing institutions of India is two-fold. First, the Government of India will have to put its house into order to defend its relative autonomy and sovereignty from powerful external centres of power, *i.e.*, whether transnational corporations or the Western State system or the global institutions like the IMF, World Bank, and the World Trade Organization. In the governance of India, political and social pressures will be exercised by the capital investing countries for getting purely economic concessions. The distinction between politics and economics was never valid, but in the new globalized system of production, such a distinction has ceased to exist. The governing institutions of India will be scrutinized by the capital exporting countries for maintaining democracy and human rights. Second, the Government of India will always remain "Big" and crucial for the Indians in the regime of liberalization and globalization for responding to the crucial demands of more than four hundred million deprived and oppressed social classes. The poor of India look towards the Government for services and succour, and the power elite of India looks with contempt towards bureaucratic arrangements of governance. The differential attitude of the social segments of society towards the government is in spite of the fact that poor are always betrayed and the elite always benefit from governmental policies. It is a myth that the so-called *Licence-permit Raj* did not benefit the industrial, trading, agriculturists and rural and urban middle classes. Only the poor did not receive attention from either the Nehru-Indira Model or any change in the model by P.V. Narasimha Rao and H.D.Deve Gowda. Further, the slogans of de-bureaucratization and decentralization are phoney because if the "Bureaucrats in Business" as described by the World Bank have played havoc during the Nehru-Indira Model, the same bureaucrats are migrating from Door Darshan to Star TV or from lucrative government jobs to private Telecom Companies.[9] How is it that serving or retired bureaucrats are immediately taken over by the Indian and foreign companies?[10]

Big Government and Development

A Frankenstein monster has been created by the local and foreign lobbyists for privatization of the economy that highly bureaucratized and centralised governance of India has brought havoc to economic development. On the basis of this mythology, a prescription has emerged that the Indian Government should de-bureaucratize and decentralize. It should also vacate its presence from the productive sector of the economy and concentrate on the Social Sector alone. The Government should concentrate on the neglected area of the development of 'Human Capital". Centralization and decentralization are always matters of degree and never of kind. There can be no decentralization without reaching a level of centralization in governance. The Constitution of India has arrived at an excellent balance between the requirements of centralization and decentralization. Many significant provisions regarding decentralization mentioned in the Constitution have not been either properly implemented or got sabotaged in the process of their implementation. Local, regional and national areas of governance require a multiple complex system of institutions and the Constitution provides for it. At the same time, while keeping in mind the regional variations, an all-India national perspective for development demands that the institutions for governance should have proper hierarchical linkages and arrangements for administrative coordination. A real effort has to be made to deepen the quality of democratic participation in governance at national, regional, sub-regional and local levels in India. The institutions for governance have to be sensitized towards democratic demands and it can be taken care of by the strengthening of elected and bureaucratic institutions at every level within the country.

Democratic Content in Governance has to be Increased and Strengthened

The distinction between 'productive-economic sector' and 'social sector' is spurious and phoney. An underdeveloped country cannot pull out of the pain of mass poverty without powerful and meaningful State intervention. The history of developed countries substantiates the fact that the State institutions have to provide effective guidance and leadership both in normal and crisis situations in the economy of a country. The U.S. President Franklin Roosevelt responded through New Deal and Big Federal Government in meeting the challenges of Great Depression. J.M. Keynes became immortal for prescribing an active role of the State and its welfare agencies in the process of reconstructing the devastated post-World War II economies of the European industrial countries. Full employment, Welfare State and State leadership in economic management as suggested by Keynes led to the recovery and prosperity of the Western capitalist countries. India has to learn lessons from the developmental experiences of highly developed countries, and history is the best guide for such learning process.

The constitutional, democratic, federal, secular and developmental State of India has to play a very big role in pulling up the downtrodden masses and establish an egalitarian social order. Globalization or liberalization or de-bureaucratization or decentralization are like fictionalized Alladdin Lamp. The Indian elite is pushing the agenda of the developed countries on India without realising the inadequacy of the Western invented agenda of Reagans or Thatchers. A meaningful welfare and developmental State cannot dichotomize "productive and social sectors". The New Economic Policy does not have any rich philosophy about society as given to us by the makers of the Indian Constitution. The Directive Principles of State Policy cannot be achieved by a "retreating" State. A Good Government in the Indian context means people-friendly and not market-friendly because in a highly stratified society the vulnerable strata depend on large governmental presence. The basic objective of Good Governance in India has to be based on the principles enshrined in the Constitution and institutions which are linked with democratic process in a significant manner. A further democratization of the existing governing institutions of India is the key to the multidimensional problems of the country. The middle of 1990s has witnessed a new discourse on governance and re-structuration initiated by the Indian elite under the inspiration of the Western ruling classes. The Indian agenda for the governance of India demands the defence of national sovereignty, deepening of democratic process and economic development for an egalitarian social order. The new agenda of the Indian elite is anti-development, anti-government and anti-national sovereignty. In reality, the market-led economy and governance in India are anti-Democracy.

REFERENCES

1. Jagdish Bhagwati, *India's Transition: Freeing the Economy*, Oxford University Press, Delhi, 1994, p. 3. Also *see:* J. Bhagwati and Padma Desai, *India: Planning for Industrialization*, Oxford University Press, Oxford, 1970, and J. Bhagwati and T.N. Srinivasan, *India*, University Press, New York, 1975.
2. P. Chidambaram, Foreword in Ajit M. Banerjee and K.A. Chandrasekhar (ed), *Renewing Governance: Issues and Options*, New Tata McGraw Hill Publishing Company Ltd., New Delhi, 1996, pp. vii:ix.
3. Marasoli Maran, "Allowing Foreign firms to set up wholly owned subsidiaries: Job-Oriented ventures welcome", *The Statesman*, New Delhi, August 22, 1996, p. II
4. *World Development Report 1996, From Plan to Market*, Oxford University Press, Delhi, 1996.
5. James D. Wolfensohn, *From Plan to Market: World Development Report* 1996, Oxford University Press, Delhi, 1996, p. iii.
6. *World Development Report*, 1996; op. cit. p. 66.
7. Mark Rupert, *Producing Hegemony: The Politics of Mass Production and American Global Power*, Cambridge University Press, Cambridge, 1995, p. 37.
8. Mark Rupert, *op. cit.* p. 22
9. *See "Bureaucrats in Business", The World Bank*, Oxford University Press, Delhi, 1995, Distributors.
10. *See* Surjit Singh, Private Jobs land Telecom En-bosses in Lamp. *The Economic Times*, New Delhi, August 23, 1996, p. 1.

14

Grappling with Globalization

The new economic policies of the Narasimha Rao Government have been strongly opposed by the BJP and the CPI(M) because they are convinced that the ongoing globalization of the Indian economy will seriously erode the national sovereignty of the country. It is alleged that the opening of the Indian market to foreign investors always leads to intervention by the governments of advanced industrial countries in the domestic politics of Third World countries which welcome foreign aid, private foreign investment and transfer of technology. The quality of political relationships among the nation-states determines the flow of resources from the private foreign investors. The foreign investors need assurances on their investments and returns of profits and the signals for this have to come from the governments of their own countries.

It is essential to understand the sea change which has taken place in the structure of global political economy and its impact on the reality of national sovereignty. The United Nations Conference on Trade and Development in its World Investment Report of 1994 has captured the new meanings of global political economy. First, the transactional corporations have global sales exceeding $ 4.8 trillion. Second, the largest 100 TNCs had $ 3.4 trillion in global assets in 1992, and 40 per cent of their assets were located outside their home countries. These 100 TNCs also control one-third of the world's foreign direct investment stocks. Third, more than two lakh foreign affiliates of 37,000 parent firms of the TNCs operate in different countries of the world. These mega TNCs have capital and technology which the developing countries require for their economic development. It may be mentioned that the TNCs make tall claims about their role in employment generation and transfer of technology to the developing countries and India cannot be an exception to this rule.

Global political and economic context determines the nature and context of national sovereignty. The governments of the advanced industrial countries, their banks and their TNCs are global economic and political leaders and the centres of economic power have more sovereignty than the peripheral countries.

Economic and military capability determines the reality of national sovereignty. India has to operate in an inter-dependent world in which a few countries are more independent than the absolute majority of developing countries. The leaders of independent India clearly understood this essence of global political economy and they followed the policies of bargaining in an unequal interdependent world. Jawaharlal Nehru had clearly rejected the policy of isolation of India and operated in the world of give and take with a view to maximize advantage for India.

Why is India making serious efforts to become part of the ASIAN countries? If the global political economy is organized around Trading Blocs, conventional thinking on economic bilateralism or multilateralism simply collapses. India's economic policies of bilateralism will be confronted by common decisions of the Trading Bloc members. Third, the end of the Cold War has brought significant changes in the policy perspectives of advanced industrial countries where economics is deciding politics. While the BJP at its National Executive meeting held at Patna from September 15 to 17 alleged that "The government's infatuation with the globalization of economy and media is undermining the sovereignty of the country," the government of the People's Republic of China was knocking at the door of advanced industrial countries for entry to GATT and its successor the World Trade Organization. Not only this; the government and businessmen of the US have made China their special and new Mecca for investments and trade.

India has entered a very difficult stage of development because it has to grapple with very inhospitable global political economy. On November 3, J.K. Galbraith in his lecture on *"The imperial syndrome"* pointedly referred to the death of the traditional concept of national sovereignty in the new global context. He maintained that the so-called sovereign countries have no right to attack another country. Further, national sovereignty does not mean absence of global intervention if the so-called sovereignty has created "sadly inhuman situations of living."

According to Galbraith, international intervention is legitimate in the case of human sufferings in Liberia, Mozambique, Somalia and Rwanda. Purely domestic laws of some countries are not acceptable to the leaders of global political economy. The US has its own laws on intellectual property rights, on patents and on missile technology. Like all sovereign countries, the Indian Parliament has its own laws on patents and related trade practices. The laws of the US Congress are considered superior to the laws of Indian Parliament if India wants to have trading relationship with the US. The ongoing globalization process of the Indian political economy has created new situations and challenges to the policy makers of sovereign India.

In the New World Order, the old definition of 'economic conditionality' of IMF has been superseded by the new definition of 'conditionality' which is based on good governance. The demands of the World Bank and the IMF for structural reform of the economy is now integrally linked with the demands for the actual reforms for good governance. This is the new meaning of national sovereignty at the close of the 20th Century.

The New World Order has brought the developing countries face to face with the new reality of powerful transnational corporations, international banks and the powerful western countries who are selling the ideology of economic liberalization and humane democratic governance. Politics and economics have become indistinguishable and the relative autonomy of nation-state is a new reality. The agenda for Indian policy makers is to follow the path of bargaining in the global political economy. Entry to global markets and investments from foreign countries will depend on the capability of the institutions of governance in India. Political and bureaucratic capitulation before the leaders of the advanced countries or empty anti-globalization will not lead India anywhere in the fast changing contemporary world.

The logic of correlation of global economic and political forces is tilted against India because our stage of development is full of domestic conflict situations. If the institutions of governance are busy in conflict management, serious agenda of economic reconstruction and development cannot be properly followed. The only meaning of national sovereignty is India's capacity to bargain in global affairs for the promotion and protection of national interests.

Since political parties in India do not have consensus on minimum agenda of political economy, the country will be in continuous difficulties while dealing with powerful Western countries. Recognition of these difficulties is essential for both the fly-by-night globalizers and out-of-date defenders of national sovereignty.

15

Political Economy: Pluses and Minuses

The constitutional framework of Indian federalism has to operate in a specific context of economy and society. During the last four decades India has witnessed many struggles to ensure that inter-state conflicts are resolved to strengthen the national market. The economic policy-makers were aware of the backwardness of the country which also aggravated regional imbalances. Many serious inter-state imbalances have persisted in spite of the proclaimed policies of economic planners of India. Based on per capita income, Punjab and Haryana are at the top and Bihar and Orissa at the bottom. Not only this; a majority of states in India are below the national average in terms of their average per capita income. While Punjab, Haryana, Maharashtra, Gujarat, Andhra Pradesh and Karnataka are 'developed' states on the basis of every indicator of economic development; West Bengal, Himachal Pradesh, Tamil Nadu, Kerala, Rajasthan, Assam, Madhya Pradesh, Orissa, Jammu and Kashmir, Uttar Pradesh and Bihar are 'backward'. India has rich, medium, backward and extremely backward states. The logic of regional imbalance operates in a socially ruthless manner and, in the process of development, while the rich states move forward with great speed, the backward states lag further behind.

All serious political conflicts arise out of the relative backwardness in terms of economic development of the different countries or the various regions within a country. India has witnessed struggle in defence of the 'sons of the soil' and violent confrontations between the insiders and outsiders.

The system of Inner Line Control and permission for entry into some of the North East Indian states is a reality because small states want to protect the 'local economic interests' against 'outside' powerful economic groups. Many states in India have fought trade wars among themselves on the basis of entry and exit tax, octroi, consignment tax, and many duties in the name of sales tax and excise duties. Some states have also imposed 'curbs' on the movement of commodities to neighbouring states. Monopoly procurement of some commodities has been attempted by some states to assert control over their special products like cotton, oilseeds, cashew nuts or foodgrains in periods of food scarcity or drought. Thus India has experience of inter-state tax wars, trade wars, and erection of artificial barriers in respect of movement of goods or human beings in search of opportunities for professions and trade.

This is one part of the story which highlights that a highly fragmented market has to be 'unified' to achieve the goals of national development and unity. Economic integration and interdependence is a pre-requisite for emotional and cultural unity of India. Regional disparities encourage disputes and a spirit of regional chauvinism. Many political movements have challenged the unity of India on the basis of underdevelopment having been caused by deliberate neglect and discrimination. One of the factors responsible for the continuing insurgency or alienation in the North Eastern states of India is the perception that resource-rich states are suffering from underdevelopment because of national neglect and policies of discrimination. The reasons for political mobilization for regional chauvinism may be real or imaginary but if hard economic reality of backwardness persists, regional political manipulators will exploit it to create conflicts resulting in secessionist movements.

Economic backwardness of a region or a state may not always and necessarily lead to secessionist movements, but social conflicts and discord are the order of the day in most backward states like Bihar. Such states have reasons for social violence which often get expressed in the form of frequent or intermittent violent and bloody inter-community and inter-caste clashes and conflicts. A potent factor for violent anti-reservation movements in North India is the absence of economic opportunities because of the extreme under-development. Every job opportunity is jealously watched because of extreme levels of deprivation. It is simplistic to dismiss that the violent anti-reservation movements are demonstrations of the upper caste reaction. The policy of reservation in Government jobs and admissions to educational institutions has emerged on the political scene of Uttar Pradesh and Bihar at a time when 'economic development' is not on the agenda of governments in those states. During 1993-94 chief ministers of almost all states were doggedly pursuing, nay, inviting foreign direct investment. While Maharashtra attracted Rs. 1,660.88 crore of equity for 136 projects, Uttar Pradesh and Bihar could attract a mere Rs. 81.09 crore and Rs. 51.97 crore, respectively for 24 and 4 projects.

The laws of the market economy bypass some regions for others, and regional imbalance gets aggravated in the process of investment choices exercised by private as well as foreign investors.

India has many favourable and positive features which can be harnessed for the total development of the country if only the Central Government had the powers, institutional capability and political vision to achieve the goals of unifying, with a national market, the relatively developed states.

The mineral wealth in the country is spread in a manner that many states get inter-linked and they become interdependent. Most of the important rivers of India flow through many states and this natural endowment can be utilised for power generation and irrigation, *i.e.*, for the economic development of those states. Regional and national power grid systems are an institutional response to the reality that large rivers flow through many states.

During the last 47 years, many important steps have been taken to integrate the national economy and the result is not only that investors are going to different states, but also that the country has achieved the goal of a single national labour market. A very positive achievement indeed! because movement of labour across state boundaries leads to the development of a higher level of consciousness and localism and parochialism get replaced by a large trans-regional loyalty. Unlike the British policy on railways, the post-Independence expansion of the railway system has a significant goal of expanding national economic opportunities and growth.

The history of political economy of the last 47 years has both success and failure stories linked with problems of economic development of the different states, interstate disputes and inter-regional imbalances. The essence of Indian experience is that India has been able to establish, at a minimum level, an all-India functioning national market and this has been possible because of the leadership and guidance provided by the Central Government. The lesson of the last 47 years is that any retreat of the Central Government from its crucial and critical role of unification of the Indian national market will aggravate conflicts between the rich and the poor states.

But unfortunately, despite 47 years of planned development, the all-India national market is still fragile because of serious regional imbalances and only the Central Government has the resources and capacity to guide, co-ordinate, harmonise and act as an arbiter in inter-state disputes.

16

Is the Indian State Really Ruthless?

Human rights groups have often raised controversies about the functioning of the democratic, constitutional State of India which they consider is the chief violator of the Rule of Law. It has been suggested by them that the so-called Democratic State of India has always operated on the basis of Draconian Laws like the Preventive Detention Act or the Maintenance of Internal Security Act or the Essential Services Maintenance Act or the Terrorist and Disruptive Activities (Prevention) Act, 1985.

But Gunnar Myrdal, a noted Swedish economist, concluded that India was a "soft" State because it did not have the institutional capability to implement its own laws. If the State is not able to provide normal services to its own citizens, it cannot be characterised as a strong State. Economic liberalisers maintain that the Indian State is inefficient because it has arrogated to itself functions which do not legitimately belong to it.

The human rights groups demand the repeal of TADA to check the arbitrariness of the Indian State, the economic liberalisers demand the retreat of the State from its present role of the regulator of the Indian economy. It has been argued that India has not been able to achieve its legitimate levels of economic growth because the Indian State 'overestimated' its administrative capabilities to direct the economy.

The non-government organisations (NGOs) maintain that the highly centralised State has imposed a model of economic development for the whole country without caring for the diversities and heterogeneities of India. The Indian State has become insensitive to the needs and aspirations of the tribals who get displaced because of mindless centralisation practised by the State functionaries in the formulation of the so-called national policies for development.

The upshot of all this is that a minimum consensus about the real nature of the Indian State has not emerged in spite of its many achievements and weaknesses.

The most important achievement of the Indian State is that it has been able to defend the territorial integrity of the country. The territorial integrity of India was not a settled fact after the transfer of power on August 15, 1947. The political leadership of the independent State of India had to tackle secessionist and war-like situations to defend the country's territorial integrity. The Indian State followed the policy of bullet versus bullet and the politics of accommodation in dealing with the secessionist movements.

This 'two-track' policy of the Indian State has paid rich dividends in resolving the issues posed by many secessionist movements. On the eve of the Mizoram Accord between Rajiv Gandhi and Laldenga, the Mizo rebels laid down arms because the latter publicly observed that the secessionist cannot challenge the military strength of the Indian State.

But this strength of the Indian State leads human rights observers to allege that it is ruthless. The Ministry of Home Affairs, for instance, has been characterised as "Super Central Police Organisation" which has created the Border Security Force, the Central Reserve Police Force, the Central Industrial Security Force, the Rapid Action Force, the Indo-Tibetan Border Force, the Assam Rifles, etc.

Yet this description of the State is one-sided and is based on ignorance of the complexities of India. It must be clearly stated here that many secessionist movements accepted the authority of the Indian State because many legitimate demands of these groups were accepted and implemented. Many armed struggles in India came to an end not only because of the intervention of army and paramilitary organisations, but also on the basis of very hard and tough bargaining between the functionaries of the Indian State and leaders of the insurgency groups.

It must be clearly stated that the social explanations for the emergence of the politics of bullet in different regions are different and varied, and many Naxal groups have also opted for participation in electoral politics of India.

The Indian State cannot be described as ruthless because in normal circumstances, it is weak and vulnerable. A few illustrations will highlight this. First, T.N. Seshan, the Chief Election Commissioner, has shown that the holding of "free and fair" elections in India has become an extremely difficult job. The legitimacy of the Indian State depends on elections, and if elections are rigged, the State becomes illegitimate. If the democratic legitimacy of the State is eroded, its capability to win over the willing support and consent of the citizens becomes very weak.

Second, serious incapabilities of the State functionaries have been witnessed in implementing the various programmes which are meant for the poor and the vulnerable strata of society. It must be clearly stated here that the powerful sections of the Indian society may be demanding the retreat of the State, but the poor defend and demand an interventionist State. And the State has betrayed them.

Third, the functionaries of the Indian State are not able to collect their taxes in a normal and routine manner. It is not a simple question of "Tax evasion." It is a deeper issue of the relationship between the State and the citizen who is a tax-payer. An average citizen who is satisfied with the normal services provided by the State will willingly pay the taxes. Disgruntled citizens show their disapproval of the role of the State by either not paying or by reluctantly paying the taxes. A harassed and humiliated citizen cannot be enthusiastic payee of taxes levied by the State.

There are many explanations for the growing weaknesses of the Indian State. Every modern, complex State creates effective institutions to deal with social problems and the Indian State has followed this practice of all modern States. India has a huge bureaucratic apparatus to implement policies of the Government. The proliferating bureaucracy of India has shown serious weaknesses while performing its tasks in the society.

The Indian bureaucracy is completely politicised and inspite of its loud protestations, it has entered a kind of *quid pro quo* with politicians. As politicisation was not enough, the bureaucracy is also getting casteised and communalised because of the political developments in the country. How can such a bureaucracy be fair and impartial while dealing with the citizen?

Further, the capabilities of the democratic State grow with the growth of the structures of accountability in politics. The democratic State of India has very weak institutional arrangements for accountability and the result is that no one can be held responsible for the faulty performance of public duties. The institutions of the State improve their performance if failures are punished and successes are recognised and rewarded. Since India has a very weak institutional system of checks and balances, the functionaries of the State neither fear punishment nor do they expect any reward for performance.

Obviously, the Indian State is in the process of establishing its hold over the society. This State has many contradictory features because its points of strength are as significant as its weaknesses.

A State which cannot deliver normal services to the citizen and which has difficulty in implementing its own laws cannot be described as authoritarian. A democratic State becomes strong if its legality is willingly accepted by the majority of citizens. And India has to go a long way in achieving its cherished goal of becoming a strong democratic State where the majority of citizens feel that it is their own State.

17

50 Years of Indian Democracy

The Post-Independence politics of nation-building, state-building and social transformation of India was integrally linked with inter-related pillars of democracy, secularism, federalism and planned economy for creating a new egalitarian society. All these goals of national transformation were based on the promises of leaders of the National Movement that new Independent India would be qualitatively and fundamentally different from the oppressive, exploitative and undemocratic British colonial rule.

What has been the experience of the people during 50 years of their democratic journey? A significant achievement of Indian democracy is that politically apathetic Indians have become very conscious, assertive and demanding. The Indian voter defended democracy by punishing Indira Gandhi in 1977 for her authoritarian political regime. The tallest leaders of the Congress, including Indira Gandhi were humiliated by the voters who exercised their electoral option against the crimes of the Emergency phase of Indian politics of 1975-77. The election of 1977 were a referendum between the defenders of democracy on the one hand and enemies on the other. The Indian voter has learnt the art of punishing political leaders for their acts of omission and commission. Further, historically neglected and oppressed marginal strata of society are actively participating in political decision making and backward castes and communities are successfully challenging the inherited discriminatory and exploitative social order. Have the politicians become more responsive and accountable to the voters because of the messages which deprived groups are sending at the time of election? The answer is a big no. The Indian political class has evolved numerous strategies to manipulate and manoeuvre the electoral process to hoodwink the innocent and poor voters. A few serious distortions of Indian democratic process deserve to be mentioned to properly reveal the ugly faces of Indian political reality. Political power has become an end by itself and political leaders are practising every stratagem to win an election and occupy a position of power in the government. The electoral process has been corrupted because political parties, groups and leaders are spending millions of rupees to win an election by buying and bribing voters and their local influential public opinion makers. Not only this, if the power of money proves insufficient to win over the electoral support of the voters, professional criminals are openly employed by political leaders to terrorise the unobliging sections of society. Democratic politics has been hijacked by politicians who employ completely "illegitimate" and "illegal" methods for winning an election. This growing criminalisation of politics in India has not only delegitimised all democratic institutions of governance, its impact has been felt at every level of public service. If criminals or leaders supported by criminals occupy seats of power in the State Assemblies, Lok Sabha or Council of Ministers, it creates a political culture of illegality and respect for criminality in society.

The system of rule of law which is a pillar of any democratic state is under serious threat in India because public functionaries are themselves practising criminality and illegality. How can such public functionaries safeguard the practice of legality in society? Jayaprakash Narayan in 1974-75 and recently N.N. Vohra, former Union Home Secretary in a report, and the Union mass media have repeatedly alerted the nation about the great power and penetration of criminals in politics. It is essential to keep in mind that if a political class is thoroughly illegitimised in the eyes of voters, the anti-democratic and authoritarian forces can exploit people's sentiment in the name of cleansing public life in India. Thus Indian democracy is threatened by those who pretend to represent the voters.

Democracy in a multi-religious society is integrally linked with the principle of separation of religion from politics. A democratic state has to deal with every citizen's rights on the basis of the principle of "equality before law" and if any religion is allowed to dominate public decision-making institutions, such a state cannot be democratic because it will not be based on the principle of equality of citizens but on discriminatory practices. Of late, the secular content of Indian democracy has been not only diluted, if not checked, it is in the process of getting eroded. For winning an election, all democratic parties have not only taken recourse to illegality, they have made compromises with religious fundamentalists and the consequence of this politics of compromises has been growing communal divisions in the country.

How can democratically elected leaders inspire confidence among various religious communities, if during the elections they show open association with priests, and religious leaders and also make appeals on the basis of religious slogans and symbols. The compromising attitude of the so-called democratic and secular parties in India has created a situation where a full-fledged communal party has emerged an important player in Indian politics. It was a total failure of democratic and secular political forces which encouraged the BJP, the RSS, the VHP and its other linked organisations to demolish the Babri Mosque on December 6, 1992. Hindu communalists gave a clear message that they have finally arrived to demolish the secular democratic state of India.

It needs to be stated here that Hindu communal politics did not occupy a significant public space in the 1950s, and 1960s because the secular political forces openly and unambiguously confronted it at every play in society. It was clearly recognised that communal politics is a product of very powerful communal ideology and the opposition secular forces have to challenge communalism at the level of politics and culture.

This was the essence of Nehru's politics and philosophy which was diluted by his successors in the Congress party who finally abandoned it in the 1990s by appeasing openly the Hindu sentiment. The point to be understood is that the present formidable challenge of communalism to secular democracy has emerged because of the serious acts of omission and commission by all secular parties.

Hindu communalism has emerged in a big way by exploiting the ideological vaccum created by the Congress. Indira Gandhi and her successors in the Congress, unlike Nehru, reduced secularism to the level of political tactics for winning elections. For Nehru, secularism was fundamental principle of Indian democracy but for his successors, winning an election by any means, became the essential goal of democratic politics.

This is our journey of the last 50 years where principles in politics for nation-building have been completely abandoned for winning political power for self or family members or friends. Former Chief Minister, ministers including a former Prime Minister are accused for criminal abuse of their political power. The total derailment of principled politics was dramatised when some formed ministers or chief ministers or very high ranking civil and police functionaries were imprisoned for misconduct while holding public office. Is it New India for which the masses fought against colonial rule?

Indian democracy is under siege because the levers of power have been captured by a minority of politically and socially powerful groups and the absolute majority of the poor, deprived and marginalised social groups have not been really empowered in any meaningful sense of the term. The Indian leadership had linked the goals of democratic nation-building with social transmigratory and developmental agenda so that the Indian masses participate not only in electoral politics, but they also get a share in the fruits of economic development. The strategy of planned development of India was promised on a belief that the right to vote was a necessary but not a sufficient condition for establishing a real participatory democratic society.

Since Indian democracy has not tackled the agenda of distributive justice in a serious of society are simply involved in a struggle for daily survival. If more than 400 million people are just struggling to make their ends meet even after 50 years of Independence, such a society cannot remain peaceful. Hence the country is witnessing different varieties of open or hidden social violence which get reflected in caste versus caste, religion versus religion and region versus conflicts. Social divisions have been sharpened because social opportunities have been cornered by a minority in society and the majority of struggling masses have become victims of benign neglect by the democratic state. This mass of alienated people are politically manipulable by casteist, communalist and regional chauvinst leaders because they successfully provide some false sense of security to the vulnerable strata of society. In such a social situation Thackereys, Imams, and criminals prosper because the mass of disempowered and disenfranchised people do not identify themselves in a meaningful manner with democratic politics.

The main thrust of the above discussion is that the democratic political process of the last 50 years has created a situation where people have become socially volatile because the process of economic development has led to regional, class, religious, caste and language confrontations because the fruits of development have been unevenly distributed among communities castes and regions. A country of gross social inequalities and deprivations provides a fertile ground for the growth of anti-democratic and anti-secular forces and this is precisely what is happening today. If corrective steps are not taken, the social crisis will become quite unmanageable. Electoral reforms elimination of criminals from politics and the agenda of secular politics linked with distributive justice is the only way to safeguard democracy. It may be mentioned here that democracy provides its own cleansing mechanisms. Hence no compromises should be made with the ongoing democratic process. The need of the hour is to launch an alternative agenda of democratic governance which is truly people-oriented, secular and socially transformative.

18

Federalism in the Age of Globalisation

The constitutional and political issues raised by the chief ministers at the meeting of the Inter-State Council clearly revealed a total insensitivity towards the new global developments and their implications for the functioning of Indian federalism. This fact was further confirmed by the conduct of the Chief Minister of Andhra Pradesh who approached the World Bank president who for aid without involving the Central Government of India. The collapse of the erstwhile Socialist State Systems and the emergence of the so-called New World Order has created an absolutely new global milieu for political decision-makers in India.

If, on the one hand, economic decision-making has been transnationalised, on the other, every state in the Third World is having to negotiate and bargain with very powerful transnational corporations for capital, technology and opportunities for exports. National policies have had to be evolved while dealing with the issues of Foreign Direct Investment or the import of technology or the flow of goods and services among the nation-states. The Indian federal state will become extremely vulnerable if the political decision-makers allow each of the 25 states of the Indian Union to negotiate directly with global economic and political centres of power.

A few important facts may be mentioned to situate India in the global power relations. The World Investment Report of 1996 informs us that the world's largest 100 TNCs are all based in developed countries, their $1.4 trillion worth of assets are in foreign countries. Out of these 100, 32 TNCs are from the United States. Further, about 90 per cent of parent firms in the world are based in developed countries, but two-fifths of foreign affiliates are located in developing countries. This internationalistion of firms has created a situation where the home governments of the parent firms are expected to promote and project the global interests of their TNCs. The Law of Patents, Copyright, Trade Practices and Multilateral Agreement on Investments have assumed a new significance because the national decision-makers in India will have dealings with the Western State Systems and TNCs.

The Centre-State relations in India will have to be evolved by keeping in mind the imperatives of the rapid ongoing process of global integration. A weak Central Government dependent on the support of the region-based political class will not be able to pursue the country's national goals while dealing with global centres of economic and political power. India failed to win a seat in the Security Council because the economic and political power of Japan is far greater than ours.

The H.D. Deve Gowda Government of 13 political groups is unequal to the task of bargaining with powerful international aid-givers and investors because this Government consists of only regional parties and leaders. Every minister in the Deve Gowda Government is a representative of his own State and is also concerned with the political and economic problems of his State. Mr. Mulayam Singh Yadav, the Union Defence Minister, has more time for U.P. than for problems facing the defence of the country. Mr. Ram Vilas Paswan, the Railway Minister, is not only interested in promoting the interests of Bihar, he has shown very clearly that the Deva Gowda's Council of Ministers consists of individual decision-makers who do not take collective decisions.

A Weak Centre Bodes Ill

The Central Government employees have received a clear message that the Railway employees will get benefits because their Minister has favoured them and other employees are ignored because of the leaderless Central Government. The settlement of river water dispute between Tamil Nadu and Andhra Pradesh was a result of goodwill of the Chief Minister of Andhra Pradesh for his Tamilian counterpart. The so-called Federal Front of TDP (Naidu), DMK (Karunanidhi), the Samajwadi Party (Mulayam), etc. have come together to manage the affairs of the Central Government and they have not given any evidence to show that they have any common national goal and perspective.

A Chief Minister, during the Inter-State council meeting, suggested that the Central Government should have only four powers, like foreign policy, defence, communications, and currency. Another Chief Minister suggested that the post of the Governor of the State should be abolished without reflecting for a moment the need for Centre-State linkages. Dr Farooq Abdullah, the new entrant to this Federal Front of the regionalists, along with other regional representatives, is demanding a kind of autonomy for the State which will lead to a token relationship with the Central Government. The upshot of the above argument is that the Deve Gowda Government is not a coalition of national parties but a conglomerate of regional groups. The consequence of this fact is that national policy framework has become marginal before regional demands and pressures.

The Common Minimum Programme of the United Front partners is merely on paper and every minister in the Deve Gowda Government as well as the State chief ministers are pursuing their own priorities without any reference to any coherent national policy agenda. Is this kind of Central Government capable of dealing with the new global pressures? The answer to this question is a big no. It is for the first time in the history of Independent India that the

World Bank president announced that the Bank officials will visit India for a half-yearly evaluation of the Bank-funded programmes. If the pace of implementation of projects has to be regularly evaluated by the fund giving agencies, it will be difficult to anticipate the future levels of foreign intervention.

A very important concern of the Central Government is to correct the existing inter-state and intra-state regional imbalances. A weak Central Government will not be allowed to perform this task because powerful rich State governments and regional parties have no concern for underdeveloped states and an all-India policy for dealing with problems of such states. Karnataka and Maharashtra on the one hand, and Bihar and U.P. on the other, or the underdeveloped Seven Sisters of the North-East have to exist together, and indifferent developed neighbouring State governments will make such co-existence very problematic. How can the Central Government abdicate its responsibilities in relation to the diverse problems of development of the states?

The upshot of the above analysis is that neither the new global developments nor the complexities of a diverse India can be tackled by a weak Centre. A weak Central Government led by Mr. Deve Gowda announced the creation of Uttarakhand without preparing itself for a chain reaction of such demands. A major difference between India and the US federation may be mentioned. A political executive of the US federal government is always in the driver's seat to protect its national interests globally and also to deal with any domestic crisis. Franklin D. Roosevelt provided a national leadership in the phase of Great Economic Depression. A modern federal government with a weak Centre is a recipe for foreign dictation and internal inter-state conflicts and ruthless competition.

19

Perils of Regionalism

The changing political landscape has brought into focus the new emerging role of regional parties. Mr. P. Chidambaram recently highlighted this fact before a distinguished group of international business leaders by observing that the regional parties are "close to the people and impatient to develop India". Not only this, the Chief Ministers, who represent the regional parties and aspirations, are "actively involved in deciding national affairs."

It is essential to demystify the reality of regional parties and politics for properly understanding the real challenges of emerging regionalism in India. Every single state in the southern, eastern north-eastern, northern and northwestern regions is involved in either inter-state boundary or river water disputes. Since every regional party is co-terminus with its state boundaries, these parties cannot negotiate with their neighbours because of the fear of alienation of local state sentiment on the basis of which these parties come to power.

Mr. Parkash Singh Badal raised the demands of Punjab and Mr. Bansi Lai of Haryana, a neighbouring Chief Minister of a regional party, vetoed Mr. Badal's demands because the regional parties of Punjab and Haryana have to take care of their respective regional sentiments. Mr. Chandrababu Naidu of Andhra Pradesh, Mr. Karunanidhi of Tamil Nadu or Mr. Mahanta of Assam may be experiencing new freedom in the context of regionalisation of Indian politics, but these Chief Ministers have not been able to find any solution of their own to either inter-state river water disputes like Cauvery or Almatti or inter-tribal or intra-tribal fratricidal wars in north-east India. Regional parties are nurtured and nourished by local sentiments and it is impossible for them to resolve inter-state disputes without a powerful arbiter *i.e.* an effective Central Government.

The regional parties represent local caste and class interest and these interests come into conflict with either the neighbouring states or with larger social goals of development of India. The Akali Dal of Punjab represents caste, community and class interest of the Jat Sikh capitalist farmer and Mr. Badal emerged as a lobbyist of his social constituency by raising the issue of the minimum support price for wheat. Further, he has issued a warning to the whole country that if the support price for wheat is not enhanced to Rs. 550 or Rs. 650 per quintal, the official procurement agencies will not be able to induce the farmer to sell his products to them and the modified Public Distribution System will not succeed in the absence of new incentives to the producers of wheat.

Mr. Bansi Lai of Haryana, leader of the Haryana Vikas Party, also jumped on the bandwagon of Mr. Badal, to win over the support of the farmers of Haryana. Many illustrations like these can be mentioned to prove that the so-called regional parties are neither socially neutral nor a great model of good governance. Fiscal deficit, populist schemes, and bankruptcy of the State Electricity Boards are the highlights of governance by the regional parties. Not only this. Many regional parties have not been able to provide an alternative of model governance as compared with the erstwhile governments of the Congress party.

The Janata Dal and the Bahujan Samaj Party Governments of Bihar and Uttar Pradesh are in no way an improvement over the Congress Governments of these states. Like the erstwhile Congress state Governments, many regional parties have consciously obstructed the development of local democratic institutions in their states. It may be mentioned that the Left Front Government of West Bengal and the Left Democratic Front or the United Democratic Front Governments of Kerala have shown many innovations in governance but the explanation in these cases is that they are regional governments led by parties which have a national perspective as distinguished from the pure regional parties like the DMK-AIADMK, TMC, TDP, AGP, Akali Dal, HVP, or the Janata Dals. Regional parties have actively followed the practice of erstwhile Congress Governments in breaking and bending the state civil services for purely partisan purposes.

The upshot of the above argument is that it is wrong to romanticize the regional parties. These parties have not shown any new quality of governance. Not only this. Many regional parties have intensified the feelings of parochialism and language fanaticism. The Kannada Development Authority is fanatically promoting the cause of Kannada language without learning a lesson from West Bengal where the policy of devaluing of the English language brought disastrous consequences for the people of that state. Bihar and Uttar Pradesh have entered the dark ages in the field of education because of the ill-conceived language policy of the Hindi enthusiasts of these states.

Jean Dreze and Amartya Sen have come to a tragic conclusion about UP by observing that "the region is characterised *inter alia* by exceptionally high levels of mortality, morbidity, undernutrition, illiteracy, and social inequality, and a slow pace of poverty decline" and their considered judgement is that the total failure of public services or governance is responsible for the present dismal situation of U.P as compared to the other backward states. The powerful regional leaders of U.P. and Bihar like Mr. Mulayam Singh Yadav, Ms Mayawati and Mr. Laloo Prasad Yadav have not shown any capacity to pull out U.P. and Bihar from backwardness.

The governance of India requires a political arrangement which responds to the needs of unity and diversity. The recent truck drivers strike is the best illustration of the existing interlinkages in India. The national market can get regionalised and balkanised if regions are allowed to manage them according to their local needs and priorities. An active role of the Central Government is essential to maintain a proper balance between the local needs of regions and the national and international priorities of India.

Europe has taken more than forty years to realise that a unified Common European Market will provide scales of economy to compete with the continental-sized economy of the US. India has a natural advantage of large size and resources which are found all over the country, and an ineffective Central Government and local-oriented regional parties pulling in different directions will lead to internal regional civil conflict on the movement of goods and services.

Punjab and Haryana have given a warning that wheat is not available except on the terms and conditions laid down by Mr. Badal and Mr. Bansi Lal. The ULFA or ASSU-AGP in Assam may follow Mr. Badal and Mr. Bansi Lal and stop the flow of oil to the country. The Deve Gowda Government was inherently fractured to manage the affairs of India with a perspective which included national and local priorities of governance. It was a sum-total of regional parties, groups and leaders and showed its weaknesses while dealing with pressures from regional parties and leaders.

Hence, individuals and leaders who are glorifying the emergence of new cooperative federalism in India are actually rationalising the ineffectiveness of the Central Government to provide an all-India perspective for national development in the context of the New Global World Order. The Telugu Desam Party chief, Mr. Chandrababu Naidu, wants that Article 356 of the Constitution should be deleted, and the Deve Gowda Government, the heroic model of Mr. Naidu, imposed President's rule in Uttar Pradesh.

The so-called Gujral doctrine and Mr. Farooq Abdullah's dreams of state autonomy can succeed only if the Central Government occupies a pre-eminent position in the governance of the country and regional formations can expect resolution of their legitimate demands only if the Centre functions in a proper manner.

20

Naxalism and the Indian State

Home Minister Lai Krishna Advani spelt out the policy framework for dealing with the Naxal problem on June 15,1998, when he attended the meeting of the chief ministers of Madhya Pradesh, Maharashtra, Orissa and Andhra Pradesh. The first component of Mr. Advani's methodology for tackling Naxalite activities is to prepare a development and security plan, upgrade the technological skills of armed police forces and further tighten the laws on the lines of the Tamil Nadu Prevention of Terrorist Activities Act, 1998. It was suggested that the 10th Finance Commission has also made separate allocation for states to improve training of their police personnel, build more police stations and develop technologies in the field of communications to tackle Left-wing extremism.

Mr. L.K. Advani's tough law and order approach is an offshoot of his belief that the tendency to regard Left-wing extremism as a socio-economic problem gives their activities a responsibility and legitimacy they do not deserve. This law and order approach devoid of a proper response to the socio-economic reasons, which give birth to such violent social struggles, has always proved inadequate and wrong. Mr. Siddharth Shankar Ray, the former Chief Minister of West Bengal, had adopted such a ruthless policy of state repression in the mid-1960s when the Naxal movement was at its peak in Bengal. But the problem was resolved only when the Left Front Government addressed itself to the whole question of agrarian social relations in rural Bengal.

It is essential to properly situate the ideological and socio-economic philosophy of Naxalism in order to deal with the issues raised by this movement. Marxist political parties interpret social reality on the basis of a theory of class analysis. It is inherent in such a party or movement that different interpretations of social reality will be made and different strategies of dealing with class problems will be evolved by leaders or groups who practice Marxism for the goal of changing human society. Different perceptions of social reality within the broad Marxist theoretical framework have been an essential feature of Marxism even when Karl Marx was alive and himself involved in struggles for interpreting social realities.

The belief of Indian Marxists, that feudal-landlord relations in agrarian

India cannot be destroyed without taking to the gun because the powerful state is a defender of feudal landlords and, that the power of the state has to be smashed by the power of the gun of the oppressed masses, has been one of the mainstream ideas of Indian Marxists. The Telengana peasant uprising resulted from such an interpretation of Indian social reality.

When the Telengana struggle came to a dead-end, Communists revised their thesis about Indian reality and accepted the challenge of participating in parliamentary democratic politics. The Communists emerged as the single largest opposition party in the Lok Sabha in 1952 and the largest number of its MPs came from Andhra Pradesh. It may be mentioned here that as a result of the Telengana uprising, the agenda of land reforms came back into the agenda of the ruling Congress and depending on the balance of social forces within the party, land reforms were implemented in states on the basis of the social composition of the State Congress party.

Even as the Communist movement launched its parliamentary journey, different interpretations of social reality plagued the Communist leadership. Conflicting party lines, or theses on India were debated and when differences became irreconcilable, the party split in 1964. Developments within the Communist parties led to a further split because a section of party leadership like Charu Majumdar, Kanu Sanyal and others rejected the party line of parliamentary struggle of the CPI and CPI (M). The old thesis that Indian feudal-landlord oppression supported by the Indian state cannot come to an end without militant peasant uprising was revived and they launched such a struggle from Naxalbari in West Bengal. Power, they said, flows from the barrel of the gun and guerrilla peasant armed struggles will "liberate" India. This "war of liberation" launched by the Left-extremists derived its ideological inspiration from the successful peasant revolution in China under the leadership of Mao. Marxism, Leninism and Maoism became the reference points of the splinter Left-extremist groups who indulged in violence not only against class enemies but also against class-collaborators, especially the cadre of the two parliamentary Communist parties.

This politics of the gun brought into sharp focus the basis of agrarian oppression and conflicts but the methodology of gun as the mid-wife of revolutionary liberation had very few takers. The Indian state ruthlessly crushed the Naxalite movement which was at its peak in the mid-1960s in rural Bengal, parts of Bihar and Telengana area in Andhra Pradesh. In fact, the whole of South-East Asia witnessed Maoist kind of peasant uprisings in the 1960s and 70s. Philippines, Burma, Indonesia, Korea, Cambodia, Malaya saw Maoist Communist peasant struggles and as in India, Mao proved a wrong prophet for resolving the peasant question in South and South-East Asia.

The Left Front Government, after coming to power in 1977, undertook large scale land reforms programme in Bengal. Its impact was felt because Naxalism soon became socially redundant. Similarly, the Communist parties in Kerala also implemented the unfinished agenda of agrarian reforms in the

1970s and Naxal ideological influence from neighbouring Andhra Pradesh did not travel to Kerala.

The above description clearly reveals that a pure law and order response to the agrarian question raised by the gun-wielding Left adventurists has limited utility. It is a well-known fact that Naxalism is operating in areas like the feudal-dominated tribal belt of Madhya Pradesh, the oppressive landlord dominated areas of rural Bihar and Telengana, and the most backward areas of Maharashtra and Orissa. Naxal-extremism is confined to pockets in states where landlord oppression is unmitigated and land reforms have been carried out in an inadequate manner. While the Naxal belief in the power of the gun should not be glorified or romanticised, the social agenda of agrarian restructuring cannot be ignored or else it will continue to provide breeding ground for the violence of both the landlords and the Naxals.

Naxal ideology is absolutely defective because democratic consciousness among the Indian masses has increased not because of the politics of the gun but due to universal adult franchise. Elections have played a revolutionary role and Indian democracy provides ample social spaces to launch struggles against landlord oppression. The politics of the gun only provides an excuse to the state to convert a socio-economic problem into a law and order problem. The social agenda of democratic mass movements will have more impact than mere physical annihilation of the class enemy. The Naxal movement or People's War Groups or the Maoists of Bihar cannot claim the credit for any structural change in land relations in Andhra Pradesh or Bihar. Gun versus gun is a short-cut to social revolution and the politics of bullet will never succeed in transforming Indian society The rural masses have to be made conscious of their rights through democratic struggles. Chief ministers of states where Naxal-inspired rural violence is taking place should answer the question: Why is such agrarian violence not in existence in many other states of India? A democratic state has to offer political solutions while dealing with social agrarian questions and policing by the state cannot be a substitute for a meaningful social reform.

21

Hindutva and the Indian State

The BJP-led government under the leadership of Atal Bihari Vajpayee and L.K. Advani has brought in an epochal change in Indian politics because the forces of Hindutva have a definite ideological orientation, which is fundamentally different than the weak and confused left-of-centre ideology of the Indian state, which was practised by different political formations from 1947 to 1998. The philosophers of twentieth century political Hinduism like Hedgewar, Golwalkar, Veer Savarkar and Aurobindo have conceptualized India as "One Nation, One People and One Culture" and all the groups of Sangh Parivar, as an inheritor of this monolithic cultural interpretation of Indian culture, are fully committed to practice and promote this brand of Hindutva by the exercise of state power.

It is not only that the forces of Hindutva have very clear goals while exercising state power, they have operationalized and concretized their programme of total restructuring of the state apparatuses to make it work in tune with the demands of Hindutva. The 1998 Election Manifesto of the BJP has devoted a lot of space and attention by spelling out a full and comprehensive Agenda for institutional rejuvenation by promising Constitutional, Electoral, Judicial, Administrative Reforms with special reference to the Reforms in the Law and Order Machinery of India. L.K. Advani asserted in an interview to the *Hindustan Times* of April 14,1998 "that the perception of India being a 'soft state' has to go". L.K. Advani as Head of the Police Ministry of the Indian state elaborated his concrete programme of "streamlining of intelligence outfits to act tough against disruptionist elements, particularly those aided and abetted from across the borders".

L.K. Advani's interview and the BJP's Election Manifesto raise some significant issues about the concepts of 'soft' and 'hard' state and their implications for the governance of a really pluralist society like that of India. Gunnar Myrdal while inquiring into the causes of Poverty in his Asian Drama described our state system as 'soft' because of the inherent incapability of the state functionaries in implementing their own laws in society. The manner and method of restricting of agrarian land relations in the 1950s and 1960s dramatized the limitation in the capabilities of the state to carry out to its logical end its own programmes.

Such illustrations can be multiplied from all the new states of Asia, Africa and Latin America. In Pakistan, the population Census cannot be undertaken without the active involvement of Army. Every day a citizen comes across the phenomenon of the limitations of the capabilities of the institutions of the state while performing normal and routine functions like the delivery of a driving license to a motorist. Since the forces of Hindutva are not well versed in the history of modern state formations a few facts may be mentioned that we are in the early stage of state formation and all modern western states have gone through the same historical process as we are witnessing these days.

The process of modern state formation in Europe is linked with Absolutist Monarchical system and the growth of mercantile capitalism from 1500 AD to 1800 AD. Every philosopher of state like Machiavelli of *The Prince* or Hobbes of the *Leviathan* who are described as votaries of Absolutism emphasized that the monarchs should make every effort to win over the willing consent of the population for obedience and acceptance of the state authority. The Nineteenth and Twentieth Century European philosophers of the state grappled with the issues of Republicanism and Democratic state formation based on social contract and consent between the citizens and their representatives in elected parliaments. European journey of democratic and willingly acceptable state system continued to face many ups and downs and the Twentieth Century witnessed a real struggle between legitimate, effective, democratic state system on the one hand, and on the other, Nazism, Fascism and other forms of Authoritarianism to establish hard and strong states in the place of popular consent-based democratic state systems.

The moral of the story is that the journey of state formation and the willing acceptance of its legality and pre-eminence by social groups is a very long and difficult task and any artificial conversion of an inherently 'soft state' by injecting excessive law and order approach to governance as emphasized by Advani, is quite dangerous and uncalled for. Further a very powerful colonial state in India had realized its limitations' while dealing with multiple Indian social groups because its efforts to control Indian society burst into an open revolt in 1857. Hence in the proclamation of 1858, Queen Victoria clearly mentioned that Her majesty's Government will show maximum respect to the ways of life of different social groups in the country.

It is not without reason that the British Colonial State abandoned its so-called civilizing and reformist agenda after 1858 and the British rule from 1858 to 1947 had great political and economic content, and its social and cultural agenda for the colonized people was put in abeyance. Maurya or Gupta or Mughal Empires constructed state-systems in which large autonomous social spaces were available to social groups, communities or in the words of Kr. Suresh Singh, an eminent anthropologist." *Biradari* code of conduct. Indian society has multiplicity of groups who follow self-regulatory code to determine their family and social way of life and it is autonomous from state and its rules and regulations.

The essence of Indian social life is that multiple levels of authority, obedience, and loyalty operate simultaneously and state is only one such institution which is expected to regulate social conduct and the state functionaries have to compete with the authority of caste, community, biradari leaders while implementing laws of the state. Tradition and modernity are coexisting and competing in the Indian society where secular and modern formal and legal public institutions have to come to terms with private domains of authority of the Elders in a village or family.

The newly modernizing societies can be managed by only democratic states, which have the capacity to exercise legal coercive powers by understanding the social forces of resistance and voluntary obedience. A very resilient state apparatus, which has democratic sensitivity, can combine the demands of generalized law and order regime with autonomous spaces where social groups do not willingly accept state regulation. It has been witnessed that the believers in law and order require lot of patience, or under the arrogance of power inject heavy doses of efficiency and legality, which in reality has meant military or civilian authoritarian state systems in the whole third world. Military Generals of Pakistan did not understand the inherent logic of the making of Pakistan society and came to grief because not a single solution offered by military dictators resolved any problem facing Pakistan. Mrs. Indira Gandhi also acted against the structural logic of Indian society and imposed the Emergency to convert 'soft' into 'hard' state and the Indian society taught her a lesson, which she never forgot.

The Sangh Parivar's total world view and belief system is an absolute negation of complex historical formation of India. The Sangh Parivar wants to implement its ideological agenda by using state power with the help of Advani as "Police" Minister, Murli Manohar Joshi and Sushma Swaraj as ideological leaders of Educational and Cultural Agenda of the Hindutva. Advani is attributing every civil disturbance in India to foreign inspired ISI agents of Pakistan. All border states are full of 'infiltrators' from neighbouring countries and to check this so called human holocaust. He wants compulsory identity Cards for multi-religious and very sensitive border states of India. Bangladeshi Muslims in India have been always a target of hate campaign by the forces of Hindutva and Advani at the helm of affairs has to stop this by converting 'soft' into 'hard' law and order police state on the borders.

The multiplication of factors which are responsible for the whole disturbed North East India have been forgotten and Hindu chauvinistic agenda of anti-Muslim, in this case so called Bangladeshi have to be tackled as a priority basis by the BJP government. AASU-AGP opposition to Illegal Migration Act has got a sympathetic hearing because for Advani it is a Hindu-Muslim problem.

Thus, behind that mask of Home, Education and Broadcasting Ministers, lies a clearly Hindutva agenda, which will terrorise the minorities and pose a serious cultural threat to pluralities of Indian society. India is a way of life and the Indian state can operate only by accepting its multi-dimensional historical antecedents which lie in its autonomous and self-regulatory social arrangements which operate as a matter of convention. In social and cultural history, certain stages cannot be by-passed and the leaders of Indian state should understand this. The state functionaries have to respect such traditional rights and make efforts to persuade the believers of traditions to adapt themselves to the requirement of formal legality of the state.

The Agenda of Modern State Formation for the Indian political classes is quite heavy because global dimensions have a direct bearing on the processes of making of the states.

A few illustrations will prove this point. The IMF has bailed out South Korea, Indonesia and Thailand by advancing a loan of U.S. $100 billion with all kind of conditionalities which every borrower has to accept. The Central Banks of these three states have to keep their 'books' open for scrutiny by foreign investors who should know about the real health of economy of these societies. Do these states have any control over their Central Bank?

India's trade regime is being reviewed by the World Trade Organization and Patent Laws of India have to be accepted by international organizations. The Trade Representative of the United States has warned India to allow more import and stop offering lame excuses of foreign exchange crisis. Finance Minister Yashwant Sinha has made pilgrimage to Washington and New York and Sikandar Bakht, the Industry Minister, feels irritated when he is reminded of 'swadeshi' and invitations by the present government to foreign investors. The BJP-Shiv Sena Government in Maharashtra accepted Enron and made a volte face because these groups while in operation had stalled Enron operations. All the above illustrations are from the first month of BJP government. Why is India a 'soft' state under the BJP while dealing with agencies like WTO?

The crux of the issue is that the forces of Hindutva are oblivious of the globalization of capitalism and its implications for our state system. Similarly, any excessive reliance on police and intelligence agencies to convert 'soft' into 'hard' Indian state by the BJP will generate social unrest in the country. The strength of any state lies in its capacity to win the consent and willing obedience of its citizenry and keep its coercive instruments of power in reserve for the emergencies.

India has a long way to go for achieving the goal when absolute majority of people identify with the state by proclaiming that it is our state. The prerequisite for achieving such a long term goal is not by strengthening police but by launching a socio-economic agenda for the uplift of the poor, who would support the state voluntarily as it is only a caring state that is considered legitimate.

22

Indian Transition

When a society moves from one stage of the material base of production and, consequentially, different social relations of production, to another historical stage, it has to go through an extremely complex and long process of dialectics of social transition. The process of birth and maturing of the new forces of production is a winding process of ups and downs because the old material forces of social production and the ideological and cultural superstructure of social relations of the 'old' persist even when the new mode of production is in the process of taking birth. While Karl Marx had alerted us that the 'New' is born out of the 'Old', the persistence and resilience of the 'Old' social relations of production continues to be an integral part of the living social realities of every society that has moved from feudalism to capitalism. The statement that a social and material transition from the old mode of production to the new takes centuries is validated by the history of the long journey of transition from feudalism to capitalism in Europe. This journey also witnessed the overlapping of the past and the emerging 'new', and, among European countries, only the bourgeois revolution of France marked to a large extent a break with the feudal 'ancient regime' and the beginning of a new journey after overthrowing the baggage of its past feudal history.

This evidence on the process of transition led many western theorists studying the post-World War II 'decolonised' societies of Africa, Asia and Latin America to examine the social aspects of developments in these societies on the basis of the 'tradition-modernity' paradigm. It was maintained that the 'traditional' societies were emulating the 'modern' western societies, and the unstated assumption was that these societies would follow the same historical path towards 'modernisation' as experienced by modern Europe. This tradition-modernity theoretical context for the study of 'old societies' entering the new world simply hangs in the air because its focus is only on the superstructural changes like the establishment of a new, modern state system where social life will be governed by secular laws and jurisprudence instead of the old traditional authority structures where living beings managed and regulated their affairs by simply following primordial loyalty structures like a hierarchical caste system or tribal practices as defined by tribal chiefs. Robert C. Allen observes:

> In the mid-20th century, the problem of Asian economic development was conceived as a problem of modernising 'traditional societies'. In fact, their circumstances were anything but traditional. Underdevelopment was the product of 19th-century globalisation and western industrial development.[1]

Western writers have projected a social agency of 'the modernising elite', who may comprise of political or bureaucratic or military generals who would be able to transform these so-called traditional societies and launch a journey of modernisation of economy and culture. This tradition-modernity theoretical structure for the study of decolonised societies focuses attention on the face-value of social changes without any understanding of the underlying material forces that are at work in shaping and reshaping the social structures of these societies. Edward Shils, C. Geertz *et al.* have focused attention on 'Old Societies and New States', where primordial and old loyalty structures were getting replaced and displaced by a secularisation process that was based on the rule of law enforced by the state and its functionaries. Talbot Parsons in his theoretical structure recognised that 'conflicts' arise during the ongoing process of social change, but he also maintained that there is never a Hobbesian war of all against all and that 'conflicts' get resolved without large-scale social upheavals. Parsons' formulations are an advancement over other western social theorists because he recognizes that 'conflicts' occur in a changing society, but he also does not relate the whole process of change with the fundamental transformations in the material foundational levels of society. The tradition-modernity approach is absolutely flawed because it delinks itself from the history of colonised societies whose growth process was arrested. Marxist theoretical intervention is based on full cognizance of the historical reality that fundamental social transformations are integrally linked with the changing nature of material forces of production in society.

Eric Hobsbawn has summed up the materialistic interpretation of history and dialectical materialism followed by Marx in his 'The Critique of the Political Economy of Capitalism', that: 'The social relations of production (i.e. social organisation in its broadest sense) and the material forces of production, to whose level they correspond, cannot be divorced.' The economic structure of society is formed by the totality of these relations of production.[2] While elaborating Marx's approach, Hobsbawn observes that 'economic development cannot be discussed except in terms of particular historic epochs and particular social structures'.[3] The current debate in India, that the increasing rate of economic growth and national gross domestic product has directly impacted the process of social transformation, especially beginning with the 1990s, is like the modernity-tradition approach, which is partially relevant because it 'masks the revelation of contradictions of capitalism' and it does not focus attention on the interests of the dominant classes, without which the complexities and contradictions of India cannot be comprehended or explained. Hence, the materialistic interpretation of history and the dialectical process of social transformation provide an important key to explore the complex contradictions of the Indian transition. Paula Allman correctly points out that the 'dialectical conceptualisation of contradiction and inner relations of capitalism as emphasised by Karl Marx help in demystifying the social forces which are at work in society at a given time and at a given stage of historical development of a society'.[4] The above framework is sought to be applied to analyses, interpret and explain the ongoing process of the grand transition of India.

INDIA'S HISTORICAL LEGACIES

India was plundered by the Robber State of British imperialists (to refer to Bukharin), and the long, bleeding process of the colonial phase of history (Karl Marx) led to the complete distortion of the material and social structure because of the complete disruption of the ongoing natural processes of material changes that were at work from the beginning of the seventeenth century. India was structurally integrated with the capitalist colonial system which not only 'extracted' national social surplus value, but also imposed an international division of labour along with unequal terms of trade for primary products required for the industrial needs of the British. The whole society was forced to produce raw materials and other primary products for serving the needs and requirements of the industrial metropolis, and its long-term consequence was that the productive system of the whole society was pushed backward and engaged in primitive means of production and social relations that were structured for the 'extraction' of social surplus value for the rent-seeking colonial state of the metropolis. Social relations and structures bound to agrarian society remained tied to the past because the oppressive landlord/ *zamindari* or the *rayatwari* system of land revenue collection in British India, and autocratic feudal/princely rule over large parts of the country froze the history of change. A very powerful and sustained anti-colonial struggle was launched by different strata of victimised and oppressed society, like the peasantry, working classes, emerging professional middle classes, and the small, medium and big bourgeoisie, with a goal to liberate the country from the colonisers, who had pushed back the whole society materially and socially by thwarting its natural and autonomous material and social development.

On the eve of independence, India had all the indicators of backwardness as a direct consequence and legacy of the colonial oppression and exploitation. 'The most important jewel in the British crown', as described by British historians, was reduced to the status of backwardness both at the level of material forces of production and social relations. The social structure of India, as a direct legacy of colonial rule, missed new opportunities provided by fundamental changes taking place in the eighteenth, nineteenth and up to the middle of the twentieth centuries, and the real journey of India as inherited a backward rural-agricultural economy and society, and public and private investments for agricultural growth were meager and minuscule because the primary goal of the colonial state, feudal-princely states, and *zamindars* and landlord classes, mostly absentee, was to extract revenues from the peasantry. Further, the infrastructure for agricultural growth also presented a story of benign neglect, since public resources were not deployed for public works development, and a large part of the agricultural and rural sector of the economy and society was just a playground for 'exploiters'—whether the colonial state or local feudal landlords.

The industrial sector during the colonial era met the same fate as the agrarian sector, and in spite of the presence of Indian-owned textile, sugar, jute, steel and heavy machine tools factories in some parts of India, preferential treatment was given to 'foreign investment' and the colonisers blocked capital for investment to Indian industrialists. The whole infrastructure for the development of big, medium and small-scale industry had to be created after 15 August 1947, because British rule led to deindustrialisation in the country and froze the history of change. The legacy of colonial rule was not only a backward agricultural and industrial economy, but the whole social structure, which was based on backward material productive forces, reflected all the features of a feudal and landlord society. A country's social structure does not hang in the air, and the caste system and ritualised religious belief system as an integral part of the inherited material foundations of society have persisted as the organising principles of social relations of a feudal landlord-dominated agricultural rural society. The medieval age is associated with social arrangements based on 'fate and faith', and they serve the interests of the exploiting feudal-monarchical and landed aristocratic classes. Even at the time of the negotiated transfer of power in 1947, 'fate and faith' belief systems persisted and continued to serve the economic interests of the exploiting propertied classes, and, in spite of the abolition of absentee landlordism and its replacement with new land-owning classes represented by middle and backward castes, they continued to exploit the landless agricultural workers, marginal farmers, sharecroppers, tenants *et al* by keeping intact the old belief system.

In *The Grundrisse* Marx has referred to a stage in which 'the co-existence and mixture of different forms' of social relations of production continues and there cannot be 'pigeon holding' of the stage of the demise of feudalism and the emergence of full-fledged industrial capitalism with new social structures as a product of the new capitalist mode of production. This concretely is the picture of the post-1947 journey of India. The post-independence journey began with scarcity of investible capital and a low level of savings rate in the economy.

> Saving at constant (1948-49) prices increased from Rs 591 cores in 1950-51 to Rs 902 cores in 1958-59 or, as a proportion of national income from 6.7 per cent to 7.7 per cent, the aggregate saving income rate increased from 5.9 in period I (1950-51 to 1952-53) to 7.3 in period II (1953-54 to 1955-56), then it rose only insignificantly in period III (1956-57 to 1958-59) to 7.9.[5]

The evolution of India's productive and social relations have continued to be quite complex beginning, with a simple bullock-cart agrarian economy which existed along with a proliferating trading sector and traditional industries.

Marxist scholars of the erstwhile USSR characterised this stage in India as 'multi-structural', where multiple modes of production existed and social relations of such mixed structures of economy clearly reflected the co-existence of pre-capitalist categories of social organisation with emerging capitalist social relations. The most important constituting pillars of the pre-capitalist stage were the caste system, and ritualised and organised religion based on 'fate and faith' and controlled by priestly classes around temples, mosques, gurdwaras and churches. This was the social picture or profile of India on the eve of independence. D.D. Kosambi has thus summed up the social situation: 'The bullock cart and village huts seen in Bharhut sculptures of about 150 BC, or the plough and ploughman in Kushamr reliefs of AD 200 would cause no comment if they appeared suddenly in some modern Indian village.' He further observed: 'Modern India produced an outstanding figure of world literature in Tagore. Within easy reach of Tagore's final residence may be found Santhals and other illiterate primitive people still unaware of Tagore's existence. Some of them are hardly out of the food gathering stage.' 'Kaaskmi and Kosambi mention the survival of the old and emergence of the new, and this stage of 'transition' witnesses 'change with continuity'. Hence the theoretical and methodological approaches followed by Marxists can be enlightening in understanding an extremely complex and contradictory story of human history in the extended phase of transition.

Two inter-related issues about the power of the state and violence in the stage of transition have always been highlighted by scholars on the basis of the historical experience of Europe, and especially the history of capitalist development of England.

> The dawn of the era of capitalist production showed diverse faces of the power of the state, which is ... the concentrated and organised force of society, to hasten, as in a hothouse, the process of transformation of the feudal mode of production into the capitalist mode, and to shorten the transition.

Further, western historical experience beginning with the fifteenth century to the end of the tweritieth century leads to the firm conclusion that 'violence is the midwife of every old society which is pregnant with a new one. It is itself an economic power'.[7] While history may not repeat itself, to a large extent the above diagnosis of Marx is applicable to India, which has experienced and witnessed various levels of the colonial state's violence and the use of State for facilitating original accumulation for capitalist industrialisation of the metropolis.

THE INDIAN EXPERIENCE

Hobsbawm has described Gramsci as a pioneer of the 'Marxist theory of politics' who, by following Marx, offered the conception of the state as an equilibrium between coercive and hegemonic institutions. Gramsci recognised that the 'material base and superstructure of ideology, state apparatuses and legal system' interact with one another, and he recognised the autonomous role of the superstructure by asserting that 'politics is an autonomous activity' in society. The post-independence state of India was not a passive reflection of the social structure and formations based on diverse modes of production, and in this specific historical situation the political superstructure played an autonomous, critical and central role in building capitalism. Without tackling the powerful pre-capitalist structure of landlordism and feudal princely state system, the emerging capitalist mode of production could not have moved forward. If the anachronistic and at the same time extremely powerful and entrenched landlord and princely feudal classes had not been confronted by the state, which was the only powerful institution available after the transfer of power, new India could not have been created. Historically, the abolition of centres of power of feudalism, the nobility and aristocracy, structured and entrenched around 625 princely states, by the democratic state of post-independence India can be considered a revolutionary step, and a landmark in the transition of India towards political democracy as enshrined in the Republican, secular, federal, democratic, welfarist Constitution of India.

The immense power of the state was derived not only from the legitimacy and popular social base of the political leaders. It deserves to be emphasised that the industrial bourgeoisie also wanted the state to play a crucial and leading role in creating the prerequisites for capitalist development. State power was exercised in the abolition of landlordism and princely state feudalism, and the powerful landlord and feudal classes battled against the Indian state; it can be stated unambiguously that without the exercise of state power, landlordism and princely feudalism could not have been weakened and vanquished.

The essence of a class state of the propertied classes is that even while confronting a segment of propertied classes, it makes compromises and does not hurt their interests beyond a point. The institution private property has been legally and constitutionally protected by the state of the propertied classes and this is the explanation for the continuance of relics of pre-capitalist social structures, because the mode of production that sustained them in the past was not completely liquidated. Even after 63 years of the evolution of the capitalist mode of production, landlordism and feudalism, the country. The Supreme Court, while dealing with the issue of land acquisition by the government, has observed that 'even though the right to property is no longer fundamental and was never a natural right, and is acquired on a concession from the state, it has to be accepted that without right to some property, other rights become illusory'.[8] Thus, India continues to be a 'property-owning democracy' where the state continues to provide protection to every stratum of property owner, whether weakened landlords and feudals, or the modern bourgeoisie and all its segments.

The story of the past continuing in the present makes a fascinating study of India in transition. It is essential to focus attention on the complex social class structure of India to properly situate the coexistence of the past and its traditions and the present. The essence of social transformation can be concretely understood by focusing on the concrete nature of the social class structure, because this is the only way to find out the concrete nature of existing social reality. Marx had observed: 'History does nothing, it does not possess immense riches, it does not fight battles. It is men, real, living, who do all this. The men make their own history.' The existing class structure can be categorised by keeping in mind that capitalist development in India has not only to grapple with social and economic divides like caste versus caste, religion versus religion, the rural and urban divide, but also that in such a situation, the levels of social inequality are determined on the basis of complex class and social relations. The summit of power is occupied by the big industrial bourgeoisie, which is globalised in its operations. When there is a coexistence of modes of production and social class formations, capitalism develops in such a manner that social inequalities get reproduced in various forms; and that is the reality of the late capitalist, developing society of India.

The above narrative suggests that the system of absolute unequal distribution continues to exist and has created social inequalities at multiple levels. The democratic state of the 'property-owning classes' in India, like all capitalist welfare states of western Europe, implements some social welfare programmers to project the human face of capitalism and to manage social conflicts so that violence-based social struggles are not generated. A high-sounding label like social market capitalism is in circulation and the reality is that

> welfare state-capitalism permits a small class to have a near monopoly on the means of production. Property-owning democracy avoids this, not by the redistribution of income to those with less at the end of each of period, so to speak, but rather by ensuring the widespread ownership of productive assets and human capital (that is education and trained skills) at the beginning of each period, all this against a background of fair equality of opportunity.[9]

Social inequality lies in the structural logic of capitalism. The second revealed the existence of sharp social cleavages where billionaires and oligarchs exist and 'the number of households today in the lowest income bracket, the poorest of all, is far higher.'[10] India was always an extremely unequal society. However, beginning with the 1990s, the inequalities have deepened and sharpened because the capitalist state does not have any 'income policy' or any commitment to distributive social justice. Of course, the governing political executive has followed pro-poor and pro-deprived policies for social sections that constitute the majority of the population because of the logic of the functioning of political democracy based on adult universal franchise. A highly competitive political democratic system in which elections are held regularly has to respond to the basic needs of the under-classes.

It is essential to focus attention on the role of the state in facilitating the growth of capitalism in the context of a functioning democracy, and in the global context of the new 'young' twenty-first century. What are the strategies followed by the ruling and exploiting classes for ruling a society where competing strata and fractions of surplus-appropriating classes are in competition with one another to maximize their own share in the social surpluses? Fractions of the ruling classes ruthlessly compete against one another in a social situation where their property interests are not threatened. This is the situation in India where propertied classes do not face any challenge from social organisations that stand for the liquidation or annihilation of the social structure of exploitation and oppression.

The Indian state as guarantor of capitalism is in the driver's seat for resolving inter-class and intra-class conflicts, and the first strategy of the ruling classes is to capture and control the levers of state power. Indian capitalists have evolved complex strategies to perpetuate their control over society and its most important instrument for maintaining its leading position is the Indian state. First, classes are actively participating in the ongoing democratic electoral process with a view to capturing the levers of state power or dealing with intra-class and inter-class conflicts. Historically, the most important conflict at present is between the strata of surplus-generating rich peasantry who are trying to dominate over the medium, small and marginal farmers, and an oppressed army of millions of landless agricultural workers. The conflict takes the shape of parties fighting for their own classes' representation. It is not without reason that the politics of representation at state government levels is done mainly by parties of the peasant classes. The central government, irrespective of ruling parties or the coalition of parties, is considered by peasant-based parties as an agency for the promotion and protection of the class interests of all fractions of the capitalist classes. And all peasant-based state-level parties find themselves in conflict with the central government, which is perceived by them as anti-peasant and pro-bourgeoisie class interests. Can it be maintained that the peasantry versus the bourgeoisie conflict represents a non-antagonistic contradiction which can be resolved democratically in a federal state system, in which the centre can look after the interests of the bourgeoisie and state governments of the peasant classes—or, can it be maintained that Indian capitalism can deal with the peasant question within a democratic constitutional framework?

Another specificity of the social divisions that emerged in the 1990s, known as the phase of economic reforms, is that the whole of rural agrarian society, irrespective of prevalent class divisions within the agrarian social structure, is left behind because the real beneficiaries of the economic rate of growth have been the urban big bourgeoisie, middle bourgeoisie, expanding service professionals and entrepreneurial classes, and even those engaged in new growth areas like real estate and surplus-generating peasants who have entered urban sources of private profit like commerce, trade and hotels. The rural labouring classes, who have been 'forced' to migrate under 'distress' to urban areas, are employed in the informal sector on low wages, and this migrant labour is not at all the beneficiary of the rising urban prosperity because their 'daily wages' are depressed in the absence of organised unions. Rural migrants make a contribution to the process of capital accumulation because their wages for labour are fixed at a low level in an arbitrary manner. The democratically elected political executive, under the logic of participatory electoral democracy, distributes financial patronage by 'fixing mini-mum support prices' for crops, and it also partially supports the funding of fertilisers, seeds, irrigation and electric power to those engaged in agricultural activities. Such state interventions have helped in smoothening social antagonisms in rural society and the legitimising of state power held by the capitalist classes. Besides operating a social welfarist system, the state receives support from the caste system and the ritualised religious belief system. The levels of social consciousness, especially when a class-in-itself becomes 'class-for-itself' and actively organises class struggles against exploitation in society, are mediated by an anachronistic loyalty structure of the past.

What is the role and relevance of the 'caste system' and 'organised, ritualised, priestly class-controlled religion' in obstructing the emergence of new levels of social consciousness? The question is, when will the under-classes understand the material foundations of the exploitative social structure and be ready to fight against exploitation? Capitalism builds itself on 'givens' and launches struggles only against those productive forces that act as a roadblock to the emergence of a new capitalist mode of production like feudalism and landlordism. Historically, it does not feel the need to confront an inherited superstructure ideological value system if its existence is not obstructive to the processes of capital accumulation. Why should the capitalist class oppose and struggle against the caste system and ritualised religion around which Indian society is organised? Marx was correct in highlighting the progressive, historical role of the bourgeoisie, but at the same time, if the real goal of the bourgeoisie is to 'accumulate, accumulate and accumulate', this class is under no pressure or compulsion to fight against social organising arrangements as long as they are not obstructing 'accumulation'. Further, if market power and political power are working in harmony with one another, and if powerful economic classes can enter the corridors of political power as a matter of right, these dominant classes do not feel any relevance for an anti-caste and anti-ritualised religious agenda. The Indian capitalist classes are actively promoting the agenda for the promotion of modern science and technology for industrialisation, but they are also engaged in the building of new temples and caste-based charitable institutions, while the material foundations of the continuation and perpetuation of a caste-based social structure are still more or less 'intact' in the agrarian economy because landless agricultural workers, and the marginal and middle strata of peasant society are producing surplus value under caste-dominated groups.

EMERGING SOCIAL TRENDS IN THE TWENTY-FIRST CENTURY

A few salient facts may be mentioned to highlight the emergence of new social tendencies in the twenty-first century. First, the post-1990s capitalist integration of India with global capitalism has resulted in class-based, caste-based, region-based and rural-urban based social inequalities; and, within the structure of class power, the leading industrial bourgeoisie has become 'oligopolistic', and is expanding quite aggressively in Africa, Southeast Asia, Europe and North America. It is a new development because, unlike the big bourgeoisie of post-independence India, which up to the 1980s was generally confined to the Indian market, from the 1990s, its frontiers of operation have expanded much beyond the territorial boundaries of India. The big industrial bourgeoisie is really occupying the summit of power in the class hierarchy, and this fact has altered the balance of power between 'capital' and the 'state'. The capitalist state of India beginning from the 1990s has, without hesitation, actively promoted the global interests of the leading powerful fractions of the ruling classes and of imperialism at the stage of 'finance capitalism'. Global finance capital has come to play an important role, dictating conditions to the Indian capitalist state.

The best illustration to substantiate the argument that the 'leading strata of the bourgeoisie' has come to play an active role in asking and demanding from the political executive to reform itself, so that economic policies acceptable to this fraction are implemented efficiently and effectively is this: fourteen 'eminent captains of industry' recently wrote an open letter to Prime Minister Manmohan Singh to clear the 'roadblocks' for industrial expansion. They observed that:

> owing to several such impediments, fresh investments are not forthcoming at uncertainties and delays in approvals are forcing many large corporate entities to seek out opportunities in other geographies.[11]

It is not only that the composition of the working class is changing, or that the character of the peasantry is changing, or that a new large middle class has emerged in society; it is also that the quest for capital accumulation is taking the big bourgeoisie wherever mineral resources or land *is* easily available for their operations. In 2006, Tata Steel bought Anglo-Dutch steel maker Corus for $12 billion, Hindalco purchased Novelis, the UB group acquired Scottish whisky maker Whyte and Mackay, and finally, Tata Motors acquired Jaguar Land Rover. This process has not stopped. If leaders of Indian capitalism look to other territories for capital accumulation, foreign capitalists are also looking at India with excitement. 'There is a renewed interest in India. Global players which are facing slowdown in their home countries are making India their pillar of growth.' During 2011, foreign companies and private equity funds invested $22.7 billion.[12]

A very important development to be noticed is that the Department of Industrial Policy and Promotion (DIPP) is focusing on crude oil, gas, iron ore and coal, and its goal is 'outward investment by the Indian private sector companies for many purposes and acquisition of raw material resources being one'.[13]

NEW POLITICS

It is not only inter-class and intra-class relations that are in a constant process of change, even the meaning of politics has altered. Hamish MacDonald, in his 'Ambani Son', observes about Dhirubhai Ambani:

> he was steadily augmenting his skills at breeding money from money and at wielding political and bureaucratic influence on government policies and their interpretation. Dhirubhai was never simply an industrialist, a trader, a financial juggler of a political manipulator, but all four in one.[14]

Finance Minister Pranab Mukerjee, while facing problems from opposition parties in Parliament or from state governments, addressed the Chambers of Industry on 1 March 2011 thus: 'I seek your support... as you have influence over state governments, you are having interactions across the political spectrum in the country'.[15] This is the new idiom or language of politics in the second decade of the 'young' twenty-first century, which clearly shows that 'the state' and 'capital' have become indistinguishable. The Indian situation is similar to that of the United States, of which Joseph Stieglitz has lamented:

> democracy ... is not just one-person-one-vote. There's the debilitating nexus between special interests, campaign contributions and revolving doors—when the same person hops between top jobs in government, the private sector and international organisations. This nexus is why the US has the best democratic government money can buy.[16]

Can democracy of property-owning classes resolve conflicts of an extremely divided society in the twenty-first century?

It deserves to be re-emphasised that Indian society was always unequal and not only has such social inequality persisted, it has been accentuated and deepened from the beginning of the 1990s. The Forbes list of world billion-arise mentions 55 Indians in 2011, up from 49 in 2010.[17] Further, an Indian CEO, on average, gets Rs 5-7 crore a year. A CEO in the US gets \$6-8 million. A Fortune 500 company CEO may get \$8-10 million.[18]

The fast-expanding, powerful modern capitalism, integrated with global capitalism, is involved in aggressive competition to extract mineral wealth, which in India is generally located in rich forest areas inhabited by poor, forest-dependent tribal populations. The ongoing process of displacement of the tribal population from its natural environment has intensified the process of social dislocation. The mineral-rich states such as Odisha, Chhattisgarh, Jharkhand and regions of Andhra Pradesh have witnessed serious conflict situations arising out of displacement of the tribal's. Not only this. If land is needed for industrial, infrastructural and multiple urban projects, disputes have arisen not only on 'compensation' for the acquired land, but also on the issue of rehabilitation of those whose land has been acquired either for state-owned or for private-owned projects. If globalised capitalism in India has given rise to 'agrarian distress' because of its hunger for minerals and land, the 'informal sector', which is making an immense contribution to the accumulation process, remains completely unregulated in spite of legislation. The informal sector of the Indian economy is not an insignificant social reality as shown by the National Sample Survey Organisation (NSSO) 2004-05. First, the labour force numbers 459 million, and 433 million of this 459 million, or about 94 per cent, is in the unorganised sector. The bourgeois state has enacted a toothless law like the Unorganised Workers' Social Security Act, 2008, which is either half-heartedly implemented by the 'employers' or simply ignored.

To recapitulate, the most advanced capitalist productive system, even including 300 robots, whirr to life every morning all over the Hyundai Sriperumbudur plant near Chennai, rubbing shoulders with 1,500 employees and 7,000 workers. Together, men and machines churn out one car in less than a minute; more than 600,000 cars roll out of the factory every year. The number of robots inhabiting the factory has increased more than ten-fold in a decade and it coexists with a primitive, pre-capitalist productive system, leading to the incoherence and incongruence of the existing complicated structure of social relations. This is precisely the situation that has been described by Marx about Germany in his 'Revolution-and-Counter-Revolution'. Of Germany, Marx wrote: 'The great mass of the nation, which neither belonged to the nobility nor to the bourgeoisie, consisted in the towns, of the small trading and shop keeping class and the working people, and in the country, of the peasantry.' Further, the small trading class and shop keeping class is exceedingly nurnerous in Germany, in consequence of the stunted development which the large capitalists and manufacturers, as a class have had in the country. 'Now in Germany, the mass of the working class were employed, not by these modern manufacturing lords of which Great Britain furnishes such splendid specimens, but by small tradesmen whose entire manufacturing system is a mere relic of the Middle Ages.' The peasantry 'class again sub-divided itself into different fractions'. The state of India's social relations is a replication of nineteenth-century Germany.

The Indian bourgeois state and bourgeois parties have, during the past 63 years, organised this incoherent and extremely fragmented society on the platform of parliamentary democracy; and, in this process, in spite of the continuance of backward-looking social formations, Indians have become politically aware and assertive, because of the functioning of a universal, adult franchise system. Political mobilisation of voters undertaken by various fractions in the bourgeois party system has to large extent inter-connected disparate social groups across the whole country and in the different regions. The management of social conflict situations through the institutions of the parliamentary democratic, competitive political system, based on the principle of universal adult franchise, has, with all its limitations, responded by accommodating the conflicting and clashing interests of various contending and competing strata and fractions of a highly fragmented and divided social structure. The weaker and exploited strata of society are still participating actively and enthusiastically in the hope that democratically elected representatives will find solutions to their 'basic problems'. It deserves to be emphasised that the limits of democracy of the property-owning classes have been recognised, but its capacity to distribute some public resources for some public services with a view to managing social conflicts has also helped in healing the wounds.

Huber and Stephens (1999: 761) observe: 'though the bourgeoisie made important contributions to the movement towards democracy by insisting on its share in political power in the form of parliamentary control of the state, they were hostile to further democratisation when its interests seem threatened'. It is further emphasised by Rueschemeyere *et al.* (1992:60) that 'any class that is dominant both economically and politically will not be eager to dilute its political power by democratisation'.[20] India is at a stage of development of capitalist relations of production where the 'internally competing disunited ruling class' is not at all threatened by any large-scale oppositional challenge by the under-classes, and in this stage of transition, democracy in India has provided a platform for the resolution of social conflicts. The dialectical social process of the stage of the grand transition cannot be smooth and historically the European phase of the transition to capitalism witnessed great social turbulence. The same story can be seen in India. The so-called left extremists (Maoists), insurgents and terrorist groups on the Indian periphery like in north-eastern India and Jammu and Kashmir, have opted out of democratic processes for the solution of their grievances. If these groups have opted for armed struggle against the oppressive and suppressive class state and the central authority of the state, the Indian state has also confronted these well-armed groups by deploying its well-equipped and professional military of 1.3 million soldiers along with another about 1 million well-armed paramilitary armed forces. Parliament and state legislatures have never hesitated to enact draconian laws like the Preventive Detention Act or Unlawful Activities (Prevention) Act, Or extra-ordinary laws safeguarding the interests of the armed forces which are deployed to crush violent armed groups.

Indian democracy has many faces. While facing challenges to the power and authority of the state, an extraordinarily strong label jurisprudence has been put in place by the elected representatives of the people on the basis of universal adult franchise, which legitimizes 'the garrison state' of India in war against the extreme leftists (Maoists), or secessionists, or even farmers or tribals who agitate when they are 'dispossessed' of their land.

Will the weak and divided fractions of the ruling exploiting classes succeed in facing the challenges of the Indian transition through the 'mix of democracy' and democratically legitimised deployment of well-equipped, modern, professional armed forces to silence the guns of the challengers? The history of fundamental transformation in societies provides evidence that people have to be prepared and organised for long-term struggles for the replacement and displacement of the class-based exploitative state and society. A prerequisite for the emergence of any popular mass struggle is that through struggle a 'class-in-itself' becomes a 'class-for-itself', and through struggles the levels of consciousness get transformed when people can recognize their main enemy and primary antagonistic contradictions in society.

The history of the anti-colonial struggle for national liberation from the British super-exploitative colonial state shows that the masses have to become 'conscious' through struggles against a visible opponent like the British colonial state. For the last 64 years, movements in India have taken place and reformist movements have been organised by parties, leaders and groups situated within the bloc of the ruling classes, and these intra-class demands raised by movements have been accommodated and positively responded to by the state. The positive response of the Indian state to movements is based on an understanding that these are movements of 'our own people and class fractions'. Full-fledged anti-state armed struggles have been responded to on the basis of a policy of 'bullet versus bullet'. The state of the ruling classes has not felt threatened because the 'basic exploited classes' have not become conscious enough to challenge the authority of those who have 'put chains around their necks'. Every strategy of 'encircling the towns' by the peasantry and establishing 'liberation zones', and gradually launching a successful armed assault against the centre of power, has been all wishful thinking and has ended in futility. If the development of capitalism is witnessing the jumping of stages with a goal to arrive at the 'post-industrial' capitalist stage, the mass movements are not thinking about any 'goals based on alternatives' to the present exploitative system. It is only socialism that can build a society and social relations on the basis of 'social equality', but this ideal of movement for socialism in India is not on the agenda of mass movements not only because of internal obstructions to the unity of the masses, but also because at the global level socialism, which inspired the exploited working classes to launch struggles, remained only relevant for the twentieth century. The global context cannot be ignored because powerful ideas and ideologies capture the minds of the people by transcending boundaries.

Socialism as an ideology had a global appeal for all those who had a living experience of the exploitations suffered under capitalism. Real-life experiences and struggles raised the levels of awareness among the masses about the real causes of inequity, and these conscious masses had an alternative of socialism worth struggling for. The twenty-first century global, authoritarian-technocratic capitalism has created an ideological vacuum by talking of market capitalism with a few palliatives or opiates for the masses by under-taking some welfare social security programmers. The twentieth-century welfare states acted like a 'midwife' for projecting the image of a 'caring' state, and the socialists committed to anti-capitalism saw through the game and launched anti-capitalist struggles for establishing a society of equal social relations.

India's 'grand transition process' has lessons for the twenty-first century because this is a journey without any grand theory and ideology. Hence, muddling through will continue for the building of modern capitalism in a situation where basic threats to the ruling classes do not exist, and a fragmented and fractured society is unable to launch a united all-India mass revolutionary struggle against the exploiters. If the anti-corruption movements, led by Jayaprakash Narayan in 1974-75 or Anna Hazare in 2011-12, can attract public attention, a political movement of a similar kind has not succeeded in dealing with the problems of the 'under-classes'. It is very difficult to project which direction this society in grand transition will take because it is the first example of transition where 'property-owning democracy' has been at work for the last 64 years.

The history of western capitalism has gone through a long process where capitalism was on the march much before real participatory democracy/ emerged. Universal adult franchise-based competitive democracy in the west is only a post-World War II phenomenon because all western capitalist citizens. This long history was based on a limited participation of its citizens, but at least five centuries of capitalist development in the west gave birth to other positive forces that impacted the levels of social consciousness, such as the French enlightenment, scientific discoveries by Copernicus, Galileo, Newton and Darwin, and protest movements against the church by Luther—all of which opened new windows of awareness among the people of these countries. The 'fate and faith'—based culture was continuously attacked by scientists, artists, writers, thinkers and organised universities, and all this contributed to the weakening of religion-based traditions inherited from the 'feudal-church dominated past' The European and North American transition experience is different from the historical evolution of India because every step forward for the creation of a new social order has to be focused on democratic politics, which is in the 'driver's seat'. If democratically elected political leaders abolished a princely social order, the capitalist order is also being established by politics. The story of transition in India is linked with the prospects of democracy and its capacity to reconcile antagonistic class interests of a divided class society.

The history of the twenty-first century is not fated to end with the capitalist social order. Contemporary history, as the history of the twentieth century, will witness socially conscious masses struggling for social equality that will start from Parliament and reach the streets. The Indian transition to end the oppressive and exploitative capitalist social order, and for achieving the goal of socialism, is bound to be long and difficult, but struggles that are the mid-wife of social democratic revolution remain on the agenda of Indian society.

NOTES AND REFERENCES

1 Robert C. Allen, *Global Economic History: A Very Short Introduction*, Oxford University Press, Oxford, 2011, p. 6.
2 Karl Marx, quoted in Eric Hobsbawm, *How to Change the World: Tales of Marx and Marxism: 1840-2011*, Little, Brown, USA, 2011, p. 134.
3 Ibid.
4 Paula Allman, *On Marx: An Introduction to the Revolutionary Intellect of Marx*, Sense Publishers, Rotterdam, 2007.
5 *Economic and Political Weekly*, Vol. XIII, No. 37,16 September 1961.
6 See, Sabyasachi Bhattacharya, *Talking Back: The Idea of Civilisation in the Indian Nationalist Discourse*, Oxford University Press, New Delhi, 2011, p. 32. Also see D.D. Kosambi, *Introduction to the Study of Indian History*, Popular Pakistan, Bombay, 1956; and *The Culture and Civilisation of Ancient India in Historical Outline*, Vikas Publishing House, New Delhi, 1970.
7 Karl Marx, *Capital: A Critique of Political Economy*, Vol. I, Penguin, Harmondsworth, quoted by Mark Nucleolus, 'War on Waste: Original Accumulation and the Violence of Capital', *Science and Society*, Vol. 75, No. 4, October 2011, pp. 506-07.
8 'Right to Property', *The Hindustan Times*, New Delhi, 9 March 2011, p. 13.
9 Quoted by Martin O'Neill, 'Liberty, Equality and Property-Owning Democracy', *Journal of Social Philosophy*, Vol. XL, No. 3, Fall 2009, p. 393.
10 *The Economic Times*, New Delhi, 1 February 2001, p. 11.
11 'Open Letter to PM', *The Times of India*, New Delhi, 11 October 2011, p. 13.
12 *Economic Times*, New Delhi, 26 December 2011, p. 6.
13 *The Hindustan Times*, New Delhi, 10 January 2011, p. 21.
14 Hamish McDonald, *Ambani and Sons: The Meaning of the World's Richest Brothers and Their Feud*, Roli Books, New Delhi, 2010, p. 48
15 Pranab Mukerjee, address to the Federation of Indian Chambers of Commerce and Industry and CII, *The Hindustan Times*, New Delhi, 2 March 2011, p. 25.
16 *The Times of India*, New Delhi, 21 February 2011, p. 16.
17. *The Hindustan Times*, New Delhi, 11 March 2011, p. 25.
18 'Indian CEO's Pay on par with Global CXO's, *The Economic Times* New Delhi, 15 February 2011, p.10
19. See Karl Marx and Frederic Engels, *Selected Works*, Volume I, Progress Publishers, Moscow, 1969, pp. 304, 305.
20 See E. Huber and J D. Stephens, 'The Bourgeois Democracy: Historical and contemporary perspective', *Social Research: An International Quarterly of the Social Sciences, 66* (3), 1999, pp. 759-88. Also see D. Rueschemeyar, E.H. Stephens and J.D. Stephens, *Capitalist Development and Democracy* Polity Press, Cambridge, 1992; Karl Polanyi, *The Great Transformation* Octagon Press, New York, 1975.

23

Maoism: Responses of the State

DEAD-END OF THE TUNNEL

An armed guerilla struggle by a section of peasantry against the Indian state was launched from Naxalbari in West Bengal. It was led by Charu Majumdar who broke away from the CPI(M) because he considered that the Communist Party of India (Marxist), formed in 1964, wasn't militant enough and its parliamentary road to establish communist rule could never succeed and the oppressed, labouring classes cannot be, 'liberated from the oppressive rule of semi-feudal, comprador, collaborating capitalist classes'.

The movement launched by Majumdar which survives in some parts of backward tribal areas even till today has declared itself as follower of Marxism, Leninism and Maoism. It has claimed to be the practitioner of the true and 'pure' ideology of communism as opposed to the 'revisionary' and 'reactionary' communist parties of India, including CPI(M). It is factually correct that CPI (M-L) or CPI (Maoist) are a splinter faction of communist movement of India and its strategies for the overthrow of anti-people, anti-labouring classes neo-colonial state deserve to be rigorously interrogated.

It deserves to be clearly stated that if theoretical and ideological premises of claimants of revolutionary politics are wrong, the strategies for achieving the goals of revolution from flawed theoretical understanding of such leadership are bound to be counterproductive. While it is correct to mention that Charu Majumdar learnt his theory and practice of Marxism from his own studies of Karl Marx and movements and struggles launched by Indian Communists of which he was an active participant, it is absolutely wrong to maintain that the practitioners of guerilla warfare for the overthrow of Indian state and exploitative social class structure were in any way followers of Maoist theories and strategies for achieving goals of revolution like the Chinese who succeeded in overthrowing the oppressive rule in their country under the leadership of Mao. The facts speak for themselves. Hare Krishna Konar, a comrade-in-arms of Majumdar in the CPI(M) from 1964-67, when Majumdar parted company from the CPI(M), had visited China and he was unambiguously told by the Maoist leadership of China that the historical context in which Maoist revolution could succeed in Chaing-Ki-Sheikh's tottering regime, was not at all replicable and repeatable in the Indian concrete situation because the Nehruvian state in post-independence India was firmly in the saddle. Not only this, the Chinese leadership was quite annoyed with Charu Majumdar, Kanu Sanyal and other leaders of the Naxalbari guerilla warfare when they had declared that 'Chairman Mao of China is our Chairman'. It is not only simplistic, even erroneous, to maintain that the Naxal strategy of moving from 'Liberated Area' to another struggle for establishing 'Liberated Area' has anything to do with Mao's strategy of Liberation followed during Long March in China. The Chinese Maoists clearly told that the People's Liberation Army created by Mao was to fight against his ramshackle enemy army. The Indian Army was a well-knit and well-organised professional army and it would be impossible to win any battle against such a formidable army by guerilla armed struggles. Hence, at its best, the claim by Naxalite and later on liberator fighting guerillas in Srikakulam in Andhra Pradesh is an appropriation of Mao to gain legitimacy and ideological acceptability, and, at its worst, it is a propaganda by the Indian State to justify its highly coercive responses to crush this movement by alleging that they are Chinese inspired because post-1962 nationalist public opinion had become completely hostile to China after the border war of October-November, 1962.

The Indian State functionaries have tried to delegitimise these guerrilla groups in the eyes of general mass by occasionally propagating that 'the Chinese made arms have been seized from these Maoists', as if Indian domestic arms-bazaar is not enough to supply arms to every kind of mercenary. The purpose of this narrative was not only to set the historical record right, but also to emphasize the fact that by delegitimising these struggles, the Indian ruling classes and the State are evading and avoiding their own responsibility to tackle the root causes of social discontent in parts of agrarian India and the tribal belt of Odisha, Chhattisgarh, Jharkhand and all the places where the movement has spread its influence especially among the most exploited and oppressed forest dwellers, tribal's and dalits. The so-called Maoist guerrilla armed warfare against the Indian state is purely 'indigenous' and 'home-product'. It is a well known fact, empirically established, that the completely unfinished agenda of agrarian social restructuring through land reforms has left out lower peasantry, tribal's and Scheduled Castes, who are living in misery. These 'dispossessed' strata of underprivileged society who are misguided, provide a fertile ground for the State to crush the so-called 'Left Wing extremism' by employing its third largest professional army in the world and highly armed paramilitary organisations.

West Bengal has a tradition of militant struggles like the Tebhaga movement against oppressive and repressive jotedars which encouraged Congress chief minister Siddhartha Shankar Ray's 'lawless and brutal' police operation to crush the guerrillas. But the lasting solution came when Operation Barga liberated millions of lower class peasants in Bengal. It is the CPI(M) led Bengal government from 1977 which appropriately responded to the land issues in West Bengal that brought the end of Naxalism. It is a well-known fact that lessons are never learnt from history and same mistakes are repeated in a farcical and tragic manner because no lesson was learnt from the success of Operation Barga, and guerilla movement spread to the areas inhabited by 'displaced, dispossessed tribal' populated area which is dramatised by the living misery in Bastar tribal district of present Chhattisgarh. The 'security centric' approach of the Indian State is completely counterproductive because armed forces are fighting against the 'symptoms' and the democratically elected political executive and its bureaucracy has practised the strategy of 'breaking the promises of development', for the last sixty seven years of post-independence India.

How could the Indian State and the democratically elected political executive deal with the 'root causes' of discontent of the tribal's and dalits, 'The Wretched of The Earth' because the class-state of India could not act against a 'relatively few affluent farmers' who had appropriated political power by sabotaging every attempt or effort at the land reforms. It is a well-known fact that the class state protects class interests; it does not cut its own throat by confronting its own fraternity. The Planning Commission's Task Force on Agrarian Relations in May 1973 observed,

> 'In the context of the socio-economic conditions prevailing in the rural areas of the country, no tangible progress can be expected in the field in the absence of requisite political will. The sad truth is that this crucial factor has been wanting...'

It is unfortunate that the same story of grave neglect by the Indian State has forced innocent tribal populations to become a part of the ongoing violent guerrilla warfare against the State and this story of lack of performance by the Indian State functionaries to tackle the root causes of serious social discontent prevailing among the most neglected areas of tribal population comes clearly in Santosh Mehrotra's edited volume[2] where well intentioned public policy makers whose hearts bleed for the poor tribal's have given lot of suggestions and blueprint to deal with forest areas populated by these tribal's so that they can breathe somewhat easy under the cruel situation of expanding and unstoppable activities of extraction of rich mineral resources by Indian and global multinationals. Every innocent life of fighters for 'equality' in a society of 'absolutely inequalities and disparities' is taking place because of the wrong ideology and strategies of the so-called revolutionaries whose guns are matched by the ruthless state apparatus. The innocents are suffering because the state's tall claims of 'development' are not matched by its actions and neither the armed might of the Indian State can suppress such an 'uprising' of the discontented nor can the gun wielding revolutionary practitioners of politics can achieve anything by fighting against the gun wielding soldiers of the Indian State. A situation of complete deadlock exists as unequal, but determined, parties to the conflict are not ready to drastically review their present strategies and goals, and this is the reason that the present impasse can't be broken. If the Maoists are not ready to accept this fact that 'spaces for social changes' are available on the basis of struggles in the existing imperfect, bourgeois democracy, they are bound to end up knocking their heads against the Chinese Wall of highly armed capitalist Indian State. It is not Marxism, Maoism or Leninism of any kind where the so-called revolutionary leadership is not worried about the death of the innocent cadre fighting for the cause of equality. A revolutionary leadership worth its salt cannot be casual or even cavalier about the death of innocents whom they are leading on the basis of an extremely flawed understanding of Indian concrete reality.

MULTIPLE AND CONTRADICTORY RESPONSES OF THE INDIAN STATE

Maoists of India have not studied the seminal theoretical writing of Mao, 'On Contradictions', where he himself identifies multiple antagonistic and non-antagonist contradictions in the Chinese society because of the presence of many kinds of social formations which existed during Mao's early phase of revolutionary activity. The message is quite clear that social contradictions have to be identified to understand the complete nature of social formations under a concrete social situation by stating that a society is divided just into two antagonistic classes of the 'exploiters' and the 'mass of exploited' and such bipolarity can never be a feature of any specific society. Historical context has to be kept in mind while identifying the existing material forces of production which determine the social relations of production and the type of changes which are taking place in the mode of production and relations of production. It becomes quite clear that many contradictions exist within the social classes and the multiple strata of capitalists and peasants of the Indian State and society which is undergoing a process of change in the existing stage of Indian transition.[3]

Hence, the multiple responses of the Indian State are determined by the nature of social class relations and political contradictions which constitute the social essence of the Indian State. The capitalist State of India, while promoting and protecting the class interests of every fraction of private property owning social groups, has to work under boundaries defined by democratic and republican constitution of India. If on the one hand, private capital and the Indian State is fully integrated and this 'integration' is not only between domestic capitalist classes and its fractions with the Indian State, on the other, the Indian capitalist State and the leading capitalist classes and the big industrial houses are also fully integrated with global capitalism, specifically finance capital.

While the Nehruvian capitalist State enjoyed 'relative autonomy' both in relation to domestic natural capital and independence from imperialist-capitalist States of the developed industrial societies of the West. This is a thing of the past. The monopoly capitalist classes and the Indian capitalist State are pursuing common class interests by integrating with global capitalism and by following the model of capitalist development based on the Washington Consensus of free-market economy. The inspiration for this New Economic

Policy of free-market capitalism came from former American president Ronald Reagan and British Prime Minister Margaret Thatcher who successfully sold their 'model' of free-market economy whose pillar was free flow of finance capital from global centres of capitalism to the developing countries of decolonised societies of Asia, Africa and Latin America. Both Reagan and Thatcher dismounted and demolished welfare capitalist state system in their countries and for Thatcher welfarism was a feature of a 'nanny state'. The social Darwinist model of free market capitalism of the type advocated by Reagan-Thatcher could not be implemented in the letter and spirit of India because of the compulsions and the logic of participatory, competitive political democracy based on fair and free elections after regular intervals with the system of holding accountable the democratically elected political executive and legislature.

Further, India has held sixteen Lok Sabha elections beginning from 1951-52 to May 2014 and the Indian voters have shown capabilities of electing and rejecting political parties and mighty political leaders with regular intervals during the last sixty-seven years of post-independence India. This fundamental contradiction is at work because if on one hand, private capitalism is guided and motivated primarily for achieving the goal of maximum private accumulation of capital and profit, on the other, political executive of the capitalist State of India gets its legitimacy only from popular masses who exercise this power on the basis of universal adult franchise and hence have to be looked after and public resources have to be invested for their welfare.

An important social and political formation of India, the Indian National Congress, which governed the country for more than forty years, on the basis of consent of Indian voters always showed its concern for social welfarism for the deprived strata of society. The illustration of combining the needs of capitalist classes and social welfarism for the deprived masses is provided by Mahatma Gandhi National Rural Employment Guarantee Scheme of 2004-2005 and Food Security Act of 2013. The social dialects of complex democratic process which is at work has always revealed it negative and positive social tendencies and a new phase in 'imperfect bourgeois democracy' of India has begun with the emergence of formidable right-wing using Hindu communal fascist forces which are in control of many governments at the state levels and presently it controls the levers of powers at the real centre of political and executive power of the Indian State.

The Rashtriya Swayamsevak Sangh guides, directs and controls the BJP government at the centre and the states of Rajasthan, Madhya Pradesh, Chhattisgarh, Gujarat etc. The BJP government has publicly proclaimed that it is 'pro-business classes' and follows real free-market capitalist economy literally on the path shown by Reagan-Thatcher in the 1980s and it is unambiguously committed to a free Indian market for free flow of foreign capital and it is committed to complete the cycle of integration of Indian capitalist state and free-loading classes with global finance capital. What happens to the democratic legitimacy of constitutional democratic capitalist state controlled by the ideologues of Hindu Rashtravaad (nationalism).

A question arises here about the 'role of ideology' in legitimising the super-exploitative system of class state in a class divided society like that of India, French Marxist Poulantzas made an important categorisation by differentiating between 'the ruling classes' and the 'governing classes'. The ruling classes control the levers of state power by keeping themselves behind the governing classes which act as public face for sheltering the class interests of private accumulation of capitalists and the focus of public attention or anger is always directed against the governing classes. The ideology of ruling classes is quite clear because it centres around the goal to accommodate and accumulate at the same time, the governing classes also need an 'ideology' to capture the mind of common public to gain legitimacy with the voters. This question of the role of ideology for legitimating of the governing classes of the exploitative capitalist state deserves to be critically analysed because the post-World War II capitalist countries of the developed industrialised West are witnessing the phenomenon of complate social consensus in support of capitalist system of accumulation and private rights of individuals to own private property. It is claimed that the states and governments of developed industrialised capitalist Western societies have achieved a level of social class consensus which supports the idea that private property is 'legitimate' and this is the reason that post-World War II Europe and North America has not witnessed any class action or class struggle because across the classes and their fractions, the private has achieved 'the public legitimacy'. This led Daniel Bell, an American, to write an influential book called *The End of Ideology* and followed by another American in the late 1980s and the beginning of 1990 to proclaim that societies have agreed to accept Western liberal values and model of capitalism and he claimed it as 'The End of History'. This convergence between the legitimate goals pursued by every strata of private property owner and the, role of State in such societies is to facilitate the orderly development of such law-bound social system. The opposite, even contrary, view is that human societies based on the fundamental social arrangements of exploitation cannot be managed or governed without a dominant ideology which makes people accept the existing inequalities inherent in class-divided exploitative societies. The real role played by ideology is to make common man, even the deprived ones, internalise the basic value system of such a society without such an internalisation of values, society cannot remain quiet and becomes impossible to govern.

IDEOLOGICAL CHANGES AND THE STATE AFFAIRS

A society based on the system of ruthless exploitation and repression of the labouring under classes cannot be ruled just by deploying the brute coercive forces of the mighty army and police forces and the State coercion has also to be legitimised on the basis of ideologies which act as a powerful tool in the hands of the ruling classes to make the oppressed believe that the State, by following some important welfarism programmes, is their own State and government. If on the one hand the State has oppressed the movement launched by those who carried the Maoist 'Red Book' in their hands to justify that power flows from the barrel of the gun, on the other, policies of welfarism were also followed to wean away the cadre of gun-wielding communists. Such 'dual' approach of the State is an open aggression policy of confrontation with gun-wielding communists. It has been openly declared by the State of the ruling classes proclaiming that the 'left-wing extremists' are enemy number one of the democratic State and they can be crushed only by deploying of the professional well armed forces by following the policy of ballet versus bullet to deal with this 'menacing challenge'.

Such a turnaround by the functionaries of the State has taken place because the Indian ruling classes are democratically elected. Political personnel of the Indian state have completely abandoned economic policy framework for national development on the basis of 'self-reliance' and the ideological driver of this new economic policy is that the 'animal instinct' of the Indian capitalists should be given freedom to pursue the goal of 'economic growth' through any means as decided by the dominant leading industrial business houses. This break with the forty year old post-independence model of capitalist development of somewhat 'human face' is the product of new social classes which are in full sense of the term 'right-wing' in their attitude and devotees of ruthless 'acquisition of wealth'. Such a right-wing social shift is also integrally linked with the emergence of Hindu-communal ideology which has come to occupy a dominant status in the affairs of the Indian State. The believers of right-wing Hindu Rashtravaad, trained in the seminary of the RSS, are aggressively committed to fight against 'atheist communists' by using physical force. The Home Minister, announced on August 21, 2014, his 'doctrine' to wipe out 'Naxal menace' and its components as operationalised by him are, a) no talks with Maoists, b) to talk when they lay down arms, c) going after the top Maoist leadership with the help of dedicated security forces, d) pushing in more security forces into worst affected areas like Bastar, and finally, e) political commitment from all Maoist-affected states, to eradicate the left-wing extremists. The purpose of this militant doctrine is to codify policy for tackling this menace.

FUTURE PROSPECTS

A solid tradition of self-criticism, self-appraisal and self-correction has been a legacy of every communist guided by the teachings of Karl Marx, V. I. Lenin, Mao and the history of 'splits' among the Indian communists clearly shows that every split took place after serious inner debates among the communists and it was always debated and thoroughly dissected about the class position of the Indian State and the stages of social and material development occurring in India. The Telangana Armed Peasant Struggle against the Indian State launched by the United Communist Party was called off and Amritsar Congress, brought out its new policy document. Unfortunately, the fraction of breakaway groups from CPI and CPI(M), have never scrutinised the limits of their ideological perspective on Indian State and society and its results are visible. They engaged in an armed struggle of annihilation of class enemies because of their theoretical formulation that the Indian State is alien and completely disconnected from the exploited labouring underclass especially forest dwelling tribal population.

Not only this. A communist struggle in India cannot be 'confined' or limited to concerns of the poor 'tribal peoples' or marginalised village—dwelling farm workers merely, because a successful class struggle and mobilisation can be achieved in short-term and long-term goals if communists have a presence in the urban areas too. Maoists' limited social reach and political praxis has failed to persuade urban proletariat and petty-bourgeois intellectuals and government sympathisers except a few civil rights' activists in urban areas who fight legal battles in defence of Maoists whenever it is felt that fighters for the cause of poor tribals should be protected from the atrocities of the police forces. If on the one hand, Maoists or Liberation groups have a limited ideological appeal as shown by its limited social base, on the other, the CPI and CPI(M), the two communist parties of India have a sizeable presence among working classes, Trade Unions, peasantry and intellectuals and the support base of these two parties is much wider than the guerrilla Maoists. The intellectuals messengers of Indian communism are school teachers, colleges and universities, and other professional classes and along with tall Communist leaders in Indian parliament and state assemblies, communist parties in India have received legitimacy for their fights for the defence of the rights of the exploited and oppressed underclass.

Is it not enough to argue that the CPI(ML) or liberation guerrilla groups require a drastic rethinking and reappraisal of their ideological and political positions? Why are the Maoists confined to tribal-populated states of Jharkhand, Chhattisgarh, Odisha, et. al. Marxism requires continuous struggle to understand the changing nature of social reality and dynamics of class formation so that the communists can adapt and adjust its tactics and strategies of confronting its class opponents and powerful class State apparatus. Further, every struggle launched under the leadership of communists is not confined to extracting a part of accumulated surplus capital by the exploiting bourgeois classes, its struggles should also help in transforming the levels of social consciousness of masses involved in social struggles. It deserves to be clearly stated that the so-called Maoists, armed guerrilla warriors, have neither succeeded in transforming the lifestyle and levels of social consciousness even in its cadres who are cut off completely from the outside social reality transcending these facts, nor have they served the cause of communist transformation because instead of 'uniting', they have divided and fragmented communists and parties. If the Maoist leadreship and cadre had not been confined and pushed back to the forests to search for sanctuary against Indian State's policy of 'gun versus gun', and if they were operating actively among the mass of people without any face of 'gun down the state', they would have been compelled to theoretically and strategically respond to the new challenges of the twenty first century capitalist-imperialist globalisation and Indian interaction with imperialism of a new kind and also for the rise of the full-fledged right wing Hindu communalism with its fascist tendencies.

That Karl Marx had clearly suggested that it is imperative to understand and conceptualize the new basic tendency and an essence of early last century for allowing appropriate theoretical implications about the minor changes in the capitalist mode of production and it suggests clearly that the eighteenth century capitalism had different essentials than the present imperialist capitalism. How can guerrilla warriors confined to thick forests of so-called 'liberated areas' understand the new global and Indian reality while themselves being cut off from the reality of society. It is a completely non-Marxist approach to characterize the sixty-seven years of post-independence State of India as comprador, neo-colonial social formulation because this is completely contrary to the social facts about the nature of society, the state and social classes of fifty years of post-independence India. How can Marxists ignore that a fundamental change has taken place from the beginning of the 1990s, both at the level of global monopoly capitalism and the capitalist state of India. How can Marxists ignore the emergence of a new reality of the rising ideological and political influence of the Hindu Sangh Parivar?

The crux of the issue is Maoists in India began with faulty theoretical and strategic approaches and they still continue to be imprisoned in categories of analysis and praxis which are not at all reflective of changing social dialects of the ground reality of India. A new social narrative exists in the twenty first century and only a 'United Front of Communist Forces' can face the challenges of the society. Indian Maoists are on the losing side of history because of their faulty theory, tactics and blind opposition to other communist social formations which they have been always disrupting.

NOTES

1. Quoted from Sumanta Banerjee, *In the Wake of Naxalism: A History of the Naxalite Movement in India,* Subarnarekha, Calcutta, 1980, p. 371.
2. ***Countering*** *Naxalism with Development: Challenges of Social Justice and State* Security, Sage, 2014.
3. C.P. Bhambhri, ''The Indain Transition' *Social Scientist*, Vol. 41, Nos. 1-2, January-February 2013, pp 69-85.

Social Scientists, Vol. 43/Nos. 7-8/July-August 2015.

24

Globalised Monopoly Capitalism and Indian Society and State

Indian capitalism in the twenty-first century seems to be succeeding in establishing its hegemony, not only over subordinate labouring classes, but also over the inherited pre-capitalist, feudal land ownership strata of society, and in its ongoing effort to integrate the whole society and every state. The capitalist classes have made full use of the Indian state power, especially after independence from the British colonial rulers. The central fact about the spread of Indian capitalism, both horizontally and vertically, is that it has achieved its present monopolistic state because of its deep harmony and control over the state. The Indian state has been the facilitator of the ongoing and unstoppable march of Indian capitalism. It deserves to be clearly stated that India had inherited a backward, underdeveloped and extremely poverty-ridden economy and a productive system which was kept almost primitive by the British colonial plunderers. The historical content of colonial exploitation of the Indian society as a whole is quite significant, because it also impacted the development of Indian capitalism, and the indigenous capitalist classes were quite weak and vulnerable to ever establish a pre-eminent class position in the society. The post-independence Indian state, while maintaining relative class autonomy, created institutions for the development of capitalism. The post-independence phase of Indian capitalism needs to be mentioned because its salient feature was that a relatively weak capitalist class with a limited capital base needed the state to carry it on its shoulders. As a result, in about less than four decades, the capitalist class, which was growing under the protective and promotional umbrella of the state, succeeded in graduating into big industrial and business classes.

The reality of the first two decades of the twenty-first century is that the infant capitalist classes of 1947 have become monopolies, and have decided to conflate themselves completely with global finance capital and imperialist transnational corporations. The capitalist classes and the Indian state began their journey in 1947 by following policies that fully protected the Indian merchants and Indian capital from the foreign capital of imperialist countries, because it was felt that the big fish will devour the small fish that has come of age. And Narendra Modi, the chief political executive of the Indian capitalist state, declared on 10 November 2015 that India, 'on the one hand [was] to further open the sectors for more foreign investments in the country and make it easy to invest in India'. Narendra Modi, during his three-day visit to Britain from 11 November to 13 November 2015, while addressing the India-UNCEO forum, observed that his government 'had confidently eased, consistently and ceaselessly worked to integrate the economy with the world'.

This story of Indian capitalist integration with global monopoly capitalism does not stop with the top instruments of the Indian state. All the 29 states and 7 Union Territories are visiting foreign capital for investment in their respective states, and this problem has further solidified the social base of foreign capital in every corner of India. The most important implication of the above narrative is that the globalised monopoly capitalism of India has merged itself with the Indian state. The salient feature of the twenty-first century is that capital and the state have completely merged with one another, and the Indian state has become a real instrument in the hands of the private property-owning industrial, business, entrepreneurial classes, whose number is about 300 million only in a country with a population of over 1 billion. Hence, one of its early characterisations that the state is a collective agency of the capitalist classes has almost become real in the past two decades of twenty-first century India. The weak capitalist class, with a low level of capital base of their own, in their class interest, wanted a relatively autonomous class-state after about four decades of the post-independence phase of capitalist development. However, the relationship between 'capital and the state' has fundamentally changed once the Indian capitalists have become monopolists and big economic players. R.K. Hangui, on 11 December 1965, had submitted a report which stated that corporate India needs to be repudiated because it had accumulated a 'high degree of concentration of power'. In 2016, we see in the *Forbes* magazine that the richest 100 Indians are worth US$ 345 billion—and Mukesh Ambani, a post-independence entrant to industry and son of Dhirubhai Ambani, has assets with a net worth of US$ 18.9 billion, as of 2015. The erstwhile houses of Birla and Tata were known as the big bourgeoisie of India on the eve of independence. With the emergence of a new brand of industrialists of the twenty-first century, they have fallen to a junior position.

It is in the new India of monopoly and globally integrated capitalist classes that the 300 million private property owning, capitalist business trading, entrepreneurial strata of society are living a 'segregated' social life, while the absolute majority population of toiling working classes, labourers in the informal sector of economy, landless marginal agricultural workers of the 'other India' are engaged in daily struggles for survival and are also serving the upper classes, in a highly unequal society. A few analytical questions arise here, because the state of the monopoly capitalist classes and their global patron is governed by seeking the 'consent' of the empowered citizens, who enjoy universal adult franchise and fundamental rights, as enshrined in the republican Constitution of India. Hence, a central issue is the 'equality and inequality' inherent in the capitalist-democratic state of the country. A basic contradiction of India has to be resolved, because if on the one hand, the monopoly capitalists supported by their own state are engaged in ruthless accumulation of profit, and on the other hand, the electorally empowered population of 700 million that constitutes the 'other India' are actively involved in the struggle to get a share in the fruits of economic growth which is contributed by these 'labouring classes', then, how can the democratic-capitalist state satisfy the greed of the private profit accumulators and the ordinary working class citizens who have the right to vote and to elect or reject the members of the political executive, the parliament and assemblies? There is a need to raise the larger issue of the role of ideology, which plays a significant role in making a large majority of people believe or accept that the rulers are working in their interests, and that therefore these democratically elected leaders of the state deserve their support and consent.

Karl Marx, in *The German Ideology, The Eighteenth Brumaire of Louis Napoleon,* and the Italian Marxist Antonio Gramsci,, in his *Prison Notebooks,* elabourated on the role of ideology in society. The Indian state, like all other modern states, whether democratic or authoritarian or military-ruled, tried to gain the consent of the governed by coercion and ideology, which is acceptable to the masses. It deserves to be clearly stated that there is enough impeccable evidence from twentieth-century state systems to substantiate the argument that only a coercive apparatus, i.e. the state, is not enough to make rulers succeed in ruling their societies, as even the fascists and the Nazis needed an ideology to mobilize people and get their willing obedience. Hence, India cannot be an exception to this general rule that an exploitative and oppressive capitalist ruling class in the twentieth century depended on state systems consisting of a coercive apparatus to crush rebellions as well as the consent of the governed, to facilitate capital accumulation for private appropriation of the owners of the means of production.

The post-independence Indian state had successfully established its quasi-ideological hegemony over almost the whole of India by following the best ideological legacies of the anti-colonial struggles of the nationalists like the Gandhi-led Indian National Congress, the Socialists and Communists. The sectarian communalists like the All India Hindu Mahasabha, the All India Muslim League or the Rashtriya Swayamsevak Sangh were neither involved in anti-colonial liberation struggles, nor were they part of the mainstream ideological value system of nationalists like the Congress, Socialists and Communists. The post-independence Indian state gained its legitimacy because it practised and verbalised the ideology of secularism, integrally linked with the agenda of equality and socialism. The ideological hegemonic project of post-independence India had two pillars of secularism and socialism, and the grand experiment of economic and social development of an underdeveloped and backward country was launched by ensuring that every citizen of the country, irrespective of religion, caste, creed or gender, is a rightful shareholder and active partner in the economic growth agenda of independent India. A composite India belonging to every resident citizen is not only equal before law, but also a participant in his or her own right, in the gigantic task of making a new India. After independence, the critical debate in the public domain was about the content and substance of socialism. However, the controversies were not about the relevance of socialism for India but the speed and pace of private property owners whether landlords or industrial bourgeoisie, in socialist India. An ideological consensus existed that the Indian state was based on the pillars of secularism and socialism and that an effort needed to be made to deepen the process of the secularisation of society and make adequate institutional efforts in order to create a socialist society based on the principles of equality and social control over the main means of production. This national ideological commitment around secularism and socialism as two sides of the same coin gradually weakened, and challenges to these twin goals of new India came from the sphere of the Hindu Right, headed by RSS, which attacked the ideology of secularism and socialism.

The relevant issue worth analysing is that the challenges to and critiques of the nationalist ideological hegemonic agenda saw the great link that existed between the ideology of secularism and socialism, and an attack was launched against these two inter-related ideological goals, along with attempt to construct an alternative ideological hegemony, by demolishing both secularism and socialism and creating spaces for a new alternative ideological hegemony, based on full-fledged capitalism and Hindutva. It is analytically significant that Hindutva and supporters of globalised monopoly capitalism could demolish the ideological hegemony of the nationalists in spite of the fact that secularism and socialism were the products of long mass struggles and sacrifices.

What is the explanation for the success, even if temporary, of the emergence of an alternative ideological hegemony of the Indian state? It is empirically wrong to suggest that the socialist project failed to deliver on the promises made to the common labouring classes because the global experiment of socialism collapsed with the collapse of first socialist country of the world. Backward Soviet Russia and underdeveloped India, while launching the socialist project of social reconstruction, had to handle a heavy burden of not only developing the new modern means of production in their societies, but also of reforming and restructuring archaic social relations inherited from the past. It was a total agenda of creating not only a new productive system, but also establishing a system of new productive social relations because the past social relations had hindered and obstructed the growth of a new material productive system in society. The transition to socialism and secularism would not have been smooth either for erstwhile USSR or for India, and in spite of many difficulties, some solid steps had been taken for the reconstruction of social and material productive relations in both these societies. However, the Indian experiment of mixed economy and planning failed to meet the expectations of the commoner who had lived in poverty for too long in history. Thus, the social and ideological forces which were selling an alternative dream to the common people, of Hindutva along with rapid economic growth, filled in the spaces which were being vacated by the practitioners of socialism and secularism. The forces of Hindutva and the Sangh Parivar have nothing to do with Hinduism and its diverse sects. In spite of this hard fact, they were able to manipulate the mass of people who were fed up with the unfulfilled promises of secular socialist torch-bearers. Socialism had given hope to the people of India and perhaps they waited too long for the hopes to be fulfilled and it was then, to quote Karl Marx, that 'Religion which is the sigh of the oppressed, hope for the hopeless', was offered as 'opium' by the Sangh Parivar. The social soil was fertile for the Sangh Parivar, and by mobilising huge priestly classes, the common Hindu was mobilised in pursuit of ritual-based Kumbh *melas* and other places of pilgrims. The Sangh Parivar established and strengthened a strong Hindu social, religious and cultural constituency for political mobilisation on the basis of the targeting of religious minorities. The idea of a Hindu Rashtra came in handy for demolishing socialism, which believed in equal rights for every citizen of India.

However, the story does not end here. It was not easy for the Sangh Parivar to establish Hindu religion-based ideological hegemony over the entire country, because of its rich cultural diversity. Hence the Hindu *Rashtravadis,* following in the footsteps of the socialist-secularist ideologies, projected themselves as champions of economic growth, which, according to them, could not rise to great heights because of the socialism of the past. Development became the mantra of Hindu ideological hegemony and it acted as tonic for these who had lost hope of better living in India. Hindutva and globalize monopoly capitalism are twin inter-related pillars of an alternative ideological hegemony of the Indian state in the first two decades. The monopoly capitalist classes and every strata of the petty bourgeoisie had shifted in their support to Hindu political parties, because it was the best bet for their future and prosperity. The Indian state is under the ideological hegemonic project of the Sangh Parivar, which is carrying on its shoulder the agenda for establishing a Hindu Rashtra and a prosperous and developed India, with the full contribution of the 300 million private property owners of the 'other India'. Social equality has no place in the new ideological discourse because the priority is to establish a prosperous and powerful Hindu Rashtra. The upshot of the above narrative is that the powerful, exploiting and regressive ruling monopoly-capitalist classes, who have successfully established their dominant position over the Indian state and its political, bureaucratic and coercive apparatus, are happy to accumulate maximum private profit even if the Hindu Rashtra is born from the ashes of the outcasts.

The Indian state in the twenty-first century is the handmaiden of private property owners and profit seekers, both Indian and transnational imperialists, and is an instrument in the hands of Hindu *Rashtravadis,* who are dedicated to the project of making a Hindu nation in an essentially plural and diverse society.

Social Scientist, Vol. 44/Nos. 5-6/May-June 2019.

25

The Making of a Hindu State

Prime Minister Narendra Modi during his first two years has sent a clear and unambiguous message to fanatically and ideologically committed anti-Muslims belonging to the RSS or stray groups like Abhinav Bharat of Lt. Colonel Prasad Purohit or Kumari Pragya that they will be fully protected by the State apparatus even if they had broken the law of the land. May 13, 2016 charge sheet submitted by the National Investigation Agency in the Malegaon Blast case of 2008 has overturned the investigations and charges filed by the Maharashtra ATS against Lt. Colonel Purohit, Kumari Pragya and other accused. Instead of Maharashtra Control of Organised Crime Act, National Investigation Agency has accused them under criminal conspiracy, murder and under various provisions of arms act, unlawful activities act and Explosive substance act. The National Investigation Agency has rejected the charge sheet based on evidence under Maharashtra Control of Organised Crime Act and on the basis of some new evidence collected by it in 2016, it "has dropped charges against Sadhvi Pragya and others, besides diluted the case against Lt. Colonel Purohit." The electronic media which is largely biased in favour of the Modi government has castigated the Congress-led UPA government at the centre for influencing investigators against Purohit and Sadhvi to condemn the RSS and Hindutva, forgetting that the same logic can be applied to National Investigation Agency Investigators in 2014 to 2016 under the Modi Government. For RSS cadre, any means to achieve its Hindutva agenda is moral. The Malegaon blast case provides the best example of investigators by the National Investigation Agency favouring the acquittal of perpetrators of violence because they are Hindus and protected by the BJP government at the centre. According to this logic, only Muslims are responsible for 'violence' and the functionaries of Indian State should firmly suppress suspected Muslim militants and protect Hindus who indulge in anti-Muslim violence. The story does not end here. The RSS and Hindutva groups are using the politics of beef to target Muslims and Christians. The Sangh Parivar has launched a mass campaign, projecting Muslims as the enemies of Hindus as they allegedly slaughter the 'Holy cow' for food. The politics of beef by the Hindutva groups is a mobilisation agenda for the Hinduisation of Indian society and it has been taken to the masses, so that the society gets polarised between Hindus and Muslims. Riots have taken place on the basis of rumours spread by Hindu Rashtravadis that a "slaughtered cow has been found" near a temple and allegedly Muslims were the culprits who were to be punished for this unholy activity. A few Kashmiri students in Rajasthan who happened to be Muslims were attacked by Bajrang Dal for allegedly 'eating beef' and police protection was sought by the terrorised Kashmir students.

Moreover, it is a well known fact that any political authority or State which is committed to promote a particular kind of ideology and belief system has to control educational institutions. It is not only by raising emotive issues like beef eating for the Hinduisation of India, but also by control of education system in schools, colleges and universities that the Sangh aims to achieve its agenda of 'Hindu India'. The Sangh Parivar feels that the intellectual dissenters in universities like the Central University of Hyderabad and Jawaharlal Nehru University, posing a challenge to this agenda are to be controlled. A fundamental difference exists between liberal philosophy of education and education for indoctrination, because in the former, dissent and free spirit of inquiry is encouraged, while in the latter, it is merely an ideological instrument, focusing on only one view point. Islamic seminaries teach theology and produce believers of Islam. The Sangh Parivar, like Islamic seminaries believe in the system of education that produces proud Hindus only. The slogan of Sangh Parivar and Modi government, including Modi himself is that "Hindu India has been a repository of knowledge" and the India of 21st century has to learn its own Hindu past and nothing else. With this in mind, the Modi government and other BJP governments in the states are working to 'Hinduise' education. The making of Hindu State is possible if the agenda of the making of Hindu citizen is implemented and pursued by educational institutions because these twin goals are 'inter-related and inter-connected'. The upshot of above narrative is that from 2014 and the evidence available up to 2016 clearly shows that the Modi government and the RSS are making every effort through control over the Hindu State apparatus to establish a new Hindu Republic in place of secular democratic republican constitution of India adopted in 1950.

People's Democracy, May 16-22, 2016.

26

The Making of Personality Cult

The Narendra Modi government decided to decisively respond to the terrorist attack on the army camp at Uri on September 18, In which 19 soldiers were killed. Prime Minister Narendra Modi led from the front and his first statement on September 24, while participating at the BJP national council meeting in Kozhikode, was that there is nationwide "aakrosh (anger)". Modi reiterated his resolve to decisively respond to the Uri attack by Pakistani terrorists, and in his monthly "Mann Ki Baat" radio address on September 25, he had observed that "I will just reiterate...that the guilty will certainly be punished". "The army does not speak, the army takes action, shows its power." Modi made it clear that his "resolve to do something" was in response to the nation's anger against terrorists from Pakistan. It was left to other BJP leaders like president Amit Shah and general secretary Ram Madhav to inform BJP delegates at Kozhikode that the Modi government is determined to hit back at Pakistan and the action came on the Intervening night of September 28/29 when the Indian Army's Special Forces launched "surgical strikes" on terrorists launching pads in Pakistan-occupied Kashmir. The Narendra Modi government announced to the people of India after the action that "successful" surgical strikes were carried out on seven camps across the Line of Control, inflicting heavy casualties on terrorists.

What is the political significance of the surgical strikes by the army for the BJP in the country? Why did the Narendra Modi government make "public announcement" of this military action claiming that the Line of Control was crossed by the Indian Army? It is not for the first time that the Government of India had taken action against Pakistan-based terrorists who had harmed the Indian Army, but the erstwhile Manmohan Singh-led UPA government at the Centre never made "public announcements" of such responses taken against terrorists across the Indian border. India has been dealing with such terrorist intrusions from Pakistan without making any public boastful statements of actions taken by the Indian Army. It is not only Modi who talked that the guilty will be punished, Amit Shah, the BJP president, on September 29, after the Army's successful surgical strike, in a celebration mode observed: "It is for the first time (that) in this frontal fight against terrorism, India under the leadership of Prime Minister Modi is feeling secure... Today's strikes signal the rise of a new India when the GOI (Government of India) doesn't get cowed down by nefarious designs of terrorists." Shah claimed Modi is a leader who believes in "walk the talk". Ram Madhav, the BJP general secretary, in the same tone on September 29 said we have got a "complete jaw for a tooth" and that "PM Modi Ji has walked the talk. Punishing the perpetrators of terror from across has begun". The BJP leadership and RSS have been working overtime to spread the message across the country that Prime Minister Modi is different and a man of immense courage because only such a leader could ask the Indian Army, in spite of many risks, to cross the LOC and attack the terrorists launching pads.

It may be suggested that such adulation of a Prime Minister in a Parliamentary democracy is normal because such an individual serves appreciation because he successfully leads the country in a quasi-warlike crisis situation after Uri. Modi's case is different because his projection by the BJP with full support from the RSS, especially its all-powerful Sarsanghchalak Mohan Bhagwat, has been on the top of the agenda of the Hindu Sangh Parlvar. Bhagwat single handedly picked Modi as the BJP's chief election campaigner and prime ministerial candidate for the 2014 Lok Sabha election. Perhaps, it was based on an assessment of the personality traits of Modi, the most important is his single-minded commitment to the idea of Hindu Nationhood. The Sarsanghchalak of the RSS was clear that Modi had the persona to lead the Indian state and achieve the goals of establishing Hindu Nation in the country and hence, deserves unqualified support by all Swayam Sevaks within or outside the BJP governments. Further, RSS believes that an organisation including the government should ultimately revolve around the personality of an individual — the Leader. The RSS organisation itself is hierarchical and the authority of the Sarsanghchalak is unquestioned and unquestionable. This is precisely the quality that the RSS supremo was searching in a leader who should be able to impose his authority on the government of the BJP and whose personality should inspire respect and fear and awe among his government colleagues and MPs. Modi's image of a strong leader was projected during the election campaign to the 16th Lok Sabha both by the army of the RSS cadre and big industrial houses and corporate business groups who controlled the media. The whole burden of election campaign of Modi was that the UPA government led by weak Prime Minister Manmohan Singh has led to serious domestic crisis and only Modi, a strong decisive leader, has an immense capacity to pull out. India which was in disarray because of directionless UPA II government. Had Modi as Chief Minister of Gujarat from 2001 to 2014 not shown his immense capacity to build a new industrial state? Hence, Modi on the basis of his tracking record of Gujarat could deliver the goods at the Centre also. This projection of Modi's personality-oriented leadership became the subject matter of normal times in 2014 to 2016 when every policy initiative of the BJP government was attributed to the great leadership qualities of Modi.

The point to be understood is that 'personality cult' around Modi has been in the making from the time he was chosen by the RSS to lead the BJP in the Lok Sabha election of 2014 and it became a normal feature of Indian politics beginning with the electoral successes in 2014 when BJP obtained 282 seats out of 543. However, beginning with the Uri attack of September 18 by Pakistani terrorists and the drama around the success of surgical strikes of the Indian Army has added one more chapter in the so-called glorious achievements of the Leader — Narendra Modi. The surgical strikes by the Indian Army is only one part of the story, the other part is that between September 18 and 29, 2016, a campaign was launched to condition the Indians to demand revenge for the killings of 19 soldiers at Uri. It is a well-known fact that much emotional responses seeking revenge can be normal 'even' manufactured and artificially maneuvered. Any student of public opinion in a democracy knows it that demagogues war mongers masquerading as nationalists and patriots can create an artificial situation where everyone seems to be speaking the same language of revenge. Modi himself in his first public statement observed on September 24 that "anger" is visible and 'sacrifices of the soldiers' will not go in vain. Modi himself set the atmosphere of emotion based on hyper nationalistic public discourse in India and big industrial houses-controlled media, representing no one, added fuel to the fire by broadcasting loaded debates. The upshot of above narration is that without reading conspiracy theories, it becomes clear that the post September 18 situation in the country should not be seen in just black and white terms because the way BJP has campaigned in the country, its political meanings cannot be ignored.

The real political significance is that Modi is riding high in public estimation and in normal political situation of 2014-2016, or during quasi-crisis situation of post-Uri events, it is only his leadership and personal qualities that matter. Another important offshoot of post-Uri situation is that the RSS brand of aggressive, jingoist, hyper nationalism is dangerously spreading its shadow over the minds of citizens of India. The post-Uri glorification of Modi is extraordinary capabilities as a leader who can courageously face a 'war-like crisis situation' has unfortunately eclipsed the role of patriotic professional Indian Army which successfully destroyed terrorist camps through surgical strikes. The whole credit should be given to the Army but the BJP and the RSS have successfully shifted the focus away from the contribution of army to the adulation of Modi as the Leader so that only he matters in public affairs.

People's Democracy, November 07-13, 2016.

27

Explaining the Rise of Rightwing Social Forces in India

The unexpected and unprecedented expansion of the right wing social forces in India in the twenty first century deserves special attention and analysis because Indian rightists and "counter social revolutionary forces" are determined to destroy the idea of pluralist, secular and democratic India and replace it by an anti-people and anti-secularist full-fledged idea of "Hindu Nation-hood". India is witnessing a kind of polarisation of society in which Hindu religious fundamentalists are trying to capture all instruments of State power for creating a social, cultural, religious and politico-economic order which is non-egalitarian and anti-Muslim and anti-Christian. The Hindu right wing is making every effort to reduce the diverse religious minorities as "second class citizens" and establish Hindu religious hegemony over the whole society in which only Hindus are considered as "first class citizens". This idea of Hindu Rashtra as believed and practised by the Rashtriya Swayam Sevak Sangh and its ideological affiliates including its political affiliate known as BJP is moving forward to influence the leadership of Hindu upper classes and the labouring lower classes with a class goal of capturing the State power to make India a Hindu state, country, society and culture. Political power is a means to establish ideological hegemony of vedic Brahmanical Sanskrit brand of Hinduism over the whole society. The goal of RSS is to establish its totalitarian control to create a state system and society which is fundamentally opposed to all the basic values enshrined in the republican, democratic, secular, pluralist, federal and social welfarist Constitutional system of governance which is a product of all tendencies of anti-colonial national liberation movements and struggles. The Rashtriya Swayamsevak Sangh established by Dr. K.B. Hedgewar and strengthened by M.S. Golwalkar was never a part of anti-colonial national struggles and hence it has no commitment to the constitution and its values. How is it that these totalitarian anti-democratic forces have succeeded in replacing and displacing the progressive social and democratic forces from the centre stage of society, politics, economics and culture in India? It deserves to be mentioned that not only in pre-independence India, even in post-independence phase, the centre stage of approximately the whole society was occupied by centrist forces represented by the all India Congress and socialists and communists and this fact was substantiated that in the Lok Sabha and state assembly elections of 1951-52. It were the Congress, the socialists and the communists who had occupied the ruling party space as well as the opposition party space and other communalists or rightists were "marginal" in the elected legislatives of 1951-52. It was the bloc of the communist and the socialist MPs which made up for the largest opposition group in the Lok Sabha and in 1959 the first Communist Party government with EMS Namboodiripad as the chief minister was formed in Kerala after the elections of 1957. The undivided Madras Presidency and later on Andhra Pradesh carved out of it had sizeable presence of communist MLA's in the state assemblies. How was it possible for the marginalised Jan Sangh or Ram Rajya Parishad or Hindu Mahasabha of early 1950s to take such a big leap forward beginning from the 1990, and eventually in the 21st century are in the control of the central and many state governments? First, it can be no one's case that social, cultural, religious tendencies were non-existent or marginal in the Indian society. On the contrary, religion has always played a dominant and even a controlling role. It is an important factor in the lives of the Indian people and because religious factor has always been crucial in mounding the attitudes of mass of people, the superstructure of politics could be built on the social soil where religion plays a crucial role in shaping the value-systems of the masses. Thus strong presence of religious faith among the majority of Muslim people made it possible for political parties, groups and leaders to build their organisation on the basis of religious mobilisation of people for politics, if such religion-based parties had desired to exercise political power for the defence of their religion. It is not without reason that religion-based socially extremist parties have always been in contestation with the secular democratic parties in the whole of 20th century India.

Religion was available as a formidable force if parties or groups wanted to build their political base on the idea of defence of religion as their goal in politics. The beginning of 1990s witnessed a new political phenomenon, like a break with the past, when the All India Congress Party not only abandoned its economic project of planning for growth and social justice in favour of just growth on the basis of following a new path of liberalisation, privatisation and decrepitation of economy preferring free market competitive economy, along with preference for the free market capitalism it did not see itself as a defence for secularism against the onslaught of RSS-BJP because it did not politically fight out against L K Advani's so called rath yatra known as Ram Janmabhoomi movement. There was complete failure of the Congress to accept the challenge thrown by Hindu communalists who were openly targeting Muslim community and succeeding on December 6, 1992 with the demolition of Babri Masjid by all the affiliates of RSS under the leadership of swayamsevakes like L K Advani, Murli Manohar Joshi et al. The RSS with all its Hindu Rashtravadi affiliates celebrated not only the demolition of the Mosque but also the fact that they had achieved their main political goal of decimating the Congress party by projecting it as an opportunist party. The beginning of 1990s was the beginning of the emergence of self-confident and self-assured right wing Hindu Rashtravadis who had succeeded in demolishing the whole structure of secularisation as enshrined in the constitution of India because they had not faced any road block or resistance from so-called divided and fragmented secular parties and RSS and its affiliates found secular Congress as an "empty shell" which failed to stand up and get counted when the moment of trial had come. The politics of Hindutva succeeded not only on the basis of its large scale mobilisation, but also because of the complete collapse of its main opponent, the Congress.

Third, besides the above mentioned explanation for the rising tide of Hindu communalism, the larger explanation of the growth of religion-based rightist forces is that pre-capitalist, feudal religious traditions were never frontally attacked by the secular modernists even during the anti-colonial struggle for independence. The social dialectical process of colonial phase of Indian history can only be understood by identifying the positive and negative forces which were engaged in grappling with the challenges thrown by the colonies. The positive aspect of pre-independence colonial phase was the struggles launched by the various oppressed and exploited strata of society by colonial exploiters and because of these anti-colonial popular people's struggles, a new India was getting born and freedom is my birth right became the significant part of social and political consciousness of multiple political struggle for freedom from exploitative and oppressive British colonial rule struggle is the mid-life of new social consciousness and the greatest achievement of anti-colonial struggles was mass awakening among peasantry, working class, lower middle classes who had made great sacrifices to win India's freedom. The negative aspect of this social dialect was that compromises were made with the cultural and religious tradition of pre-capitalist feudal part and post-independence India was an inheritor of all cultural traditions which were integrally linked with religion, rituals. The devout Hindus, Muslims, Christians, Sikhs continued with their rituals of worship and temple mosque, Churches, gurudawaras continued to be considered as "sacred" and their custodian, the religious priests, commanded respect and authority and the religious believers were expected to "obey" the priestly class. This religious inheritance has been further solidified because the idea of Indian secularism, i.e. co-existence of all religions and equal respect for religious beliefs of all communities made people accept religion and challenge to religious beliefs or rituals was considered as "hurting the religious sentiment" of various religious communities. It is not without reason that for political purposes, the Sangh Parivar brings shankaracharyas and other preachers of Brahmanical rituals in public-political debate to win over the Hindu voters.

The social consciousness of the masses is indoctrinated with the values of Hindu religion and the Sangh parivar is successful in playing on religious sentiments of Hindus against the "other" i.e. Muslims and Christians. It is not only that a Hindu party is able to win over the loyalty of Hindu religious believers with the help of Hindu priests and by projecting Muslims and

Christians as the "other". The ruling or petti-bourgeoisie, or lower middle class or "basic classes" like the labouring class which are in sizable number were also brought under this influence. Even the grip of religion, and in spite of exploitation by the ruling classes in a capitalist system of India, belief in religion cuts across class lines. Thus, the BJP-RSS affiliates have been able to create a solid Hindu. constituency for their goal of Hindu nationhood, all other formations are "fragmented" and because of this "fragmentation" united anti-Hindu hegemonic ideological platform of struggling "basic classes" has not become strong enough to throw an effective challenge to Hindu rightwing reactionary forces in India. The recent "trade union strike" at an all India level in the first week of September shows that anti-exploitation struggles can be successfully launched, however, unity among the exploited and oppressed is threatened by otherwise "religious politics" of Hindu Rashtravadis. Hence the agenda and platform of mass struggle can succeed if medieval religious legacies are challenged by combining it with struggles against exploitation.

People's Democracy, September 28-October 04, 2015.

28

Fight the Attack on Constitutional Values

The constitutional head of the Indian State Pranab Mukherjee on October 7, 2015 observed that "we can't allow the core values of our civilisation to be wasted." The president further elaborated that "...the core value is what over the years civilisation celebrated diversity, promoted and advocated tolerance, and plurality." This statement or warning of President Mukherjee has been made in a specific context of the role of Sangh Parivar and the BJP government which is leading to a complete polarisation of society on religious basis, a phenomenon which is spreading hatred and instilling intolerance in society. The Sangh Parivar and BJP while making every effort to push their project of Hinduisation of society and marginalisation of religious minorities has led to the erosion of basic values enshrined in the republican constitution of India, like democracy based on tolerance of dissent and respect for plurality of opinions and viewpoints as guaranteed in the chapter on fundamental rights of the constitution. Why has the president of India thought it appropriate to remind Indians about the civilisational values of plurality and tolerance as enshrined in the constitution?

These constitutional values should have become integral to the way of life of every Indian during the last seventy years of the functioning of competitive parliamentary democracy based on universal adult franchise. A country which is never tired of pro-claiming from housetop at the global level that it has held sixteen free and fair Lok Sabha elections and the voters have freely exercised their right to vote and elected and rejected political par-ties. The verdict of the votes has been accepted by every competing party and governments have changed on the basis of voters' choice. The need to defend the "basic structure of the Indian Constitution" and the freedom guaranteed by the constitution to every citizen of India has arisen because the Sangh Parivar and BJP while pursuing their ideologies of Hindutva are subverting the democratic institutional and value system of the constitution. While winning the elections, the focus of Hindutva in government, is inherently the "agenda" of Hindu Rashtravad which is a complete "negation" of the basic values of the constitution. Democracy is threatened by forces which are using democracy to come to power and work against the letter and spirit of democracy. The longest serving RSS supremo MS Golwalkar, addressed as "Guru ji" by all RSS swayam sevaks including present chief ministers, ministers and prime ministers, had defined in 1940 that the goal is "One flag, one leader, and one ideology of Hindutva". Golwalkar to Bhagwat, Vajpayee to Modi are pursuing this definition of India and this goal of Hindutva as defined here has something to do with the constitution of India. The high ideological priest of the RSS, Golwalkar, while defining the essence of Hindu Rashtra, has emphasised on homogeneity, uniformity and unity.

In respect of diversity and plurality, the objective resolution moved by Jawaharlal Nehru himself on the floor of the Constituent Assembly while concretising the "objectives" of the constitution of India, and the preamble of the constitution, stands for a complete rejection of the idea of Hindutva and Hindu State. The preamble begins with "We the people of India....secure to all its citizens justice, liberty, equality and fraternity." Not only this, "We the people, in our constituent assembly this twenty-sixth day of November 1949, do hereby adopt, enact and give to ourselves this constitution." Is this constitution of the people of India, in letter and spirit, acceptable to the votaries of 'One Nation' minus plurality and diversity of the people inhabit this country? The answer is a big no. A few facts need to be mentioned here to substantiate the argument that the ideology of Hindutva of RSS-BJP in government is not at all in tune with the philosophy of the constitution and this is the reason that a time has come to defend the democratic values in the constitution from its enemies who are fundamentally opposed to such values enshrined in the constitution. First, the RSS established in 1925 kept itself completely away from anti-colonial struggles whether led by the Indian National Congress or Socialists or Communists and the RSS did not associate itself with peasant struggles or working class movements which were launched during the 1920's to 1940's in opposition to offensive laws made by the colonial rulers to extract "rent" from the labouring and toiling masses of India. Anti-colonialism was not the agenda of the RSS and VD Savarkar, a great inspirer of RSS's Hindutva ideology, offered "apologies" to the colonial rulers and begged for his release from prison. Savarkar and Hindu Mahasabha leaders were the only "apologist collaborators" of the British Raj while other leaders, groups and sections of society were fighting for freedom from the oppressive colonial rulers and their beneficiaries the Zamindars, money lenders et al. These were not the concerns of their founder, KB Hedgewar. How can RSS accept the letter and spirit of the constitution which had the imprint of "struggles for independence" when it has not at all been a part of those struggles?

Second, the logic of RSS leadership not participating in anti-colonial struggles was that they were not at all represented in the Constituent Assembly and they had no role to play in any activity connected with the making of constitution. It does not mean that fringe Hindutva elements were not present in the Constituent Assembly because Hindu-type Congressmen and fringe Hindu Maha sabha were representing Hindu demands such as anti-cow slaughter bill or Hindi as mother tongue of India. This fact was also noticed in

1937 when the Congress ministry was formed in the British Province of UP, a few Hindu minded Congressmen had made anti-cow slaughter, Hindi as national language and Vande Mataram as public issues. However, in spite of these individuals, anti-colonialism was a powerful issue and Congress Ministers resigned in 1939 on the issue of Britain joining war and making India a party to this decision without consulting the Congress.

The fact of the matter is that anti-colonialism was a supreme agenda of freedom fighters in India and RSS was not at all part of this mainstream of Indian struggle. The idea of Hindu nationhood was pursued outside and away from real struggles for freedom from colonial rule and the result is that the RSS-BJP does not share the nationalist sentiment underlying the constitution made by freedom fighters. The RSS cannot appropriate this constitution because up to 1947, it maintained a distance from the focus of nationalism which was: struggle for independence and the right of free Indians to make their own constitution as they desired. Hence this constitution has to be defended from those who have always opposed the basic postulates of Indian nationhood of plurality.

Third, it should be kept in mind that the Atal Bihari Vajpayee government from 1998 to 2004 had appointed a National Commission for the review of constitution and if the BJP led government had been formed after the Lok Sabha election of 2004, the BJP would have re-written this constitution of 1950. Anti-republican constitutionalism has been an agenda of the Hindu Rashtravadis and the Vajpayee government had wanted to implement its agenda of "rewriting" the whole constitution on the lines of 'One Nation, One Flag, and One Hindu religion' as the essence of New Hindu India.

The Modi government unlike the Vajpayee government has not felt the need to "formally re-write" the constitution of India, because it is using its State power formally under the constitution to achieve its goal of making India a Hindu Rashtra. Every inter-religious community violence or riot is meant to convey a message to Muslims that in Hindu India, Muslims are second-class citizens and they have to live in ghettos. This is the Gujarat model of Narendra Modi and post Godhra riots of February-April 2002 where Muslims were massacred and those who survived were forced to move to refugee camps and made to live in Muslim ghettos in Gujarat and this is an all India agenda of the Sangh Parivar that Muslims have to live separately in ghettos as second-class citizens. The full reading of Article 48 of the constitution is necessary because it states "The State shall endeavour to organize agriculture and animal husbandry on modern and scientific lines and shall, in particular, take steps for preserving and improvising the breeds, and prohibiting the slaughter, of cow and calf's and other milk and draught cattle." Hence anti-cow slaughter as an agenda of Hindutva has nothing to do with the letter and spirit of Article 48 of the constitution where it is linked with agriculture and animal husbandry. The BJP has taken this out of context and has started a movement against "beef eating and cow slaughter" by identifying Muslim community as sole consumers the of cows' beef, a mother to Sakshi Maharaj. What has cow slaughter to do with Indian Muslims? Why pick on anti-cow slaughter as mentioned in Article 48 in isolation and proclaim it as the most important duty of the Indian State? Hence the constitution and legality is being used by Hindu governments to pursue their political agenda of "isolating Muslims" as culprits for cow slaughter. The Constituent Assembly debate on Hindi as national language and the issue of "cow slaughter" clearly shows that a very thoughtful and full of passion was shown by the members while debating these "issues". The RSS was not part of the Constituent Assembly and so does not show the arguments for and against which were advanced by members while debating each and every clause of the constitution. Constitution is in the hands of those who were "outside" the four walls of the constituent assembly and were not participants, not only in constitution making but also in struggles of those who were given the tasks of making this constitution. The above discussion clearly reveals that those who never owned the real legacies of anti-colonialism cannot be entrusted for safeguarding the constitution which is a collective effort of freedom fighters excluding the RSS.

People Democracy, October 19-25, 2015.

29

Communalisation of the State Apparatus

A myth has been spread by the bourgeois writers of democracy that the state and its apparatuses are "neutral agencies" and the rule of law is implemented in an impartial and unbiased manner by all managers of the capitalist democratic state. This non-historical and non-empirical view has been challenged and contested because the state in a capitalist country is an "executive agency of the ruling exploiting classes" and it has also been historically established that the "class state" of the capitalists governs society on the basis of "an ideology" to legitimise the oppressive and exploitative system in a capitalist country. If on one hand, advanced monopoly capitalist systems rule over the mass of people by establishing its ideological hegemony on the basis of adult franchise and representative systems of democracy in which people elect their political representatives, on the other, in "transitional societies" like India the emerging capitalist state systems are engaged in establishing an "ideological consensus" for hegemonising the whole society. Such an ideological consensus is yet to emerge in India and this is the reason that capitalist classes and strata of private property owners including big businesses, property holding professionals, upwardly business classes, surplus producing land owning peasantry and the large trading classes are still struggling to evolve any "consensus" on an ideology for the governance of the whole of India, and one stream of such an "ideology" which is making every effort to capture the imagination of the whole society is that of "religion-based" social and political order which is based on ancient traditional religious values of Vedic-Brahmanical Hindu religion and the goal of this stream of ideology is to establish Hindu Rashtra or Hindu Nationhood in the country.

The struggle is to capture state power with an aim to make India a Hindu State and political agency of Hindu rashtravadi Rashtriya Swayamsevak Sangh (RSS) and its 45 affiliates including Jan Sangh/Bharatiya Janata Party. This ideological programme of 'Hinduisation' of the whole society and knitting the whole India around the ideology of Vedic-Brahmanical Hinduism has been carried by the Sangh Parivar during the last almost seventy years of post-Independence India and the RSS, the "fountain source" of Hindutva, has participated in politics to win elections and penetrate in the state apparatus and the Jan Sangh and BJP have successfully used electoral democracy, especially from 1967, to win some state Assembly elections.

The main purpose of the Jan Sangh/BJP government either at the Centre or in the states of India is to push forward its agenda of Hinduisation by appointing or nominating its own ideological followers of the RSS at crucial and critical levels of state apparatuses like bureaucracy, police forces, and as school, college and university teachers. It's a myth that if Jan Sangh/BJP get defeated in an election, the impact of their ideology also gets wiped out after the electoral defeats. The state functionaries with BJP and Sangh Parivaar ideology continue to serve Hindu cause whether they are in bureaucracy or police or educational institutions, and this process has continued in an uninterrupted manner beginning from 1967 to 2015. It deserves to be mentioned that during the early years of post-Independence India, police had to inquire into the "antecedents" of personnel entering the civil or police services and especially the candidates with "Communist" background were blacklisted by police and their entry was barred. The RSS which is gaining strength has opposed the system of police scrutiny of entrants to the civil and police services with RSS background.

How can state apparatuses be neutral while dealing with the citizens if they are committed to carry forward the ideology of Hindu Rashtravad which is in reality based on the idea that Hindus are first-class citizens and other religious minorities like Muslims and Christians are second-class citizens? This is the context which explains the present public debate on the communalisation of the Indian state apparatuses where Hindu Rashtravadis are openly following their ideology of Hindutva while in government job or while wearing Khaki uniform. The skeletons have come out in the public domain and hidden fact of creeping communalisation of state apparatuses beginning with 1967 when Jan Sangh governments came to power in some states, even for a brief period, has assumed dangerous proportions because some facts which have been highlighted by judicial commissions appointed to investigate inter-religious riots especially after December 6, 1992, when the BJP and the army of Sangh Parivar demolished Babri Mosque in Ayodhya. The post-Babri Mosque demolition led to a series of inter-religious riots especially in Mumbai in December 1992 and January 1993. Justice B N Srikrishna who investigated the "riots in Mumbai" had clearly identified "police-in-uniform" as biased and prejudiced against Muslims and they actively created a situation where Hindu mob targeted the life and property of innocent and helpless Muslims because Mumbai "police" had not provided protective umbrella to the besieged Muslims. This is a fact as mentioned by Justice B N Srikrishna on the riots of December 6 to 10 in 1992 and January 6 to 20, 1993 and later on bomb blasts of 12th March 1993. Justice Srikrishna in a later interview on August 1, 2015 observed that "there does appear to be a cause and effect relationship between the two riots and the serial bomb blasts". Justice Srikrishna further observed "if the state is complicit in the communal riots, police will take a Nelson's eye towards the real aggressor and round up the real victims, as happened in Mumbai riots and Delhi riots".

How can prosecutor be free to put facts before a judge when the communalism has taken over the state apparatus? Justice Srikrishna laments "as long as the inherent state bias is not removed, there would be no change in the situation". Has state bias come to an end or has it grown further in communalisation of state functionaries? The post-Babri Mosque violence, was repeated in post-Godhra riots of Ahmebadad in 2002 and more than thousand innocent Muslims were killed and more than 3,00,000 Muslims fled from the villages to secure themselves in refugee camps. Justice Manmohan Singh Liberhan while investigating the Babri mosque destruction "indicted" many senior BJP and RSS leaders and mentioned that it was "Hindu terror". Kalyan Singh, the then chief minister of Uttar Pradesh, who presided over the destruction of Babri Mosque on December 6, 1992 has been "rewarded" by governorship of Rajasthan by the Narendra Modi government. The Hindu activists involved in anti-Muslim riots in Muzaffarnagar in 2013 have been rewarded by the BJP and such identified persons are BJP MPs and MLAs.

The moral of the story is with the BJP in government and RSS membership not a "disqualification" for public service, the neutrality of the state while dealing with citizens as equals before the law is a pipe-dream. A former home secretary of the UPA-II government just after retirement joined the BJP and is a BJP MP in the 16th Lok Sabha. The civil bureaucracy, the men-in-khaki uniform, and numerous functionaries of the government at every level are getting "indoctrinated" in the ideology of Hindu Nationhood and in its process, minority communities are getting alienated from the mainstream of secular Indian democracy. This is a challenge before India. Fundamentals of Indian constitutional democracy are in danger because the Hindu Rashtravadis do not accept this constitutional philosophy because for Hindu Rashtravadis India has "two kinds of citizens": 'Hindus', the first special category, and 'Others' like Muslims and Christians as second-class citizens and functionaries of the state are treating citizens on the basis of "first-class" and "second-class".

People Democracy, August 23, 2015.

Index